The Daily Telegraph

Book of the

TOUR DE FRANCE

The Daily Telegraph

Book of the

TOUR DE FRANCE

edited by MARTIN SMITH

Aurum

First published in Great Britain
2009 by Aurum Press Ltd
7 Greenland Street
London NW1 0ND
www.aurumpress.co.uk

Photographs: p 1, Jacques Anquetil, 13 July 1963, courtesy of Rolls Press/
Popperfoto/Getty Images; p 15, Tom Simpson, July 1967, courtesy of AFP/Getty
Images; p 43, Brest, 1974, courtesy of McCabe/Express/Getty Images; p 63, Greg
LeMond (*left*) and Bernard Hinault (*right*) on Alpe d'Huez, 21 July 1986,
courtesy of AFP/Getty Images; p 101, Marco Pantani (*left*) and Miguel Indurain
(*right*), 13 July 1995, courtesy of Patrick Kovarik/AFP/Getty Images; p 167, Lance
Armstrong on the final stage of the 92nd Tour de France, 24 July 2005,
courtesy of Jack Guez/AFP/Getty Images.

A catalogue record for this book is available from the British Library.

ISBN 978 1 84513 484 6

1 3 5 7 9 10 8 6 4 2
2009 2011 2013 2012 2010

Typeset in Spectrum by Saxon Graphics, Derby
Printed by MPG Books, Bodmin, Cornwall

For my mother and late father,
who bought me my first, second, third and fourth bikes

CONTENTS

INTRODUCTION   ix

CHAPTER 1: 1903 – 1963   . 1

CHAPTER 2: 1964 – 1969   15

CHAPTER 3: THE 1970s   43

CHAPTER 4: THE 1980s   63

CHAPTER 5: THE 1990s   101

CHAPTER 6: THE 2000s   167

INTRODUCTION

For 11 months of the year, the best jobs at *The Daily Telegraph* are indisputably wine correspondent, restaurant critic and travel writer, and not always in that order. For the month of July every year, the position of cycling correspondent suddenly becomes the most coveted. That's the month of the Tour de France – that gastronomic, grape-fuelled adventure through the wonderful French countryside, with a bit of sport thrown in for good measure – when the role of cycling correspondent blends all three elements. No wonder the post was held for nearly half a century by just two men; once secured, you would be a fool to give it up lightly.

Just tracing the route for the following year's race when it is announced each autumn is enough to make you take the red Michelin guide down from the shelf and plan your next vacation. The mind wanders to scenes of endless fields of sunflowers, quaint little villages, chateaux on the hillside, and a slower pace of life. Now you are drifting through the wine regions of Bordeaux and the Bourgogne, Champagne and Chablis, the Loire and the wine lakes of Languedoc-Roussillon, the Rhône and Savoy: take your pick from rosé, sparkling, *blanc* or *rouge*, Premier Cru or cheap plonk. Then there is the food: the fresh seafood on the coasts, the assorted breads and cheeses, the pâtés, the terrines, the obscene but delicious things the French do to ducks and geese, the rich sauces, the regional specialities, the tartes, the gateaux — *l'addition, garçon, s'il vous plait!* You are almost there, the mouth watering in anticipation.

Through the middle of this idyll bursts the Tour de France, the biggest annual sporting event in the world, if you accept the self-publicity. It is an Olympic Games on two wheels, combining the climbers, the descenders, the sprinters, the time-triallists, the middle-of-the-roaders, in a mad, mad marathon race for the finishing line on the Champs-Elysées. More than that, as more than one *Telegraph* writer has noted over the years, it is a way of life for the French of all generations, of all classes; the excuse to go *en fête*.

It took the British a long time to cotton on to what was going on across the Channel. *Telegraph* readers, though, were made aware of the race from day one, back in 1903, thanks to a paragraph at the very end of the weekly Paris Day by Day despatch, sent 'by special wire' from 'Our Own Correspondent'. Under the mystifying headline 'A Mad Hippopotamus', our sadly anonymous correspondent reported that the annual review of troops at Longchamp was being postponed a few weeks so the King of Italy could watch it during a state visit. But, the writer consoled, the Parisians would not have to wait long, and in the meantime 'they can keep up the July fête with the customary liveliness'. There will be, the columnist said, 'dancing in the streets, illuminations, and fireworks'. It was almost a template for the Tour de France. The Tour itself, the writer concluded before a wheel had turned, sounded like a tremendous race. Before long the parties would be for *Le Tour,* and soon everyone would forget Italy ever had a king.

There were sporadic mentions of the race in the *Telegraph* in the next few years, reproduced further on in these pages, either in the Parisian diary or in a Saturday column entitled 'Motoring and Cycling', which highlighted news of events forthcoming or past. It was a sign of the times that within a few years the column had spread its wings, so to speak, scrubbed 'and Cycling', and become almost a full broadsheet page of 'Motoring and Aviation'.

If a keen follower of the sport wished to keep abreast of the new-fangled Tour, or the other massed-start road races that differentiated 'Continental' cycling from the domestic track and time-trial variety, he would not find it in the parochial British press of the time, not even the slightly less jingoistic *Telegraph.* Indeed, J.B. Wadley, the first reporter to be bylined from the Tour, though not until the early Sixties, used to subscribe as a young man to the French sports paper that founded and sponsored the race, *L'Auto.* His newsagent in Colchester, Essex, apparently thought it slightly bizarre and extravagant that anyone would pay 1½d a day for a journal in a foreign language about a lot of cyclists with funny names pedalling around France. After all, the first British riders – Charles Holland and Bill Burl – did not compete in the race until 1937, neither finishing it, and it was not until the mid-Fifties that Brian Robinson followed in their tyre tracks. Indeed, it would be the man from Mirfield, in Yorkshire, who became the first Briton to win a stage, in 1958.

However, it was the emergence of Tom Simpson, in the wake of Robinson's success, that finally inspired the *Telegraph* to stop taking occasional Reuters or Associated Press wire reports on the Tour, rewriting them with a 'local' angle, and send their own man to France. The previously mentioned John Borland Wadley, better known as 'Jock', had continued his deep interest in overseas cycling into adulthood, working for and founding several specialist magazines, and it was he who was first employed as a freelance by the *Telegraph* to cover the 1964 race, though he was certainly the 'Special Correspondent' two years earlier. J.B. was still sending back reports, aged 65, in 1980, less than a year before he died.

So what did the readers of *The Daily Telegraph* and its competitors miss in the 50 editions of the Tour de France run between 1903 and

1964? They certainly missed the most colourful period in the event's history: tales abound of mystery, intrigue, cheating, Herculean feats and larger-than-life characters. The fact that there was not a television camera, hand-held by a motorcycle pillion rider, inches from the face of the man in the yellow jersey, arguably helps embroider some of the story-telling. That and the fact that, for at least the first two Tours, much of it happened in the dark because night-riding was a feature of the stages.

Maurice Garin, the first winner, is characterised in shorthand form as a chain-smoking chimney sweep, which makes him sound like a French Alf Tupper, who brushed the soot off his clothes, climbed on his pushbike and pedalled 2,500 kilometres around the countryside fuelled only by a flagon of wine and a packet of Gauloises. In fact, Garin was the Lance Armstrong of his day, around the turn of the last century, the winner of just about every race that mattered. He found the inaugural route 'grey and monotonous' and said he 'suffered on the road, I was hungry, I was thirsty, I was sleepy, I cried between Lyon and Marseille'. From the start, he said, he felt 'like a bull pierced by banderillas, who pulls the banderillas with him, never able to rid himself of them'.

The second race was even worse. Supporters of rival competitors felled trees to block the road and beat up riders, including Garin. 'I'll win the Tour de France provided I'm not murdered before we get to Paris,' he said. There were frequent reports of tacks being strewn on the route to cause punctures, allegations of cheating by 'taking a tow' from motorcycles or jumping on trains and claims of riders being poisoned. One rider even brandished a revolver at an accuser. Garin duly arrived ahead of the rest in Paris but, along with the next three behind him, was disqualified after being accused of receiving illegal assistance.

Henri Desgrange, the Tour's founding father and director, was an autocratic dictator and made few friends among the competitors. He had a long-running feud with Henri Pélissier, the winner in 1923, most notably about the conditions endured by the riders.

'You have no idea what the Tour de France is,' Pélissier told a journalist after he had abandoned the race in 1924. 'It's a Calvary. And what's more, the way to the cross only had 14 stations – we've got 15… They wouldn't treat mules the way we're treated.' He then revealed, with tongue gently in cheek, what the riders needed to take with them just to get by: cocaine 'for our eyes', chloroform 'for our gums', horse liniment 'to keep our knees warm' and three boxes of assorted though unspecified pills. 'In short, we run on dynamite.' When Desgrange introduced the first serious climb into the Tour in 1910, the Col du Tourmalet in the central Pyrenees, the first rider over the top of what was little more than a goat track was Octave Lapize. He was pushing his bike, and as he passed Desgrange at the check-point, he spat: *'Assassins!'* Nonetheless Lapize won the race, and has a statue on the summit recalling his place in history.

The Tourmalet was also the backdrop to a scene that illustrates just how tight a rein Desgrange and his team of scrutineers kept on the race. Eugene Christophe, the outstanding favourite to win in 1913 after finishing runner-up the year before, found his front forks had snapped on the descent, but managed to grind to a juddering halt. In between bouts of weeping, he put the bike over his shoulder and stumbled for two hours to the nearest village, Ste-Marie-de-Campan, ten kilometres away. Once there, he sought out the forge and, being a skilled mechanic, set about repairing the damage himself. Which was just as well as the strict rules of the Tour forbade riders receiving assistance. However, with the bike frame in one hand, and a hammer in the other, he had to accept the help of a seven-year-old boy called Corni to work the bellows that fanned the fire. For that, the jobsworth working for Desgrange penalised him ten minutes. Added to the overall delay, Christophe's lead and his chances of winning the Tour had disappeared. Until the arrival five decades later of Raymond Poulidor, the eternal bridesmaid (he finished second three times, and third in five others), Christophe was probably the unluckiest rider on the Tour. Lightning struck him not once, not twice, but thrice: his forks also snapped on the cobbled streets of Valenciennes, close to Belgium, in 1919, and again on the descent from the Galibier in the Alps in 1922. On all three occasions he was in contention for a title he was destined never to win.

More fortunate was François Faber, of Luxembourg, who, in the middle of winning a remarkable five stages on the trot in 1909, suffered a broken chain one kilometre from the finish in Lyon, and pushed the bike all the way to the finish. He still won that day's racing, and ultimately the Tour, having led from the second stage. But six years later he died in the Battle of Artois at Carency, near Arras. Some say he was shot by a sniper as he jumped for joy after receiving a telegram announcing the birth of a daughter; more credible, though, are reports he was shot while carrying an injured colleague back from no man's land. Hugo Koblet also died an unexplained death, though six years after he had retired from the sport, killed when his car spun off the road into a tree in perfect driving conditions. Some suspected suicide. Koblet, a handsome young man given the nickname *Pédaleur de Charme*, stunned everyone when he won the Tour in 1951 ahead of legendary riders like Fausto Coppi, Louison Bobet and Gino Bartali. No one should have been surprised after his performance in the stage from Brive into Agen, though. At first the *peloton* (the main group) thought it was an opportunist break — Koblet was trying out his legs — and let him go. But as the gap increased from one minute to two, two to three and four, they realised their mistake. Koblet crossed the line in splendid isolation, stopped his watch, and famously took out a comb and fixed his hair while waiting for the next man. The wait lasted 2 m 35 s, by which time his hair was perfect.

The death of Tom Simpson resonates throughout the pages of this book, in both the build-up to the fateful day on Mont Ventoux in 1967 and the shock waves that continue to this day. It was not, however, the first death in full-on competition. That befell the

Spaniard Francisco Cepeda during the 1935 Tour when he plunged into a ravine, as he hurtled down the Col du Galibier, and fractured his skull.

Twenty years earlier, the opportunities for the unfortunate Eugene Christophe to gain that elusive win were limited further because of the four races lost to the First World War (coincidentally, the 1914 Tour started on the day Archduke Franz Ferdinand was assassinated, but continued uninterrupted). The same was true for Gino Bartali and Fausto Coppi, whose careers were interrupted by the Second World War. Indeed, Bartali's two Tour wins, in 1938 and 1948, represent the largest gap between one success and the next. Many believe Coppi, despite the presence of Bartali, would have won more than his two Tours of 1949 (when nearly 30) and 1952. In the latter, Jacques Goddet, Desgrange's successor as race director, had to increase the prizes lower down the order to keep the other riders interested because Coppi was so dominant.

Coppi was one of cycling's most colourful characters: he conducted an affair with a married woman that shocked Italian society right up to the Pope, was a prisoner of war, and died, aged 40, after contracting malaria on a hunting trip in what is now Burkina Faso. Though earlier riders had used drugs to help them overcome the rigours of the Tour – strychnine and heroin were early favourites – Coppi is often recognised as having introduced the 'modern' evil to the sport. Bartali always had his suspicions. Indeed, in a television interview after he retired, Coppi was asked outright if he had used amphetamines. 'Yes,' he replied, 'whenever it was necessary.' And when was it necessary, the interviewer asked. 'Almost all the time,' he said.

––––––

When Henri Desgrange and Geo Lefevre adjourned to continue their conversation about the possibilities of putting on a round-France cycle race to boost the circulation of *L'Auto,* back in 1902, they headed out for lunch at the Taverne Zimmer on the Boulevard de Montmartre in Paris. The restaurant is now an outlet of the international franchise TGI Friday's. It would be no surprise, though, if the building had the green cross of a chemist's shop outside, or had become the headquarters of a multinational pharmaceutical group. The Tour de France has been riddled with drugs almost from day one.

It did not help that Desgrange thought the perfect Tour would involve only one man surviving. He wanted his winner to be not just the best cyclist, but a superhuman athlete as well. The route was drawn to that end. Unfortunately the man who can sprint like a cheetah, climb like a monkey and keep going, day after day, on minimal sustenance like a camel has yet to be born. Though Henri Pélissier was half-joking when he listed the essentials in a Tour rider's tool-box, it did not take his contemporaries long to recognise that they required a little extra 'help' to get through the world's greatest endurance race. Not that the Tour itself ushered in the use of illegal or dangerous drugs: there were instances of doping in the late 19th century. Nitroglycerine, which was used to revive patients after heart attacks, and which helped riders with their breathing, was an early stimulant. The original Tour riders would consume large quantities of alcohol and some took cocaine. Amphetamines, prescribed to American GIs in the Second World War to fight fatigue, took over in the second half of the 20th century as the drug of preference. No rider, said Jacques Anquetil, the great French champion of the Sixties, 'could manage simply on mineral water'. Then Tom Simpson died on Mont Ventoux, a heady cocktail of amphetamines, heat and exhaustion proving fatal, and that should have meant closure for doping at the Tour de France. It didn't; Tom Simpson died in vain.

The pages of this book are pock-marked with more and more instances of drug usage, and attendant suspicious minds, denials, always denials, police raids, suspensions and court cases, punctuated by only the odd confession. If Simpson and 1967 failed to spell the end for the dopers and their suppliers, the Tour should surely have pulled out of the trough represented by the 'Tour of Shame' in 1998. Paul Hayward's long essay at the height of *l'affaire Festina* reads like a cross between the plot for a cheap thriller and a thesis by a medical student. Quite how the race reached Paris remains a mystery; how the sport had been allowed to plumb such depths is another unanswered question. Yet despite all the hand-wringing and soul-searching, the message doesn't seem to have got through to the men at the sharp end: the riders, team sponsors, managers and *soigneurs,* the travelling masseurs. If the cheating wasn't bad enough, the damage done to the athlete himself certainly is. Amphetamines had given way to anabolic steroids, which could bring on acne and premature baldness and significantly alter body weight, but also lead to impotence and heart and liver problems. Even worse was to follow: an injection of EPO, or erythropoietin, like amphetamines, delays the onset of fatigue. By stimulating red blood cell production, it means that more oxygen can be delivered to the muscles and the body can keep going, beyond its normal limits. On the downside, as one former rider put it, it can turn blood 'to strawberry jam', clog up the arteries and have lethal consequences. Indeed, the cemeteries of Belgium and Holland are packed with young cyclists who suffered heart attacks after taking the in-vogue designer drug.

The trouble is, no one seems to be looking and learning. It is bad enough that the majority of our heroes from the past, be they Fausto Coppi, Jacques Anquetil, Marco Pantani or even David Millar, took performance-enhancing drugs. But there can be no excuse for the present-day cheats. No excuse for Floyd Landis testing positive for testosterone on the very stage in which he made his surge for victory in 2006, and being stripped of his title within days of standing on top of the podium on the Champs-Elysées. No excuse for the entire Cofidis and Astana teams needing to be kicked off the Tour in 2007, or Michael Rasmussen having to be removed by his own Rabobank team, while wearing the yellow jersey, for lying about where he was when the random dope testers called. And no excuse for Manuel Beltrán, the former team-mate of Lance Armstrong, who was expelled from the 2008 Tour after testing positive for EPO. 'When are these idiots going to learn that it's over?' asked Pat McQuaid, president of the International Cycling Union. When, indeed. It would help, for starters, though, if McQuaid's organisation stopped quarrelling with the organisers of the Tour de France, and both sides sung from the same anti-doping hymn sheet and adopted a united front.

It is with a certain trepidation that you hope the new blood on the Tour, like 2008 winner Carlos Sastre, his predecessor Alberto Contador, Cadel Evans and Britain's Mark Cavendish, represent a 'clean' era. The planned return, after a four-year retirement, of seven-time winner Armstrong adds piquancy to the 2009 race. Armstrong, who survived cancer, has never tested positive, no matter how many tests he has taken, or how many smears have been attempted by the media and fellow competitors. He is either very clever or he really is the colossus on a bike his results make him out to be. His presence will give the Tour the lift it needs after the recent tainted races. However, you almost wish that, like the former champion boxer who won't lie down, he had retired for good at his peak: you don't want to see his reputation besmirched by ignominious defeat. Or worse.

––––––––––

While the advent of Tom Simpson precipitated the interest of *The Daily Telegraph* in the Tour de France, and J.B. Wadley was handed the opportunity to reach a wider audience than he could with his cycling journals, it was Channel 4's sponsorship of the newspaper's race coverage in 1989 that was the catalyst to elevate it to another level. Suddenly more space was afforded the Tour, and features and specially commissioned articles, including several from Jacques Goddet, the veteran race director, started to appear. For most subsequent years, Phil Liggett, who took over from Wadley in 1981, was accompanied for at least part of each year's race by a succession of feature or colour writers. Michael Calvin, Ian Ridley, Paul Hayward, Sarah Edworthy, Martin Johnson, Andrew Baker and Brendan Gallagher have all done a tour of duty or two, and helped enhance the coverage in their own inestimable ways. In addition, the *Telegraph* has been able to attract top-class articles from specialists such as Samuel Abt and William Fotheringham, riders such as Chris Boardman, David Millar and Allan Peiper, and James Cracknell, who was prepared to swap a rowing boat for a bike and ride up the infamous Col du Galibier in an attempt to show just how tough it was.

However, perhaps the most heroic attempt to illustrate for the layman the difficulty of becoming a Tour de France rider came when Brendan Gallagher was given the dubious privilege of riding a leg of the 2004 Tour on the invitational *L'Etape du Tour* for amateur riders, which takes place on the Tour's rest day. Modesty forbids disclosing the identity of the person who commissioned the quest, but the telephone exchange described by Gallagher in the first of a series of articles setting out his preparations, and included in these pages, is vaguely familiar. Cycling experts wrote in and said Gallagher, an overweight, fortysomething, rugby-following lump, was mad to attempt it. In the end, he didn't: he succumbed to injury – Gallagher (groin) – and reluctantly had to fall on his pen, but not before making a decent stab at trying to reach the start line.

This book is not only a tribute to the men who pedalled to fame and fortune on France's roads; it is testimony to the fine writers the *Telegraph* has employed over the years, particularly under the stewardship of long-time sports editor David Welch. The Tour has come alive through these writers' words, all produced under the pressure of an imminent deadline. The best job in the world, though? Like any job, the reality can be a little different – but we can dream.

You've seen the newspaper, now read the book.

———

Like any rider in the Tour de France, the editor of a book such as this requires a good team around him. Consequently, thanks must go to Keith Perry, one of my former sports editors at the *Telegraph*, for coming up with the idea in the first place; to Caroline Buckland, Head of Books and Entertainment, for commissioning it; to the always helpful Gavin Fuller and his team in the *Telegraph* library for facilitating the research; to Graham Coster, Sam Harrison and Dan Steward, my editors at Aurum, for keeping the show on the road; to my trusted former colleague Andrew Baker for his excellent advice; to my wife Jane for her support, particularly in helping to input acres of copy, of which this is only a fraction; to the writers, the men and woman with the best jobs in the world, who saw it and described it so evocatively; and, not least, to the many members of what we now call the 'production team', a veritable peloton, who performed the original editing, and wrote the headlines, when the copy landed via copytaker or laptop in the bowels of Fleet Street, South Quay, Canary Wharf or Victoria. Without these unsung *domestiques* the man in the yellow jersey would never have reached the finishing line.

Martin Smith
March 2009

CHAPTER I
1903 – 1963

2 JULY 1903

PARIS DAY BY DAY

By Special Wire from Our Own Correspondent
Paris, Wednesday Night

Sixty cyclists left Villeneuve Saint Georges, a southern suburb, this afternoon, under a scorching sun, for a tremendous race, called the tour of France. The total course mapped out is 1,506 miles long. It is to be covered in six stages, and within 19 days. The energetic cyclists are tonight travelling due south, and will reach Lyon tomorrow. The next stage, which will provide a warm journey, will be to Marseille. Those of the racers who are not roasted by then will work up from Marseille to Toulouse, thence to Bordeaux and to Nantes, and, finally back to Paris, where the finish will take place on the Parc des Princes cycling track at Auteuil, on 19 July.

---

4 JULY 1903

CYCLING AND MOTORING

The great French road race, the 'Tour de France', began on 1 July, and will finish on 19 July. It is being run in stages, the finishing points of those sections being Lyon, Marseille, Toulouse, Bordeaux, Nantes and Paris, the total distance amounting to 1,500 miles. Sixty cyclists started on Wednesday for the first stage, among them being such well known roadmen as Maurice Garin, Pasquier, Auconturier, Muller and Joseph Fischer. Garin was the first man to reach Lyon, covering the 285 miles in 17 h 45 m 13 s. This gives an average speed of over 16 mph, a fine performance for an unpaced rider. The veteran Garin was expected to distinguish himself, but the surprise of the race was provided by a novice, Pagie, who was less than a minute behind the leader. The next stage to Marseille will be run tomorrow.

---

11 JULY 1903
CYCLING AND MOTORING

The 'Tour de France', of which the third stage from Marseille to Toulouse has just been concluded, has furnished the remarkable experience of a neck and neck finish between four men at the end of a journey of 284 miles. Garin took a wrong turning, which lost him, and those who were close upon him, about a quarter of an hour. He made a tremendous effort to overtake the leaders, with the result that Brange, Samson, Garin and Pothier finished in the order named, five lengths covering the four. The winner's time was 18 h 27 m 26 s, or 14½ mph, a good speed, without pacing, against the 'mistral', which was blowing strongly.

———————

23 JULY 1904
CYCLING AND MOTORING

Evidently long-distance road-racing in France has a great sporting future awaiting it. During the recent Tour de France, among the minor episodes, barely worth mentioning, were the strewing of the road with nails and foul riding among competitors, while more inter-esting events were an attack by roughs at St Etienne upon the leaders, and another at Nîmes, each incident being an attempt to favour local men, who were being beaten. In the latter case revolvers were drawn in defence of the riders. Bullet-proof suits for racing cyclists should soon be on the French market.

———————

2 AUGUST 1909

GREAT CYCLE RACE

PARIS DAY BY DAY

By Special Wire from Our Own Correspondent

Paris, Sunday Night

The great cycle race called the Tour de France, which is probably the biggest event of the kind in the world, and which has survived the heat of earlier days, was concluded today. The distance covered by the competitors was 4,487 km in 14 stages. The final run was from Caen to Paris, the distance being 251 km, and although a comparatively new champion, Jean Alavoine, finished first in the last stage, François Faber is first in the general classification, and he wins a prize of 5,000 francs. The great tour around France began on 5 July, and no fewer than 250 entries had been received. It is needless to say, however, that scarcely more than fifty were qualified for the final run, but even this is a remarkable proportion.

––––––

28 JUNE 1961

SIMPSON OUT OF TOUR DE FRANCE

Tommy Simpson, one of Britain's big hopes, is out of the Tour de France cycle race. The 23-year-old rider from Doncaster abandoned the race during the third stage of 122¾ miles from Roubaix, France, to Charleroi, Belgium, yesterday.

Simpson had been troubled by a knee injury, which he hoped would heal if he took things easily during the early stages of the Tour. But he was ten minutes behind the leaders by the halfway point and he arrived at Charleroi in an ambulance. He said: 'I abandoned because I could not pedal any more.' A doctor who examined Simpson's knee told him an operation was almost certainly necessary, and that virtually spells the end of racing this season for the plucky Simpson, who suffered terribly before he quit.

Yesterday's run over the cobbled roads of western Belgium proved disastrous for the British team, although Shay Elliott, of Dublin, and Brian Robinson again rode splendidly. Both were only five seconds behind stage winner Emile Daems, of Belgium. Two other Belgians, Aerenhouts and Van Aerde, were second and third. Robinson was the best placed British rider, finishing ninth, and Elliott, 27th, retained fourth place overall. Elliott is 5 m 27 s behind the race leader Jacques Anquetil, of France. The British team of 12 was cut to seven, as Ian Moore and George O'Brien both abandoned the race during today's run and Peter Ryalls was eliminated for arriving outside the time limit.

————

17 JULY 1961

ANQUETIL AS GOOD AS HIS WORD

Jacques Anquetil, of the French national team, yesterday won the Tour de France for the second time and fulfilled a pledge given before the start in Rouen on 25 June that he would lead from start to finish. One of Anquetil's team-mates, Robert Cazala, won the 167-mile, 21st and final stage from Tours to Paris. France also won the two other major awards, the team prize and the individual points classification, which went to André Darrigade.

The total distance ridden on the 48th Tour was 2,372½ miles. The winner's average overall speed was 22.383 mph. The best British rider was Shay Elliott, of Dublin, who was 47th and a total of 1 h 51 m 5 s behind Anquetil.

————

25 JUNE 1962

LETTER FROM PARIS

Our Own Correspondent

Paris, Sunday

For the next three weeks France's attention is being switched from Algeria, nuclear striking forces and other weighty matters of state to the 150 men pedalling their bicycles around the country in the 49th Tour de France.

With the resilience born of centuries of political crises and military adventures, France enters its summer carefree as a sandboy. In such a mood the Tour assumes major proportions. Only a presidential visit can bring out the same crowds in the cities, towns and villages along the route, despite the acknowledged fact that the now highly commercialised Tour is slipping in popular appeal.

The great names of the past — Italy's Bartali and Fausto Coppi and France's Bobet — are with us no longer. But there are new idols: Bahamontes, the Spanish eagle, Charly Gaul, the stout-hearted Luxemburger, Anquetil, Anglade and Darrigade, the French aces, and the Englishman Simpson. These will furnish our midsummer triumphs and disasters. So it will be, too, for Belgium, Italy, Spain, West Germany and Holland. This cycling Common Market was born long before tariffs were lifted at European frontiers.

———

27 JUNE 1962

SIMPSON CLIMBS TO FIFTH PLACE DESPITE PUNCTURE

Our Own Correspondent

Amiens, Tuesday

Last night, after the second day's racing, André Darrigade (France) had the right to wear both coveted jerseys of the Tour de France:

the yellow one signifying overall leadership on time and the green as the rider with the best points score for daily placings. Now he has only the green, the yellow being back on the substantial shoulders of Rudi Altig.

He won a 40-up sprint here this afternoon and the one-minute bonus awarded to stage winners was enough to put him back in the lead, which he lost yesterday to Darrigade. The Frenchman, this time, was 'cooked' after a hard day and was placed fifth.

Enormous crowds lined the streets at the start in Brussels and it was the same throughout the 130 miles to Amiens. This stretch of country is known in cycle racing circles as the 'Hell of the North' because of the rough cobbled roads, coal-dust-covered cycle paths and treacherous tramlines.

Although not as diabolical as usual it claimed among its victims Tom Simpson, who punctured before crossing the frontier and then found his front forks on the point of snapping. Had the rider fallen it would, of course, have been serious. Fortunately he stayed upright and it was merely a minor incident for the 1962 Tour de France, but a reminder all the same of the early Tours when a rider with similar trouble had to find the nearest forge and repair the damage himself. Simpson's team car had him quickly on the spare machine and he was soon back with the main group. Simpson climbed another two places on general classification and is now lying fifth.

With a strong crosswind blowing this was not a day for sensational improvements and, although there were minor skirmishes through the 1914–18 theatre of war, there were no big pushes to report. At Amiens on the Somme, however, France lost the battle for the yellow jersey when Altig beat Darrigade.

———

2 JULY 1962

SIMPSON NOW LIES SECOND

Our Own Correspondent
La Rochelle, Sunday

Half a million Frenchmen lined the 26 miles between Lucon and La Rochelle today to applaud the riders on the first individual time trial of the 1962 Tour de France. They saw last year's winner, Jacques Anquetil, storm back to form with a winning ride which confirms Tom Simpson's opinion that the rider from Rouen will again prove the overall winner.

The tension at La Rochelle's small cement track was great as Simpson finished his ride in 56 m 23 s. If he could beat Darrigade by 2 m 47 s then he would be the first British rider ever to take over the yellow jersey as Tour leader. At the halfway mark the Englishman led Darrigade by 1 m 20 s. A strong second half with a sprint at the end would have brought success. But it was Darrigade who found that little extra in defence of his jersey. Although Simpson was the faster by 1 m 55 s, he failed by 51 seconds to take over from the Frenchman.

---

6 JULY 1962

SIMPSON HURT BUT TAKES YELLOW JERSEY

Our Own Correspondent
St Gaudens, Thursday

A great landmark in Britain's progress in top Continental cycle racing was reached today when Tom Simpson, of Doncaster, took over the famous yellow jersey of leadership – the first Englishman ever to do so.

Simpson is the fifth rider to have held the *maillot jaune* in the 1962 race, but by common consent he is the most worthy. His prede-

1903 – 1963 | 9

cessors have been temporary race leaders through winning big sprints and earning a limit of bonus time, or by successfully joining in surprise breakaways.

The Doncaster rider, however, came to the top in the tradition of such illustrious Tour names as Louison, Bobet and Fausto Coppi. He prepared the ground with splendid riding on the long Sunday session of mass-start and time-trial riding. Today he finished off the job in the mountains, arriving here so far ahead of the overnight leader, Schroeders, that the presentation ceremony was completed and he was already wearing the new jersey of leadership when the Belgian crossed the line.

Not for years have the Pyrenees sorted out the field as effectively as they did today on the 129-mile stage from Pau, which twisted and doubled to include the climbs of the 7,000-foot Tourmalet, Aspin and Peyresourde passes. At the foot of the Tourmalet Simpson was brought down when a Belgian rider fell, damaging both wheels of his machine, which were quickly replaced by the team car. He hurt his shoulder and knee.

Simpson rode hard over the remaining climbs which both began in brilliant sunshine and ended in the clouds. He finished in the leading group with Dutch rider Geldermans, who is 30 seconds behind Simpson. Although well behind Simpson, Alan Ramsbottom came through his encounter with a major climb in good style. He finished nine minutes after Simpson, who had treatment for his damaged knees, which he does not think will affect his riding in future stages.

———

18 JULY 1962

ANQUETIL WINS DESPITE CRASH

SIMPSON FINISHES IN SIXTH PLACE

Our Own Correspondent

Paris, Sunday

Jacques Anquetil today won his third Tour de France, and Tom Simpson finished sixth. They held those positions, first and sixth, when the 94 riders started this morning on the final stage of 168 miles from Nevers to Paris. But whereas the last day is traditionally a 'promenade' with nothing much happening until the final miles into Paris, the 1962 race proved an exception.

After 100 miles there was a crash involving six riders, including three of the most notable men in the race: Charles Gaul (Luxembourg), Anquetil and Simpson. Fortunately none was badly hurt and they were quickly on their machines again, but it was an anxious moment for Anquetil and Simpson, who nearly had three weeks of great work wiped out.

The finishing sprint of the stage at the Parc des Princes is usually an exciting sight with riders jockeying for position on the steeply banked track. Today the stage finished in near chaos. Three riders came in with a one-minute lead over the main group with Beneditti (Italy) winning. The main pack of 80, however, slithered all over the rain-soaked track and Anquetil all but landed with his leader's yellow jersey in a pool of water. Simpson cautiously rode the stipulated lap on the grass inside the track.

'Now the hard work starts,' said Simpson on dismounting as his manager handed him his programme of races for the rest of the month. After his feat in taking over the *maillot jaune,* Simpson is a man in demand in a series of remunerative road and track races.

———

24 JUNE 1963

RAMSBOTTOM SURGES IN TO GAIN THIRD PLACE

Special Correspondent
Epernay, Sunday

There may be only one Englishman in the Tour de France, Alan Ramsbottom, but he is a real rider. He had to be to finish third in the opening stage of the jubilee race which finished here this afternoon.

The first stage of any Tour de France is always hard and fast. Today was particularly tough. First, the wind was behind the 130 riders, giving them every incentive to attack. Second, the Belgians were out to provide race favourite Jacques Anquetil with a rough ride in the hope that he would lose valuable minutes in the opening stages.

The Belgians were as good as their word. From the moment the flag was lowered at Nogent-sur-Marne, on the outskirts of Paris, they attacked, and so fierce was the pace that 16 km were covered in the first 20 minutes – a 30 mph send-off to the Tour.

If anybody wondered if Anquetil was serious in this Tour, from which he so nearly scratched, the answer came in the opening hour. During that time Anquetil crashed and fought back to the main group, with the aid of his team colleagues, and then went immediately to the front to lead a fierce chase after seven riders who had broken away. As these included the men he feared most, Van Looy and Poulidor, one can be certain that Anquetil has not entered this Tour just to satisfy his sponsors who urged him to ride. He means to win for the fourth time.

With the Van Looy-Poulidor attempt smashed, other breaks followed quickly on the switchback road towards the Champagne country. Sooner or later one of these moves had to succeed. It was about 40 miles from the finish when Bahamontes, from Spain, began what was to be the 'paying' break of the day. He was quickly joined by Pauewels and Sorgeloos (Belgium) and Ramsbottom (England).

One wondered whether Sorgeloos would 'work' and do his share of the pace-making since he is a member of the Van Looy team and might have been instructed to wait for his team leader to come from behind. But he battled hard and fast with the others and it was clear that, barring accidents, they were due to fill the first four places.

Despite an attempt by Bahamontes to get away on his own, the four were all together at Epernay, where the Belgians took the first two places, with Ramsbottom third. The Lancashire rider was surprised at his fine form.

'When Sorgeloos went to follow Bahamontes I was on his wheel. I did not feel so good. But when we really got going I felt better and was strong at the end. I had studied the finishing section carefully and thought it was one long straight. Two hundred yards from the finish two sharp bends unsettled me and I did not risk a sprint on the final straight on the loose dirt road. I believe Brian Robinson was third in the opening stage of the 1956 Tour. He finished 14th on final classification. I shall be pleased if I do as well as Brian.'

---

26 JUNE 1963

ELLIOTT'S STAMINA EARNS HIM YELLOW JERSEY

BRILLIANT RIDE WINS THIRD STAGE

Special Correspondent
Roubaix, Tuesday

Shay Elliott, of Dublin, pedalled into another page of cycling history on the windswept track today when he not only won the tough 136-mile third stage from Jambes in Belgium, but took over the yellow jersey of leadership as well. He now has the distinction of having won stages in the three biggest marathon races in the world – the tours of France, Italy and Spain.

That Elliott was in form was evident in yesterday's racing from

Rheims to Jambes. Near the end he 'countered' an attack by Van Looy, but, on the instructions of his team manager, did not persist with the effort.

A bigger plan was in mind, one which involved Elliott's team colleague and friend, Jean Stablinski, of France. It was put into operation today on the twisting, undulating course which finally got to Roubaix by way of the outskirts of Brussels and Tournai.

After 50 miles a group of 11 riders formed at the front which was not only to be the 'break' of the day, but may well prove to be one of the decisive moves of this Tour. Among the 11 were Elliott, Stablinski and Anglade, who finished second in the 1959 Tour.

Stablinski wanted to gain back the five minutes he somehow lost yesterday, Elliott to press on to try to win the stage. But they are both team-mates of Jacques Anquetil, the race favourite, and had no right to help the dangerous Anglade gain time. Fortunately for them Anglade and the other members of the breakaway group worked hard. They were soon well clear of the main pack and the lead mounted to nearly nine minutes. Twice Elliott punctured on the rough roads but each time he sprinted back strongly to the group.

Minds went back to last September when Stablinski and Elliott were together in the decisive stage in the world road championship. It was Elliott who made the 'suicide' move which enabled Stablinski to win. Today we wondered if the Frenchman would repay the move. He did not need to, the Irishman being strong enough to win under the power of his own pedalling. Four miles from the finish he attacked, his opponents had no fight left and the Dublin-born rider who now lives on the outskirts of Paris arrived at Roubaix as stage and race leader.

One of the countless spectators who were on the roadside today was Tom Simpson, yellow-jersey hero of the 1962 Tour. He held the lead only one day. Elliott may keep it longer, but he has no serious hope of winning the Tour. 'I don't climb well enough for that,' he said.

CHAPTER 2
1964 – 1969

PUNCTURE PUTS SIMPSON OUT OF RECKONING

J.B. Wadley

Toulouse, Monday

The happiest man in the track centre here after the 115-mile stage from Andorra, was Edouard Sels. In scoring his third stage win of this Tour, the Belgian took over the green jersey as leader on points classification. The unhappiest men were Tom Simpson and Raymond Poulidor, who can now be written off the list of direct challengers to Jacques Anquetil. But it was not through loss of form that this came about – each was a puncture victim.

Punctures come thick and fast in the Tour. The rapid changing of wheels by mechanics is a routine matter and such incidents are hardly ever reported. Those of Simpson and Poulidor today were exceptions to this rule.

After climbing the 8,000-foot Col de l'Envalira on leaving the Principality of Andorra, Simpson was ahead of Anquetil and a group of others when he punctured on the tricky descent. Whether delayed by the thick clouds at the summit is not at the moment known, but Simpson's team car with a spare wheel was not in sight. Impatiently Simpson had to wait by the roadside while Anquetil and Company shot by. At last help came not in the shape of the team car but Simpon's team colleague, Mastrotto, who jammed on his brakes, slipped his own wheel out and quickly transferred it to Simpson's machine.

Meanwhile Anquetil, who had not been going too well on the Col de l'Envalira, was recovering and chasing strongly after a leading group comprising Bahamontes, Poulidor and Jimenez. In his pursuit of these three dangerous men Anquetil and a few others gradually drew away from the bunch of 30 with whom Simpson was now riding. With 15 miles to go Simpson's group was two and a half minutes behind Anquetil, who had now caught the runaways.

The situation was now desperate for the Englishman. Then, in the front, it was Poulidor's turn to puncture. Instead of the usual wheel change, the mechanics slipped him a complete bicycle and in a matter of seconds the Frenchman was back in the saddle, but the mechanics' over-anxious shove sent him crashing on the road. By the time a broken wheel had been replaced, half a minute was lost. Poulidor chased madly but in vain.

Two and a half minutes after Sels won the stage (slightly ahead of the Anquetil group which also included race leader Groussard) the Simpson-Poulidor bunch of 30 arrived. Simpson was understandably furious on dismounting. 'At Briançon I lost one and a half minutes through my team car not being there. Today I have lost two and a half more and any chance of getting near Anquetil. I'm fed up and have completely lost interest in the Tour,' he said.

---

15 JULY 1964

ANQUETIL CLINCHES FIFTH VICTORY BY 55 SECONDS

J.B. Wadley
Paris, Tuesday

There never has been a finish to a Tour de France like the one Jacques Anquetil won here today – his fourth successive victory in the world's greatest road race, and his fifth in all. It was only by summoning every bit of his remarkable ability and courage that he was able to resist the desperate challenge of Raymond Poulidor in the 17½-mile time trial between Versailles and the Parc des Princes.

Anquetil won the battle by 21 seconds and, with his 20 seconds time bonus added to the 14 seconds he had overnight, takes the Tour by 55 seconds, the smallest winning margin in the 61-year history of the race.

After the short morning stage of 74 miles from Orléans to Versailles had been won by the world champion Beheyt, the 81 riders had a break before the Versailles-Paris time trial began. Starting two and a half minutes in front was Poulidor and, so far as the 40,000 crowd waiting at the Parc des Princes stadium here and the estimated 1,000,000 lining the road from Versailles were concerned, they were the only two men in the race.

The art of taking time checks by radio has never been so effectively illustrated as today. All the expertise of three rival French radio stations was marshalled to this end. After one kilometre of the 27½-km course had been covered, Anquetil led Poulidor by two seconds. Kilometre by kilometre the news was flashed through and when the halfway point was reached with Anquetil's lead increased to 12 seconds, it seemed that the Poulidor threat had been mastered.

Ears glued to transistors, the waiting crowds gasped as they learned that the margin had dropped to three seconds. Then began the descent to the Seine and a succession of fast roads. Advantage to Anquetil, who began to pull away again. Poulidor entered the Parc des Princes to an explosion of applause, sprinted the last lap and free-wheeled to a halt. He did not see Anquetil's arrival through the track tunnel, but he knew all about it through the renewed shout from the 40,000-strong crowd. And he knew that it had come too early for him to have won the Tour.

No great performances, then, by the British riders; Tom Simpson finishing in 14th position. Two years ago he was sixth.

---

25 JUNE 1965

LE TOUR – FRANCE'S MIDSUMMER MADNESS

J.B. Wadley

For British motorists the worst part of the 1965 Tour de France is already over. The race started last Tuesday in Cologne, the riders have been pedalling through Liège, Lille, Rouen and Caen, and today's 140-mile stage finishes at St Brieuc in Brittany. The often impenetrable barrier of the Tour route has therefore been rolled up behind them, and after tonight, from St Malo and all ports east, the GB driver can head south contentedly on his own tour de France.

West of St Malo, however, he had still better look out. If he doesn't he may suddenly find himself in a solid line of cars a mile from a town centre. He will wonder at first why the line does not move, until he realises the cars have no drivers. They are in the main street watching the fun. A U-turn? Not a hope. Cars are now jammed behind his, their occupants slamming the doors in their haste to get there too – old ladies who first cheered Lapize in the 1910 Tour, their grandchildren who are Poulidor fans today.

If our motorist hates sport, crowds and noise, he had better sleep in his car for a couple of hours. If not, he should take this unexpected chance of a look at the Tour de France, the great international cycling contest which for three weeks dominates the sporting press of Belgium and Italy as well as France.

One astonished British sports writer has said the Tour is like a Test match, the Cup Final and Wimbledon rolled into one. In fact, it is a little more. Except at some stage-finishes one doesn't need a ticket: there are free grandstands both sides of the road, from sea level to 8,000 feet, for nearly 3,000 miles. Moreover, rain never stops play and somebody always wins, although last year the 51st Tour was nearly drawn when Anquetil beat Poulidor by 55 seconds.

That duel between the two Frenchmen was the bitterest the Tour has known. After Poulidor finally managed to 'drop' Anquetil on the Puy de Dôme mountain his overall time for the 2,500 miles then covered was only 14 seconds less than Anquetil's. The showdown took place two days later on the last day of the race, on 14 July at that, on the 17-mile time trial between Versailles and Paris. Three-quarters of a million holidaymakers lined the roads and untold millions on the Continent followed this Bastille Day battle on radio and television.

Britain was not among the 12 countries taking the direct Eurovision service. Perhaps if Tom Simpson and not Poulidor had been Anquetil's opponent it would have been different. Yet public interest in cycle racing is steadily increasing, and we have just completed our own 'Little' Tour of Britain, sponsored by the Milk Marketing Board, and which includes trophies and awards given by *The Daily Telegraph* and *The Sunday Telegraph*. It is little in the sense that it costs £40,000 to put on for 14 days against the £500,000 for the 21-day Tour de France. It is little in that fewer people go especially to see a stage of the Tour of Britain than will be found on one mountain summit of the Tour de France.

Along the 1,400-mile Tour of Britain route one will find a few thousand enthusiasts, who know every rider in the race and probably what kind of ten-speed gear he uses and the measurements of his bicycle frame. On the whole, though, the surprisingly big crowds watching the Tour of Britain are casual customers, holidaymakers at Paignton or Bridlington who are pleasantly surprised to find additional free entertainment with a cycle race finishing on the prom. They are thrilled at the sight of 30 riders in vivid jerseys charging for the line in a 35 mph sprint, the winner throwing his arm up in triumph. But ask a spectator if the yellow jersey was in the bunch and he would probably be as bewildered as if you took a Frenchman to Lord's and asked him if he thought it would take spin.

The Tour of Britain is an important event in the international calendar and its claim to be the world's greatest all-amateur stage race is a serious one. But it is run off under certain difficulties. Unlike French Chambers of Commerce, those in Britain do not compete to be *villes étapes* (towns where stages start and finish). Some county constabularies are hostile, others welcome the Tour, but obviously they cannot close their roads to other traffic. Severe time penalties are imposed on riders straying over the white line, slipping across on the red or failing to halt.

All this is bewildering to Continentals who are used to racing on closed roads, and to some extent explains why they do not always live up to their reputations when racing over here. Using all the road, with riders in staggered formations to combat cross-winds, switching suddenly from one side to the other to make a surprise attack – these are part and parcel of road sport. Halving the area of operations is like playing doubles on a singles court.

There is a much more solid reason, however, why Continental riders coming to Britain are not always impressive. It is simply that our riders are good. Tactics are less important in the long run than well-trained hearts, lungs and legs, and a determination to get there ahead of the other fellow.

About a quarter of Britain's 10,000 racing cyclists are really serious, and perhaps 1,000 of these dream of 'doing a Simpson' and becoming a leading Continental professional. 'Continental professional' it has to be, because there is no such thing in England, although there are a hundred Independents (semi-professionals) with British Cycling Federation licences.

The pattern is therefore for the ambitious British rider to save £200, pack his bags and go to the Continent. But only a few reach the top. Brian Robinson, of Huddersfield, was the first: in 1958 he was the first Englishman to win a stage of the Tour de France. The handful of others who are capable of doing battle with Poulidor and Anquetil are Shay Elliott (Dublin), Barry Hoban (Wakefield), Alan Ramsbottom (Clayton-le-Moors), Vin Denson (Chester), and, of course, Tom Simpson (Doncaster) himself, who in 1962 was the first Englishman to wear the yellow jersey of leadership in the Tour de France.

This year a number of British riders are off to the Continent, many with good chances of success. But how many Simpsons do we need before cycling breaks through seriously in Britain?

———

13 JULY 1965

WRIGHT WINS 20TH STAGE AS SIMPSON RETIRES

J.B. Wadley

Auxerre, Monday

Sooner or later two things had to happen to two of the three Englishmen in this Tour de France and they both happened today. Michael Wright won the stage from Lyon to Auxerre – the longest of the race – and Tom Simpson retired. The success story is the logical result of a gradual building up of form as the Tour reaches its closing stages. The retirement is the inevitable outcome of a rapid collapse by the injured Doncaster rider.

For several days I have been talking to Wright about that elusive win. He is a realist and decided that instead of waiting for a big bunch sprint and 'only' finishing second – as he has done once this year and twice in 1964 – he would take a chance with an earlier attack. That chance came today 12 miles from Auxerre. Like Darrigade before him, Wright was hoping for some kind of reinforcement from behind, because it takes an Anquetil to keep away on his own from a fast-moving bunch in the final 30 minutes of a stage.

Things worked splendidly. Only one rider, Grain (France), went with him and the pair gradually drew away. On the last 200 yards the pair were still together, but Grain had no answer to the final attack by Wright, who freewheeled over the line with hands high in the air. Wright was immediately surrounded by radio and TV reporters and happily chattered away in French with a strong Liège accent. When he was five he moved from Bishop's Stortford to Liège with his widowed mother and hardly speaks a word of English.

Wright's is the third stage success for an English rider, Brian Robinson winning at Brest in 1958 and Chalons in 1964. While Wright was riding his lap of honour laden with flowers, Simpson was climbing out of the race ambulance in which he had spent the last eight hours.

Lyon was only a few miles behind when Simpson lost contact with the bunch, following a skirmish that involved among others race leader Gimondi and challenger Poulidor. After a mile on his own he retired. Simpson was in tears as his machine was hoisted on to the dreaded 'sag wagon'. In the ambulance he was given treatment for the damaged hand that had caused a sleepless night.

This injury only partly explains his collapse during the last week. I believe that a hard early-season programme followed by two marathon rides, London to Holyhead (270 miles) and Bordeaux to Paris (360 miles), just before the Tour left him with little or no reserve to face the Alpine stages last week.

––––––––––

30 JUNE 1966
TOUR RIDERS STAGE A PROTEST WALK
J.B. Wadley
Bayonne, Wednesday

A track finish that was almost a repeat performance of yesterday's at Bordeaux ended the ninth stage of the Tour de France here today. This time Karstens (Holland) just edged Planckaert (Belgium) out of first place. Altig (West Germany) keeps the yellow jersey as race leader.

These are the facts that will go in the record book. But 29 June 1966 will be more vividly remembered as the day when 122 riders went on strike against overnight dope tests at Bordeaux – the first to be made in the professional Tour de France. Three miles after the start, after the field had dawdled along in the sun, they all got off their machines and walked slowly for 100 yards. Race director Jacques Goddet immediately called Antonin Magne, the president of the Team Managers' Association, from his car to bring the protest marchers to reason.

When Magne, who won the Tour twice, did so the riders got back on to their saddles and pedalled away. Felix Lévitan, co-director of the Tour, said it may be a turning point in cycling history. Lévitan is the President of the Race Organisers' Association, who some months ago announced they were considering the possibility of confining all the classic races, including the Tour de France, to amateur riders. This was merely taken to be a threat to certain professionals, their managers and the firms sponsoring them who have in recent years taken a dictatorial attitude to the organisers of the events from which they get their living.

Today's strike is particularly serious because the organisers were conforming to French law: a bill was recently passed forbidding the use of certain products in sporting events. Contravention entails the risk of heavy fines and imprisonment. All the riders were warned before the start at Nancy that tests would be made. Last night two doctors, accompanied by a police official, visited team hotels and took samples from riders at random (not the first three in the stage as in the Tour of Britain). Those tested included Raymond Poulidor, one of the race favourites. The international commissaires are holding an inquiry into the affair and severe action is threatened if the ringleader can be identified.

When the big sprint was over at Bayonne I asked Tom Simpson his opinion of the incident. The world champion, who had fallen 40 miles from the finish and bruised his right thigh (the one broken last winter), was not a supporter of the protest. 'I think it was stupid and I never took my feet out of the toe straps. It is French law and it is pointless protesting,' he said.

———

8 JULY 1966

BRAVE BURST BY INJURED SIMPSON

J.B. Wadley
Briançon, France

While Jimenez (Spain), the stage winner, and the new race leader Janssen (Holland) were the centre of attraction at Briançon after splendid racing in the Alps, a tired and dejected Tom Simpson was taken to hospital and had five stitches put in his arm. He had fallen on the steep descent of the Col du Galibier and severely gashed an elbow and thigh. The accident delayed Simpson no more than 13 seconds, but he lost several minutes on the upward side of the Galibier in a gallant failure. It was his aggression that laid the foundation for a showdown in the mountains between Anquetil and Poulidor, who are now moving steadily towards the head of the general classification table.

Only 92 miles, the roundabout route from Bourg-d'Oisans to here included two first category mountain climbs, the Col de la Croix and the 8,000-foot Col du Galibier. The first saw the field climbing steadily in one pack until half a mile from the summit when Galera and Jimenez and Bitossi (Italy) sprinted for the mountain prize points. The descent was a mass of loops and hairpins.

On the descent Simpson fell but on the ensuing ten-mile main-road stretch in the Arc Valley he went into a lone attack. At the foot of the giant Galibier climb Simpson had a one-minute lead over the strung-out main group. Jimenez went off in search of the impetuous Englishman. After three miles' climbing, Simpson was caught but not dropped. The pair took a two-minute lead over the field. But the Spaniard soon sprinted away from Simpson and kept on his own until the finish.

Three miles from the summit, Simpson was caught and dropped by Anquetil and Poulidor, then by Huysmans and a dozen others, including Janssen. Those last two miles to the summit of the Galibier were the toughest of Simpson's career;

then came the heavy fall caused by a motorcyclist on the descent.

---

9 JULY 1966

DISTRESSED SIMPSON GIVES UP

J.B. Wadley
Turin, Friday

The Tour de France has arrived in Italy for a two-day visit and with a stage win by Franco Bitossi the home crowd is happy. So are the main visitors, the French, for Lucien Aimar has taken over the race lead from Jan Janssen, of Holland. But the British have nothing to celebrate. For, following Vin Denson's overnight elimination, Tom Simpson retired less than an hour after this morning's start from Briançon.

It was obvious from the outset that things would be difficult if not impossible for Simpson. On a flat course his injured arm would not have been so great a handicap, but this 17th stage of 100 miles began with the Col de Mont Genèvre immediately on leaving Briançon. The world champion was 'off the back' within a few miles.

At the summit of the 6,000-foot test Simpson came through with difficulty two minutes down on the main bunch, and the group which immediately followed him was composed entirely of motorcyclists, their press and radio reporter pillion passengers hovering around because *'l'abandon de Simpson'* was almost certain to be the first news story of the day.

However, an even more dramatic incident came first. After only a few hundred yards of the descent Simpson was suddenly left on his own as he sped past a badly injured rider being tended by the roadside. It was the Italian Guido de Rosso who, at the back of the main group, had struck a rut on the road and was catapulted from his machine. He had severe head and shoulder injuries.

So de Rosso – who won the Tour de l'Avenir in 1961 – entered his native land in an ambulance and only a mile across the border another was stopped to pick up the distressed Simpson. 'Downhill was the trouble,' Simpson told me. 'I just could not hold the brakes on for more than a few seconds, the pain shooting right up the arm to my shoulder. I was scared of falling off again and seriously injuring myself. I am bitterly disappointed. I know I could have been a nuisance to the leaders in the last week of the race.'

---

11 JULY 1967

GIMONDI THE FAVOURITE TAKES TENTH STAGE

SIMPSON FIGHTS ILLNESS

Briançon, Monday

Felice Gimondi, of Italy, today won the first Alpine stage of the Tour de France cycle race, the 151-mile tenth leg from Divonne-les-Bains to here. But Roger Pingeon, of France, kept the yellow jersey as overall leader.

Britain's Tom Simpson, fighting sickness, finished 16th in today's lap, losing six minutes to Gimondi, but remains seventh overall. Exhausted Simpson twice had to stop, but he came down the 19-mile long hill to the finish in an eight-man group faster than many. One of his main rivals, Dutchman Jan Janssen, was in the group with him, but also in front was Lucien Aimar, of France, who was 1 m 46 s ahead.

Simpson said: 'I had a tummy upset which gave me hell. But I'm hoping a good night's rest will put me right.'

SAMYN 'SITS IN' ON CHASE AND POUNCES FOR STAGE

J.B. Wadley
Digne, Tuesday

After being alone in the lead for 95 miles, Georges Chappe, of the French B team, was caught five miles from the finish by three riders. One of them was his team colleague, José Samyn, who had contributed nothing to the driving force responsible for Chappe's downfall, but just 'sat in'.

When the sprint came, the comparatively fresh Samyn beat Foucher (France) and Schutz (Luxembourg) to the line with poor Chappe trailing in fourth. The main pack arrived one and a half minutes later, all the chief candidates for overall victory being present, and Roger Pingeon will wear the yellow jersey for at least another day.

There were glum faces in the British camp at Briançon at the start of the 122-mile stage. Although Tom Simpson had passed a good night and got rid of his stomach trouble, Michael Wright, hurt in a crash on Sunday, was not there to answer the starter's call. 'Poor Michael couldn't even ride a bicycle 100 yards from his hotel to the start,' said team manager Alec Taylor, 'let alone ride a 122-mile stage with two big mountain passes in it.'

When Tom Simpson was seen to be in the second group following Aimar's attack on the Col d'Allos, it seemed that he might be in trouble. But he said at the finish that he knew there would be a general regroupment on the long descent and did not fight too hard to keep with the leaders.

Arthur Metcalfe was Simpson's equal on both the climbs today and came back like a Tour veteran after a quick wheel change on the crazy Allos descent. Colin Lewis and Barry Hoban were riding steadily five minutes behind and bringing up the rear was Vin Denson, who now is the Tour's 'tail-light Charlie'. Today Denson climbed both cols 'off the back', and his chances of getting back with Lewis and Hoban on the final flat miles were spoiled by ear trouble, which delayed him a further five minutes.

---

13 JULY 1967

RIOTTE SLIPS GROUP TO TAKE MARSEILLE STAGE

SIMPSON SECOND IN PACK

J.B. Wadley
Marseille, Wednesday

The riders pottered along at touring pace under the scorching sun nearly an hour behind schedule despite having started today's 129-mile stage from Digne to here 20 minutes before the advertised time. With 40 miles to go, a group of seven riders raised the temperature even higher by breaking away from the pack. Then Raymond Riotte (France) slipped away, while his team colleague Lematayer 'looked after' the other five.

Riotte topped the final climb of the day on his own and swooped down to Marseille to win the stage on the fine Municipal Stadium. Last week Riotte wore the yellow jersey for race leader for one day. Second place looked an easy number for his friend Lematayer, and that is how he finished, but only after Basso (Italy) had been relegated to last place of the next little group for too liberal use of his elbows. A minute and a half after Riotte, in came the long, colourful line of 100 riders on to the track, with the white-jerseyed Tom Simpson in second position.

That Simpson was 'having a go' in a massed sprint was an indication that he is now in much better health. A lap and a half later on the finishing line Simpson was still second, beaten only by Karstens (Holland) and satisfied with his form. The other members of the British team were all in the big bunch, and like everybody else very hot, tired and thirsty.

If the cycling racing specialist's notebook contained nothing of importance for most of the day, that of the human interest writer was full enough. The route was loaded with colour and variety, taking the riders from snow-cooled Alpine freshness at Digne to the Mediterranean by way of the hot, sandy hills of Provence on winding roads, climbing and rambling among the views, olive groves, lavender fields and patches of golden corn.

The riders were performing all the antics Tour men have been up to on the heat-wave stages since 1903; hopping off their machines, splashing their faces in village fountains, filling bottles from the same source or raiding cafés for beer or mineral water. Some roadside picnickers had bottles snatched from under their noses. The photographers' field day included a shot of Raymond Poulidor, usually the master but now – following his accident and considerable loss of time – the *'domestique'*, pacing his colleague Aimar back to the group after one of these incidents.

Nobody was surprised at the day's leisurely pace. The riders are understandably tired after 13 days' riding and they also had in mind that tomorrow's stage includes the 5,750-foot climb of the Ventoux mountain. Even with air-conditioning, climbing this 'giant of Provence' on a bicycle is hard enough. In the prevailing heat, and in battle order, there are likely to be heavy casualties to report tomorrow night.

---

14 JULY 1967

BRITON DIES IN TOUR DE FRANCE

Our Correspondent
Carpentras, Thursday

Tommy Simpson, the British professional cyclist, collapsed while racing on the Ventoux mountain in today's stage of the Tour de France. He died in hospital at Avignon where he was taken by a police helicopter.

Simpson, aged 29, had kept with members of the leading group of riders, including the race leader, Roger Pingeon, of France, until three miles from the summit of the 5,750-foot mountain, known as the 'Giant of Provence'. The Englishman then dropped back and was seen to be pedalling with extreme difficulty. Eventually he fell by the roadside.

The British team car, driven by Ken Ryall, a cycle dealer from Twickenham, was immediately behind, and Harry Hall, a mechanic, went to help Simpson. Simpson said he wanted to continue, remounted and rode a further half-mile under the scorching sun – temperatures were in the nineties. He fell again and when the Tour doctor arrived within a minute or so Simpson was unconscious.

At the start of today's stage, Simpson was seventh in the overall placings. Mr Alec Taylor, British team manager, said tonight that the British team would race tomorrow.

Tommy Simpson was the most successful road racing cyclist Britain had produced, winning the world professional road championship in 1965. His other victories included the 'Bordeaux–Paris', 'Tour of Flanders', 'Milan–San Remo' and the 'Tour of Lombardy' classic races.

---

14 JULY 1967

TRAGEDY OVERSHADOWS ALL ON DAY OF SORROW

J.B. Wadley
Carpentras, Thursday

The tragic death of Tom Simpson, who collapsed while climbing the Ventoux mountain and died later in hospital in Avignon, cast a shadow over everything else in today's 131-mile stage from Marseille to Avignon. The stage was won by Jan Janssen (Holland) who out-sprinted a small group which had been the strongest on the mountain test.

It was hot enough at Marseille at the start of the stage and, as the route struck north towards the Ventoux country and left the Mediterranean breeze behind, temperatures went even higher. In such conditions it was not surprising to find the field pottering along again, with water-bottle filling the chief occupation.

Then, after only ten miles, there was a serious accident when a dog dashed into the tightly-packed bunch, at that moment travelling downhill quite fast, bringing down a number of riders. Two of them had to be taken by police helicopter to hospital at Marseille where Mugnaini (Italy) was found to have a double fracture of the arm and severe shoulder injuries, and Peffgen (Germany) a broken collarbone.

The field of 100 kept together for the next 80 miles as the great hump of the Ventoux loomed out of the haze, and at the village of Bedoin came the sign that the summit of the 'Giant of Provence' was 23 km ahead.

It had been freely stated that Poulidor (France) would not bother if the Spanish rider, Jimenez, went off on one of his solo raids, but would protect Roger Pingeon as he did on the great Galibier climb on Monday. Poulidor, however, went into an early attack on the early slopes of the mountain with the obvious intention, once again, of forcing the Italians to chase, while Pingeon followed.

Poulidor was caught, but attacked again, taking Jimenez with him. There were then two groups behind, one containing race leader Pingeon and Gimondi, the second including Janssen (Holland), Aimar (France) and Simpson. After riding with this group for a mile or two, Simpson dropped off the back and eventually collapsed.

Jimenez topped the summit of the 5,750-foot Ventoux on his own but was caught by the stronger of the two chasing parties which had regrouped on the final 10-mile flat road to Carpentras where Jimenez won the sprint. Pouldior, spent from his early efforts, could not keep with this group and finished many minutes down, but had the satisfaction of knowing his action had helped Pingeon retain the yellow jersey.

————

14 JULY 1967

SIMPSON: JUST AT PINNACLE OF HIS CAREER

OBITUARY

David Saunders

Tom Simpson's death at the age of 29 and at the height of his racing career has shocked the whole cycling world and has brought a terrible sadness to British fans everywhere. His name had become a legend among cyclists in this country, and the measure of his achievements are hard to evaluate in the cold light of day. Always a fighter, sometimes foolhardy and impetuous, he brought an entirely new look to the Continental idea of an Englishman. His cycling life was dogged with bad luck throughout. Even in his amateur days crashes upset his chances. A spill in the World Amateur Championships in 1958, when he dislocated his jaw, possibly prevented him from taking his first world title.

Simpson's courage was beyond question at all times and he fought through for another seven years before his dream came true and he won the world professional road title at San Sebastian in 1965. Even then the fates were against him for, only three months later, he broke his leg in a ski-ing accident. His world title win made history, but that was just another chapter for this splendid rider. He had already made his mark in the pages of sport by being the first Englishman ever to hold the yellow jersey in a Tour de France, to win the Belgian Tour of Flanders, the Italian Milan–San Remo and Tour of Lombardy classics, and countless other events both home and abroad.

He began his cycling career at the age of 14 with the Harworth and District Cycling Club, in Nottinghamshire. Although born in Durham, he lived most of his life near here and was always determined to be a great rider. His first real chance came in 1956 when, at the age of 18, he rode for Britain in the Olympic Games in Melbourne. He gained a bronze medal in the team pursuit event, and back in Britain, went from strength to strength, eventually winning the British pursuit title in 1958, and then moving to France to seek fame and fortune the following year.

His first appearances abroad were sensational, and he won no less than 60 events that season, culminating in his turning professional and finishing fourth in the world road championships. After victory in the French Tour of the South-West in 1960, he rode his first major Tour without any great success.

Despite all the other major races and his countless victories, it was the Tour de France which was always the centre of attraction for him. I remember him telling me not long ago that it had always beaten him in the end, but one day he would win it. That day will never come now, but, knowing him personally, as a friend for many years, I think he would be happy at going the way he did. In his own humorous way he would surely have commented that he had abandoned for the third successive year.

He leaves a wife, Helen, and two small daughters. He will be sadly mourned in cycling circles the world over and it will be a long time before this country can produce an equal both in terms of ability and courage.

FIELD LET HOBAN TAKE 14TH STAGE AS FINAL TRIBUTE

J.B. Wadley
Sète, Friday

Interviewed by a cycling magazine last winter about his plans for 1967, Barry Hoban – so often unlucky with punctures and crashes in the big classic races – said: 'Next season I am going to win a really big race.'

Today Hoban kept his word by taking the 125-mile stage from Carpentras to Sète, but it is a race in which he would rather have finished last. He arrived at the Mediterranean port five and a half minutes ahead of the main pack – which had not made the slightest effort to chase after him following his slight acceleration 30 miles from home.

Almost unanimously, a hundred riders had decided before the stage started that they would like one of the British team to win, as homage to their friend and rival, Tom Simpson, who died yesterday. A few Belgian riders, I am told, wanted to take up the chase, but the 'doyen' of the field, ex-world road champion, Jean Stablinski (France), went to the front to take command and there was no further dissent. Barry Hoban pedalled into Sète the unhappiest winner the Tour de France has known and, in tears, he nearly broke down when surrounded by photographers, reporters and radio commentators.

The gesture of the other riders was deeply touching, and if the manner in which Hoban won was far from the way that Tom Simpson scored his great victories, there was nothing prearranged about the sprint for second place. The hundred riders charged for the line in the kind of massed 'gallop' Tom Simpson loved so much. Guido Reybroeck (Belgium) won from his compatriot Van den Berghe, the latter being the man who beat Simpson into second place in a stage finishing here at Sète last year.

This morning Hoban and the three other British riders left in the Tour, Arthur Metcalfe, Colin Lewis and Vin Denson, were the first to be called to the line, where in obvious distress, and wearing black armbands, they and their colleagues heard Jacques Goddet, the race director, speak movingly of Tom Simpson, the champion and the man.

A minute's silence was then observed, before the flag was dropped to start the saddest 14 July in the history of the Tour. The field's sympathy was soon apparent when Lewis was manoeuvred into position so that he could win a special 'prime' of 500 francs (£35).

---

24 JULY 1967

PINGEON STORMS HOME IN TOUR DE FRANCE

J.B. Wadley
Paris, Sunday

Roger Pingeon, the man who last year could not make up his mind whether to be a racing cyclist or a plumber, was in no doubt today. He had just ridden his final lap of honour as winner of the Tour de France and should be £20,000 richer for it by the start of the next racing season.

At Fontainebleau this morning, Pingeon put on his 16th yellow jersey in 17 days. The odd day was when Riotte, his team colleague, took it over at Strasbourg. He lined up this morning with the field of 87 for the 65-mile stage to Versailles, finishing three hours later in the big bunch sprint, elbow-to-elbow with his only real rival in the race, Julio Jimenez, of Spain.

Before the laps of honour the three British riders finishing the race, Barry Hoban, Colin Lewis and Arthur Metcalfe, with team manager, Alec Taylor, stood on the podium while the great stadium was silent for a minute in memory of Tom Simpson, the

British rider who died during the race. Hoban's ride during the final stages brought the British team's total prize money to almost £1,000. The British cyclists left in the Tour after Simpson's death decided that a share of their prize money would be sent to Mrs Simpson.

The return to national teams in the Tour was a great success from the public's point of view and an announcement will shortly be made as to whether the same system will be used next year. One thing, however, is certain. The 1968 Tour de France will not finish at the Parc des Princes. Work will begin tomorrow on demolishing the back straight of the cycle track to make way for a motorway.

-----

4 AUGUST 1967

DRUGS 'CONTRIBUTED' TO SIMPSON'S DEATH

Alexander MacMillan

Avignon, Thursday

Tom Simpson, the British cyclist, was not killed by the drugs he had taken, but they contributed to his death, it was officially announced in Avignon tonight. M Palavesin, an Avignon magistrate, issued a communiqué giving the cause of his death during the Tour de France as 'cardiac collapse, attributable to an exhaustion syndrome'.

The report said that contributory factors were 'unfavourable atmospheric conditions (heat, lack of oxygen, atmospheric humidity); intense physical overstrain; and the use of medicines of the type found on the victim which are dangerous'. Traces of amphetamine and methyl-amphetamine were found in Simpson's bloodstream, urine and intestines. These drugs were also found in the pharmaceutical products Simpson had in his pocket when he collapsed on Mont Ventoux. The dosage taken by

Simpson was insufficient in itself to kill him, the report said. But as a result of them he 'exceeded the limit of his physical capacity', and brought on other conditions which caused his collapse.

It is not yet known whether a judicial inquiry, with a view to a possible prosecution, is to be held by the examining magistrate. The organisers of the Tour de France have not disclosed whether the conditions of next year's race will be altered as a result of the findings on Simpson.

---

22 JULY 1968

JAN JANSSEN CLINCHES IT – BY 38 SECONDS

J.B. Wadley
Paris, Sunday

Next year a Hollywood company is to make a $1 million film with a Tour de France background. Whatever scenario is planned might well be replaced by today's cliff-hanger finish in which Jan Janssen, of Holland, snatched victory in the final half-hour of the 35-mile time trial.

The Dutchman's task was against 17 seconds on the overnight leader Herman van Springel (Belgium A) in today's racing. In the morning 85-mile event they finished together in the main group so the afternoon time trial decided the issue. After 17½ miles Van Springel, who was struggling, and Janssen arrived here at the Piste Municipale to a tremendous welcome, not only the winner of the stage but the Tour de France as well.

The 38 seconds which separated him from Van Springel is the lowest winning margin in the 55 Tours de France. This race has been called the Good Health Tour because of the strict daily dope tests. The cleaning up of the Tour has given an entirely new slant on things, particularly for British riders. Despite having the *'lantern rouge'* in John Clarey and the team also last, our riders had a good

Tour on the whole with about £2,500 in prize money to prove it. About £750 of this went to Barry Hoban in one great day last week when he won his second Tour stage – and only a flat tyre prevented Michael Wright winning at Auxerre on Saturday.

I believe in two or three years Britain will have a first-class Tour de France team capable not only of winning stages, but of playing a leading role in the battle for the yellow jersey.

------

16 JULY 1969

MERCKX PULVERISES HIS RIVALS ON BIG CLIMBS

J.B. Wadley
Moureax Ville Nouvelle

Like a world champion boxer picking his punches in an exhibition bout with the local fighter, Eddy Merckx yesterday hit his rivals where and when he liked. The chosen spot was halfway through the 134-mile stage from Luchon, which embraced four major climbs in the Pyrenees.

After taking a lead of five seconds at the top of the Col du Tourmalet, Merckx just rode away on his own to finish the stage nearly eight minutes ahead of the next group of riders. Merckx accordingly almost doubled his overall lead on Roger Pingeon, while Raymond Poulidor goes up to third place.

When the first two climbs (the Peyrespourde and Aspin) had passed, with Galera of Spain topping each ahead of a group of 30, it seemed that Merckx at last might be riding a defensive race. Then came the savage, 6,500-foot Col du Tourmalet. A mile from the top of the ten-mile climb, only Merckx and nine others remained at the front. Here, Merckx accelerated, and together with team colleague, Van den Bossche, rode through a huge cheering crowd with a five-second lead. Then, in the manner he has made his own, Merckx followed up this 'feint' with the real thing, a spectacular and daring descent on the crazily dropping road.

By the time the groups behind had sorted themselves, Merckx was away on another 'solo'. Immediately the Tourmalet descent was over, another great col reared up, the Aubisque. At the top, Merckx had no less than seven minutes in hand. Downhill again at a tremendous speed and the lead remained at seven minutes.

This would have frightened every rider in the world except Merckx, who put his head down and pedalled on. He had finished half a dozen radio and TV interviews by the time Dancelli led in the little group with whom he had parted company on the Tourmalet. Felice Gimondi came in four minutes later. Finally, half an hour after Merckx, the main bunch arrived. The last man in on this scorching day in the Pyrenees was Derek Harrison. He crashed near the bottom of the Aubisque, damaged his bicycle, and had to wait ten minutes for a service car.

---

21 JULY 1969

MAGNIFICENT MERCKX SWEEPS THE BOARD

J.B. Wadley in Paris

There were no surprises on the final day of an outstanding Tour de France. Eddy Merckx, who has stood out like a giant on all terrains, won the final 23-mile hilly time trial into Paris yesterday afternoon with another great display of unpaced riding. In doing so, he helped himself to a further minute's lead over the two Frenchmen, Roger Pingeon and Raymond Poulidor, who finished second and third on overall classification.

Usually, at the end of the Tour de France, the photographers line up the race leader in his yellow jersey, the points winner in green and the winner of the Grand Prix de la Montagne. This year, the amazing Merckx deprived them of the traditional shot by taking all three competitions. And Merckx and his nine Faema colleagues — eight Belgians and an Italian — also won the team contest.

Their total winnings, with bonuses, will probably be around £40,000. British promoters of road and track events who would like to have Merckx on their programme next season should start saving up immediately. He has already signed 60 contracts for such personal appearances at an average of £600. Some promoters, it is being said, are willing to pay £1,000 for a single race.

Cheers rang out as the various teams rode their laps of honour at the Stade Municipale in Paris. There was tremendous applause every time Merckx appeared — 50,000 Belgians were on the time-trial course or in the stadium.

In contrast to the moving scene in the same stadium a year ago, when he won the Tour in the last ten miles, Jan Janssen, of Holland, was given a roasting by the Belgians. Janssen said in a recent television interview that Merckx's month's suspension, for an alleged doping offence in the Tour of Italy, should not have been lifted to allow him to ride in the Tour de France.

The three British riders, Barry Hoban, Michael Wright and Derek Harrison, were warmly applauded for their fine ride. So was Joaquim Agostinho, the Portuguese rider, who took two stages and might one day win the Tour — if Merckx stays at home.

CHAPTER 3
THE 1970s

MERCKX, CHAMPION AGAIN

J.B. Wadley in Paris

Eddy Merckx, of Belgium, yesterday won the Tour de France for the second year in succession and joined the distinguished company of Fausto Coppi, of Italy, and Jacques Anquetil, of France, who are the only other men to have won the Tour and the Giro d'Italia in the same year.

Merckx finished the Tour as he began it 23 days ago – with a time-trial victory. Yesterday's ride, however, was much more difficult than the five-mile sprint at Limoges. The course between Versailles and the Stade Municipale, on the east side of Paris, covered more than 33 miles of difficult country.

The Belgian won by almost two minutes from Luis Ocaña, of Spain, with Gösta Pettersson, of Sweden, another half a minute behind in third place. It brought Merckx his eighth stage success, equalling the 40-year-old record of Charles Pélissier, of France.

Merckx's formula for overall victory was similar to that of 1969 – aggression all the way, although he had to stay on defence for two days in the Pyrenees after a bout of stomach trouble.

Last year, Merckx's nearest challengers were the experienced Pingeon and Poulidor, of France. This time, the chief opposition came from two new professionals, Joop Zoetemelk, of Holland, and Pettersson (Sweden). Walter Godefroot, also of Belgium, won the points classification and led his Salvarani colleagues to team victory. Merckx was again the overall winner of the Grand Prix de la Montagne competition.

---

9 JULY 1971

OCAÑA RACES NINE MINUTES AHEAD OF MERCKX

J.B. Wadley in Orcières-Merlette

After two days probing the defences of the 'unbeatable' Eddy Merckx, Luis Ocaña yesterday launched a devastating attack to which the Belgian star had no answer. The Spanish rider arrived under a scorching sun at this 5,500-feet winter sports station nearly nine minutes ahead of Merckx, who led in a group of ten, who included the overnight leader Joop Zoetemelk (Holland). In between the triumphant winner and the beaten ten, little Lucien van Impe (Belgium) rode with great tenacity to take second place in the stage.

Although he had been riding practically on his own over mountainous country for more than 70 miles, Ocaña was remarkably fresh on completing his great ride. Now holding the race lead by a comfortable margin and with no racing today, the 26-year-old Spaniard, who has lived in France for 16 years, has a great chance of winning the Tour.

The Portuguese rider Joaquim Agostinho started the day's remarkable story by attacking soon after the start of the 83-mile stage from Grenoble and reaching the summit of the 3,000-foot Cote de Laffey 15 seconds ahead of Ocaña, Zoetemelk and Van Impe, with Merckx already two minutes in arrears. The four riders, with Ocaña doing most of the pacemaking, continued to gain over the Belgian, whose efforts to whip up the pace were hindered by three of Ocaña's team colleagues. This climb was quickly followed by a 'hot spot' sprint which Ocaña won.

With severe mountain climbing ahead it seemed likely the four would keep together, but Ocaña meant business in a big way and forged ahead at the foot of the difficult 5,000-foot Col du Noyer. With a tremendous display of climbing, fearless descending and strong time-trialling on the few flat sections, Ocaña rapidly drew away from his companions.

It was not surprising to find all rival riders in the Merckx group leaving the pacemaking entirely to him. Merckx accepted his lot with dignity and courage and made new friends by the way he took his defeat. Even when not at his best Merckx is still a great rider. After doing all the work chasing after Ocaña he was still strong enough to win the mountain sprint for third place.

---

13 JULY 1971

MERCKX TAKES OVER AS OCAÑA CRASHES

J.B. Wadley in Luchon

Even in Spain, yesterday's Pyrenees stage victory by Jose-Manuel Fuente will pass almost unnoticed against the tragedy of Luis Ocaña, knocked out of the Tour when wearing the yellow jersey and with every chance of winning in Paris on Sunday. As the race crossed the frontier for a 12½-mile visit to Spain, where the name Ocaña was painted in huge letters on the road, the national hero was being transported by helicopter ambulance to St Gaudens, unconscious and suffering from chest injuries.

It was a distressing end to a tremendous battle which Ocaña had been fighting with Eddy Merckx for the last six days. Both fell on the dangerous descent of the 4,000-foot Col de Mente during a blinding rain storm. Merckx was quickly on his feet and back in the race, but Ocaña was still lying on the road when he was run into by Joop Zoetemelk (Holland), who was unable to control his cycle because of a puncture.

Almost from the start of the 134-mile stage from Revel, Merckx had attacked Ocaña, on the flat, up hill and down, but each time the Spaniard replied confidently. The ferocity of the duel split the pack to pieces, and of the leading challengers only Zoetemelk and Lucien van Impe (Belgium) were finding enough to stay with them.

Among those who failed was Gösta Pettersson (Sweden), third last year, but obviously feeling the effects of his winning Tour of Italy ride earlier this season. He retired before the end-of-stage climbs began, and was in the ambulance called for the unfortunate Ocaña.

While groups of riders were handicapped on the dangerous Col de Mente descent – under rushing flood-water in many places – Fuente, nearly two hours down on overall time, was able to pick a path and increase his lead. After being first to the top of all four cols, the Spaniard arrived at Luchon more than seven minutes ahead of the next party, from which Merckx won the sprint for second place.

Merckx, who overnight was nearly seven and a half minutes behind Ocaña, automatically takes over the yellow jersey. 'I hoped to win it from Luis during the next three days, but I am distressed it should have happened like this,' he said, adding that he would not wear the jersey as a mark of respect to Ocaña.

———

23 JULY 1973

OCAÑA COMPLETES OVERALL VICTORY IN FINE STYLE

David Saunders in Paris

Luis Ocaña became only the second Spanish rider to win the Tour de France when he finished the 20th and final stage of this 60th Tour at Vincennes, on the outskirts of Paris, yesterday, with the main field. Federico Bahamontes, the 'Eagle of Toledo', was the first in 1959.

Earlier in the day Ocaña had won the ten-mile time trail in Versailles, again crushing the opposition to record his fifth victory of the event. He covered the course at an average speed of just over 28 mph. The French champion, Bernard Thevenet, was second, but, even in the short distance, he lost 25 seconds to

Ocaña, who again won on the new British-built Titanium racing machine he has ridden for the last ten days. Thevenet went one better on the afternoon's 55-mile final run, winning the stage with a tremendous burst of power just ahead of the main pack, to the roars of appreciation from the packed stands in the Stade Municipale.

Britain's Barry Hoban, who produced a magnificent sprint on Saturday to win the 19th stage into Versailles, his second stage victory of the Tour, was not well placed as the bunch swept into the stadium, led by Thevenet. Even so, he took 11th place. Hoban, though, will no doubt be satisfied with his performance, which helped his Gan-Mercier team to win the team points section of the race, while Ocaña's Bic team were the overall winners. Hoban finished fifth in the points classification and second in the 'hot spot' sprint, and has earned himself more than £1,000 for his fine riding – a reasonable share for one man from the total prize list of £110,000.

The amount has increased this year, but even so the riders failed to race for it with any real degree of animation, and apart from Ocaña, or perhaps because of him, it was a dull Tour. This can easily be seen from the average speed over the three weeks of racing, just over 21 mph, the lowest recorded in the event since 1952. One must say that the riders were hardly to blame.

The Belgian champion, Frans Verbeeck, put the point over succinctly enough just before he crashed and retired last week, when he said: 'We are treated like animals in a circus, and I shall never ride the Tour again under these circumstances.'

He was referring to the many miles of travelling riders had to do in order to reach their hotels after some stages ended, and also to travel to the start the next day. This all necessitated teams having to be on the move sometimes at six in the morning. A good example was last Saturday's stage when the field had to travel by train from Clermont Ferrand to the start of Bourges, a distance of 120 miles.

30 JUNE 1974

HARD-WORKING HOBAN GAINS SPRINT BONUS

David Saunders in Plymouth

Dutchman Henk Poppe won the second stage of the Tour de France at Plymouth yesterday on the first occasion of the event in Britain, where over 30,000 packed the roadsides to witness the world's best riders in action for just over 100 miles. The race covered 14 laps of a seven-mile circuit around the Plympton by-pass and the early morning rain, which must have kept many away, was replaced by warm sunshine for the stage.

The man everyone wanted to win was, of course, Barry Hoban, who rides for the French Gan-Mercier team, but although he was well in evidence throughout, victory eluded him on this important day. Hoban worked hard a number of times, no doubt spurred on by the large crowd, and he gained eight seconds' bonus time from winning one of the day's two 'hot spot' sprints and coming third in the other. This helped him to move up to ninth place, overall while Dutchman Gerben Karstens, who was also prominent in the sprints, gained even more through taking fourth place in the mass sprint for the finish, contested by 128 riders, and this moves him to a third place overall.

The race leader, Joseph Bruyère, of Belgium, a team colleague of the great Eddy Merckx, was never far from the front, and so Britain's first sight of the most famous sporting event in the world proved a resounding success.

––––––––

22 JULY 1974

MERCKX TRIUMPHS TO EQUAL 1964 RECORD

David Saunders in Paris

Eddy Merckx, of Belgium, won the Tour de France, which ended in Paris yesterday, for the fifth time, and equalled the record set by Frenchman Jacques Anquetil in 1964. Merckx was the eventual winner of the 22nd and final stage of 91 miles from Orléans to the stadium at Vincennes, on the outskirts of the French capital, although he finished second in the big bunch sprint behind Patrick Sercu. There was a protest by another Belgian, Gustave van Roesbroeck, that Sercu had switched his line in the final 50 metres, which he certainly did, and Sercu was put down to third place for the infringement, which gave Merckx another victory.

Merckx had tried desperately to create a record of nine stage wins, having equalled the present record of eight wins back in 1970. But the odds proved too much for him after he won the first section of Saturday's stage of 73 miles from Vouvray to Orléans. The Belgian was hoping to win the time trial over 25 miles at Orléans later that day, but his chances were ruined by ten seconds, which was the margin between him and a young Belgian rival, Michel Pollentier.

Pollentier won the stage but – more important – veteran Raymond Poulidor, who took fifth place on the time trial, moved to second overall position as a result of a much better time than the Spanish champion, Vicente López-Carril. It left only one second separating the two men at the start of the final day and with bonuses to be won at the two 'hot spot' sprints on the stage, the Gan-Mercier team not only protected Poulidor but got him a second place in one. This meant he ended with a five-second advantage over the Spaniard while his British team colleague Barry Hoban carried off the overall prize in the 'hot spot' section. That, plus his stage victory, was a fine achievement by the British rider.

HOBAN'S EIGHTH STAGE

David Saunders in Bordeaux

Britain's Barry Hoban won the eighth stage of the Tour de France yesterday, 84 miles from Angoulême to Bordeaux, with a superbly timed effort, taking victory by about half a wheel in a big group finish. This was Hoban at this best, using his vast experience to deliver a telling blow to the hopes of the other big-time sprinters who contested the finish.

'Nobody knows this track better than I do,' said a delighted Hoban to me after the finish. He is certainly right there because he won in Bordeaux in 1970 and it was back in 1964 when he finished second in a stage here in his first Tour de France. But now he is riding his tenth Tour and yesterday was his eighth stage victory, executed with all the dash and fire of a man much less than Hoban's 35 years of age.

Once the field came on to the track I thought Hoban had no chance. Boxed in and lying about 14th as they swept over the line with a full lap to cover it seemed too much to ask of him. Italian Francesco Moser broke clear in the back straight, followed by Belgian Walter Godefroot, the latter with a torn jersey and a nasty wound on his right arm after a crash ten miles from the start.

Gradually the field closed on them and as they came out of the final bend the big group were together. Suddenly Hoban unleashed his finishing burst and reached the front exactly as the line came up. 'I knew Moser had gone too soon,' Hoban told me. 'This is a big track, 500 metres, and there's still nearly 200 metres left when you come round the last bend. Once we were together I knew I had a chance.'

---

12 JULY 1975

MERCKX ATTACKED BY SPECTATOR ON CLIMB

David Saunders in Clermont Ferrand

Eddy Merckx, Belgian's star rider, claimed he had been punched in the stomach by a spectator during the last 200 yards of the Puy de Dôme mountain climb on yesterday's 14th stage of the Tour de France. Merckx crossed the line and collapsed against a crush barrier, vomiting and racked with spasms, clinging to the barrier and supported by newsmen.

Police said that Merckx recognised his attacker as he rode back down the mountain. He called a policeman and had the youth's name and address taken, and would start legal proceedings against the youth, whose name was not disclosed.

Although Belgium's Lucien van Impe won yesterday's stage of the Tour, the main interest centred on the man who finished second on this 108-mile ride from Aurillac to the summit of the Puy de Dôme — Bernard Thevenet, of France. Thevenet lost 15 seconds to Van Impe, but gained 34 priceless seconds on race leader Merckx, who finished third.

----

21 JULY 1975

THEVENET HOLDS OFF AMAZING MERCKX

David Saunders in Paris

Bernard Thevenet became the first Frenchman to win the Tour de France for eight years when he finished with the main field at the end of the 22nd and final stage on the Champs-Elysées yesterday, watched by an enormous crowd. Estimated at around 250,000, they jammed the famous thoroughfare for the whole of its near-four-mile stretch, which the race had to cover 27 times to total 102 miles. It was a superb spectacle. Belgian Walter Godefroot won the sprint to take the stage victory, with Britain's Barry Hoban fifth after there had been many attacks and brave lone efforts during the stage.

This has been a very hard Tour, and Eddy Merckx, although second overall, has come out of it with as much publicity and acclaim as if he had won. His decision to stay in the race against doctor's orders has made him a hero all over Europe.

Usually Merckx has all the luck, but this year it deserted him just when he needed it most. The crash when he broke his cheek-bone was the last straw, but I am sure he would have tried to regain the lead more decisively than he did. Even though in pain, he made the occasional assault but it was no use – not even yesterday when the crowd was electrified by his sudden bursts of speed. But the race leader was never far behind.

One cannot end without some words of praise for Thevenet, who throughout the race has ridden with fire and determination. Perhaps a little fortunate to find Merckx not at his best, Thevenet is a worthy winner and his ability to fight and his courage cannot be questioned.

Britain's Hoban, although finishing 68th overall, again made his mark on the race. A stage win at Bordeaux, second in the 'hot spot' sprint section and fifth in the points was another good ride. His French Gan-Mercier squad took the overall team victory, Hoban's contribution in the early days being an aid to their success. The 2,500-mile race was much more mountainous than usual and accounted for 54 men failing to finish the course.

MONEY-SPINNING CYCLE WHEELS IN TOUR DE FRANCE

Anne Sington in Paris

The Tour de France, one of Europe's most famous sporting events, started life as cycling with the addition of some advertising; today it has transformed itself into advertising with the addition of some cycling. Advertising revenue from the 100 vehicles in the 'advertisement caravan' which follows the Tour competitors has been estimated at £400,000. But this is peanuts compared with the investment made by the 18 big companies who invest in prizes.

This year they have contributed over £1.3 million for motives in which philanthropy vies with enlightened self-interest – and loses. The Miko ice-cream company, which offers the daily prize for the leading competitor (giving the right to wear the famous yellow singlet), makes an outright contribution of £700,000 to the organisers of the Tour – the popular newspaper *Le Parisien Libéré* and the sports paper *L'Equipe*. In return, the contract gives it the right to have its trade name appear in sports news photographs in each of the publications three times during the three-week Tour. These are taken on the podium, as the victor shrugs himself into the prized garment at the end of each day's lap.

Miko's name is blazoned fore and aft on the singlet of the winner, who is naturally the centre of attention for 13 million Frenchmen who line the route to cheer on their heroes. The same people then go home and watch it all over again on television – and there's no prize for guessing what the camera is focusing on either. M Ginez, Miko's director of publicity, estimates that each year's Tour gives him up to three hours of television time at moments when viewers are not dashing to kitchen or bathroom. He still hasn't finished working out what this is worth in terms of 15 or 30-second publicity shots.

Companies who finance a team, as opposed to merely buying

advertising space on the backs of those travelling salesmen, are operating on the Tom Tiddler's ground between sport and big business, and the gold and silver picked up indicate that the latter has the upper hand. Raymond Poulidor, for instance, who rides in the team sponsored by Miko and Mercier bicycles, earns nearly £1,200 a month the year round, and may pocket a further £50,000 or more in fees for appearing in events for which his Tour de France name has made him a draw.

Big money also changes hands over the exact route followed by the race. Local townships queue up for the privilege of spending a minimum of £14,000 to lure the Tour their way. Local business gets most of this back in hotel and restaurant bills and related spending, but the real prize for many places is that the Tour puts them on the map. In 1971, a new ski resort, Orcières-Merlette, went into debt to raise the money to play host for one night. The gamble paid off. It was there that one of the most dramatic incidents of any Tour took place, when Luis Ocaña deprived the champion Eddy Merckx of the yellow singlet. Suddenly, the name of Orcières-Merlette was on the lips of cycling enthusiasts throughout Europe. If the point of advertising is not that it is whitest or fastest or yummiest but just that you remember its name, then the Tour de France is the perfect medium.

---

25 JULY 1977

TESTS OVERSHADOW THEVENET'S VICTORY

David Saunders in Paris

Bernard Thevenet, of France, won the 1977 Tour de France yesterday when he finished in the main field after one of his rival compatriots, Alain Meslet, won the second section of the 22nd stage, a 56-mile road race around the Champs-Elysées.

But overshadowing everything was the news on Saturday that

Joop Zoetemelk had been found guilty of taking stimulants, and yesterday that four more riders – the Spaniards Menendez, Mendes and Ocaña, and Portugal's Agostinho – were also named as having been found positive through the new system of drug testing. Professor de Backere, of Ghent University, experimented all last winter and it is believed he has now perfected the tracing of pemoline, an amphetamine-based drug, which some riders thought could not be detected.

Zoetemelk, who has always been a correct and courageous rider, maintained his innocence throughout and said he had no idea how the drug came to be in his sample, taken after he won the stage at Avoriaz a week yesterday. The Dutchman, who has been second in the Tour three times, said: 'I tried to win into Versailles on Saturday but still provided a sample for second place, just to prove I was not taking anything. I have been tested over 200 times in my professional career and I have no idea how it could have been given to me.'

At least the rumours that were spreading fast within the Tour entourage are at an end, though there are those who say that others are still to be named. Each rider involved receives a ten-minute penalty, is fined £250 and is suspended for a month. The four announced yesterday made little difference to the top overall placings, but Zoetemelk dropped from fifth to eighth as a result of the penalty.

---

15 JULY 1978

NINETY-NINE ANGRY RIDERS GO 'ON STRIKE'

J.B. Wadley in Toulouse

Everybody who finished Tuesday's eleventh stage of the Tour de France was a hero. How could twelve- or ten- or even nine-stone men force 18 lb of bicycle over the snowflaked 6,900-foot Col du

Tourmalet, descend at 50 mph and finish by sprinting the last cruel steps of a Pyrenean Devil's Staircase?

Of all this year's Tour heroes none can compare with Bernard Hinault who, in Tricolore, Champion of France, colours, got within one minute of taking over the race lead. On form, Hinault, from Brittany, should be wearing the yellow jersey on Friday – Bastille Day. An adventure story writer could not do better.

Millions saw the battle of the Pla d'Adet on television and thousands lined the streets of Valence d'Agen yesterday to give the riders a hero's welcome at the end of the morning 92-mile half-stage from Tarbes. They knew from their transistors that the race was one and a half hours behind schedule, but appreciating the punishment taken overnight on the mountains had no complaints. Indeed, the finishing-line spectators thought, the slower the stage the faster the finish.

But instead of a massive sprint we saw the unprecedented spectacle of 99 riders dismounting 50 yards from the finishing line, arguing with officials for several minutes and then pushing their bicycles to the line. The 'Giants of the Road', tamers of mighty mountains and headwind gales, were protesting because they had to get up a bit earlier than usual. One of the ringleaders of the protest, it is alleged, was Hinault, who with some difficulty tried to explain to the puzzled crowd what it was all about.

The facts are these. In the early days the Tour itinerary was a continuous line circling the country representing as many as 3,600 miles. Since the War the International Cycling Union have restricted the length to 2,500 miles. Rather than make it a smaller but continuous 'circle' the organisers prefer to keep it large to neutralise certain sections.

A Tour rider's lot is not an easy one and grumbles were to be expected, but I do not believe they, and least of all Hinault – making his debut in the great race – would have stopped the show on their own volition. Whatever the cause the effects cannot be good for the Tour image. The organisers announced that the morning stage was cancelled and that the prize money would be given to a local charity.

---

17 JULY 1978

TOUR DE FRANCE LEADER IS DISQUALIFIED

Michel Pollentier, of Belgium, was disqualified from the Tour de France yesterday, accused of cheating on the medical doping test after he had won the 16th stage, a 150-mile mountain haul from St Etienne to Alpe d'Huez. He had also taken the overall lead. Race officials said Pollentier had been caught with a test tube containing an old urine sample taped under his armpit and had tried to substitute that for the sample taken after the race. It was announced that Pollentier had been relegated to last position in the stage, had suffered a further ten-minute penalty and had been fined 5,000 Swiss francs. But later it was announced that he had been disqualified from the race.

---

24 JULY 1978

HINAULT TRIUMPHS AT FIRST ATTEMPT
J.B. Wadley in Paris

A choir of a million voices, 200,000 of them on the Champs Elysées-Place de la Concorde finishing circuit, chanted 'Ee-no, Ee-no' yesterday as Bernard Hinault in the yellow jersey rode the last 100 miles of his victorious Tour de France.

Hinault – competing in his first Tour – is a member of the Club Olympique Briochin, the Brittany club who the late Tom Simpson joined when he began his Continental career 20 years ago. From his first races Hinault was hailed as a rider of the Simpson type, always stirring up the pace, afraid of nobody, determined to smash any 'Mafia ganging-up', winning races on his own, in sprints, time trials and up steep hills.

Yesterday, to mark the finish of the 65th Tour de France, 20 previous winners joined in the celebrations on the Champs-Elysées. Inevitably comparisons were made between some of them and Hinault. Whom does he resemble most?

Louison Bobet? Very much in his 'completeness'. Bobet, however, had five years of failure before he finally scored the first of his three successive victories, whereas Hinault won at his first attempt.

Eddy Merckx? Not by 600 miles. I do not mean that Hinault has not Merckx's basic class. But whereas young Merckx was brought up in the hurly-burly of international racing, on three Belgian indoor tracks, Hinault is still practically a track novice.

Jacques Anquetil? Though different in build and riding style, Hinault has much in common with the master time-triallist from Normandy, who while not an ace climber was never decisively dropped by a direct rival in the mountains.

---

23 JULY 1979

HINAULT HOME IN STORY-BOOK FINISH

J.B. Wadley in Paris

An enormous crowd watched a story-book ending to an outstanding Tour de France yesterday on the Champs-Elysées, when Bernard Hinault and Joop Zoetemelk, who for nearly a month had dominated the race, arrived together well clear of the field to contest the final sprint.

The result was logical. First: Hinault. Second: Zoetemelk – with the rest of the field well beaten as they had been throughout 2,300 miles of exceptionally hard competition. Zoetemelk, 3m 7s down overall on starting the final 113-mile stage, made a last desperate attempt on one of the many hills in the Chevreuse Valley. Hinault was quickly on his wheel.

As 'defender', Hinault could have left the pace-making to Zoetemelk, in which case the pair would soon have been caught. But Hinault, who overnight had scored his sixth stage victory, was determined to round off his splendid Tour by winning on the Champs-Elysées. He therefore continued to 'work' with Zoetemelk, each doing about 200 metres of pace-making before swinging out to let the other through.

It was a splendid lesson to amateur racing cyclists. There are no greater rivals in the sport than Hinault and Zoetemelk, but now they were briefly allies, resisting the efforts of the pursuing field. For the 200,000 crowd lining the four-mile Champs-Elysées-Place de la Concorde circuit, which had to be covered six times, it was too good to be true. Often the yellow jersey is hidden in a bunch of 100. Yesterday he was out in front with his valiant challenger for nearly an hour on the most famous circuit in the world.

On the last home straight up the Champs-Elysées the pact ended. Hinault and Zoetemelk were enemies again. Zoetemelk did his best, but Hinault was over the line first, winner of his seventh stage, overall winner on time for the second successive year, winner on points and leader of the winning team. Poor Zoetemelk was second for the fifth time.

Two minutes later British supporters had the unexpected thrill of seeing Paul Sherwen finish third in the 50-up big bunch sprint. Sherwen's overall place was low but he arrived in Paris in much better form than when he started.

CHAPTER 4
THE 1980s

SEAN KELLY TAKES STAGE AT LAST

J.B. Wadley in St Etienne

Sean Kelly has at last won his stage of the 1980 Tour de France. But like a good Irishman he did so in the unexpected way, in the 85-mile run from Voreppe yesterday. Instead of out-sprinting a big pack of riders with a devastating ten-second effort, the County Tipperary star rode a 20-mile individual time trial into St Etienne.

Technically it was a 'two-up' time trial since Kelly was accompanied by Ismael Lejarreta, of Spain. But Lejarreta was a passenger nearly all the way. It was not that he would not work. He simply could not follow the fast pace that Kelly was setting. Kelly had reason to be in a hurry because the main pack was closing in fast. Only 20 seconds after he had free-wheeled over the line ahead of a very tired Lejarreta, the sprint for third place was won by the champion of Belgium, Jos Jacobs.

The Irishman's victory was generally popular. Kelly narrowly missed winning several times in this Tour, and now he has proved that he is not just a sprinter, but a fine all-rounder. Indeed his winning move included the climb of a difficult second-category hill, the last big obstacle of the Tour.

———

FINAL TRIBUTE FOR WADLEY

Before the riders in the Tour de France descended the Col de Glandon yesterday, seven British cyclists paid their final tribute to John Wadley, cycling correspondent of *The Daily Telegraph,* who had followed the race on 23 occasions and who died in April this year.

Complying with the wishes of his wife Mary, his ashes were spread on the route of the Tour at a point where he passed on his

59th birthday. The spot, chosen by Neville Chanin, a renowned long-distance cyclist, was taken from *My 19th Tour de France,* a book John completed after following the race that year on his own bicycle.

———

20 JULY 1981

HINAULT'S GLORY UNDIMMED BY MAERTENS'S SPRINT

Phil Liggett in Paris

Freddy Maertens, of Belgium, won the final stage of the Tour de France, but it was Bernard Hinault who earned the cheers of the 500,000 spectators thronging the Champs-Elysées in Paris yesterday.

Hinault, the French world champion, was the overall winner for the third time in his career. He finished a massive 14 m 34 s ahead, and was the fastest winner of all time. Maertens won his fifth stage of the Tour when the 2,424-mile marathon was concluded with the 24th stage from Fontenay-sous-Bois. He headed home a pack of 118 riders.

The last day in the Chevreuse Valley was one of truce, and the field arrived to complete six laps of the Champs-Elysées in a compact bunch. This, at last, gave the sprinters a chance to win, and Maertens made no mistakes, striking the front in the last 100 yards.

Graham Jones, from Manchester, was the only Briton to finish, and his 20th place overall was the best recorded since the late Tom Simpson, who finished sixth in 1962. France had an enviable record of wins since Bernard Thevenet broke the grip of Eddy Merckx in 1975, and Hinault made up for last year when he retired injured.

Peter Winnen, 23, of Holland, who won the Best Young Rider award, finished fifth in his first Tour, and he has all the attributes necessary to win the race in another two years. Hinault showed himself to be fallible in the Alps, where Winnen won the hardest stage, and it was only in the four time trials that Hinault was able to build up such a winning margin.

Next year the organisers must reduce this individual racing, which leans heavily in the favour of Hinault who, as with Jacques Anquetil 15 years ago, has the ability to conserve his gains when the race enters the mountains. An average speed of 23.7 mph beat Anquetil's record, and the 121 riders who finished were the largest number in the history of the event.

J.B. Wadley, who followed the Tour for 23 years as a journalist for *The Daily Telegraph* before his death three months ago, was again remembered at the start of the last stage, when Jacques Goddet presented the British journalists with the medal of the Tour for his wife Mary.

---

24 JULY 1981

FARM-BOY HINAULT REAPS RICH HARVEST

Sporting profile by Phil Liggett

Bernard Hinault, 26, winner of the Tour de France for the third time in four years, is now reaping the rewards throughout Europe. He will, for the next month, race daily and be paid between £2,000 and £2,500 each time.

The dark-haired Breton has made the most of his natural ability as a cyclist but, had he come from Aquitane in the West, the French say his talent would have developed as a champion at tennis or rugby.

As a schoolboy, Hinault dreamt of the day he would move to Paris and earn enough money to return to the farmland and buy his own house. Now, as a millionaire, he has built a property with his petite wife Martine in her village of Quessay, two and a half miles from his own family home in Yffiniac.

Hinault's requirements from life are simple. When he is not away racing – which means all of the summer – he spends his time in the garden and fields. Married in 1974 at 19, he has two sons, Michael and Alexander, who are still too young to appreciate their father's achievements.

'I remember my first race when I was a cadet,' said Hinault. 'I promised my mother that the winner's flowers would decorate the dining table in the evening, and they did because I won the race by eight minutes.'

Hinault has been described as proud, stubborn and solitary, but above all he is supremely confident. 'I find success natural, but it is still a consequence of hard work,' he said. 'My popularity stimulates me in an unbelievable fashion. In my first season I won 12 races from 20 starts, but that was hardly enough to concentrate on a future as a professional. I carried on with my simple life of no smoking and alcohol and turned professional in 1974.'

Until his marriage, Hinault lived with his parents, two brothers and sister in the drab onion-growing village of 3,000 people. His parents were proud to admit that they never owned a car and Hinault used to ride the 757 pedal strokes to St Brieuc, where he studied with average academic ability.

'My parents were not rich; they are still not and never will be. But we have had everything we wanted by working hard. I remember the days when we had no meat, and we just had cabbage and potatoes for dinner.' In 1974 Hinault married and turned professional for £110 a month. Now his earnings can be estimated at £25,000 per month, although an electric saw and garden rotovator indicate Hinault's wants in contrast to a fast car.

Hinault, by his presence, commands attention. During the 1978 Tour de France he was the instigator of the first strike in the event's history. He led the riders walking across the finishing line in Valence d'Agen, protesting against their use as 'commercial animals'.

He dislikes comparisons between himself and the great riders. When asked such questions, his enduring smile disappears and his face clouds: 'I am a stubborn and aggressive Breton, who does not resemble anyone. Certainly, I think of Eddy Merckx and Jacques Anquetil, who have both won the Tour five times, but that ambition is not yet in my order of the day. Merckx and I are made of the same material, but I sincerely do not race to equal his achievements.'

Merckx, who followed the Tour de France as a reporter, said: 'I have never been surprised by Hinault's results. He is a complete champion and, although Anquetil and I have our five wins, it is possible he will pass us.'

Hinault's attitudes to his wife and family have never changed since the day he won his first race. When his career ends in, perhaps, eight years, he will certainly return to Brittany and assume a farmer's life. When he won his first Tour, his parents travelled to Paris and sat next to the President of France, appearing uncomfortably out of place in new clothes.

Now, with three wins, Hinault is a superstar. Yet, during this year's Tour, he was visited by the worried mother of a sick boy and asked if he would write a letter to her son who idolised him. Hinault did more than that. He visited the boy in hospital and gave him a Renault-Gitane racing jersey – after racing one of the hardest days of the race.

---

16 JULY 1982

SEAN KELLY CRACKS MOUNTAIN EXPERTS

Phil Liggett in Pau

Sean Kelly, the Irishman who has failed to win a stage in this year's Tour de France during his favourite flat terrain, yesterday shocked the mountain specialists with an outstanding victory in Pau after 156 gruelling miles across the Pyrenees from Fleurance.

It was an emotional finish for Kelly, who, after coming second three times, had begun to wonder if he would ever be in a position to try for a win. It was his fifth stage victory since 1978. Wiping away the sweat of almost seven hours' racing, Kelly said: 'I told myself this morning that I was strong enough to win, so why not try in the mountains. I owed the victory to myself and my team.'

After crossing the Pyrenees giants – the Col du Souler (4,853 feet) and the Col d'Aubisque (5,607 feet) – Kelly showed determination to remain in contact with the climbers, which marks his progress generally this season. 'I caught them on the final climb, and although they dropped me slightly, I rejoined on the way down,' he said. 'Once away from the mountains I was confident my sprint finish would see me through.'

---

9 JULY 1983

REFEREES HAIL SHERWEN SHOW OF COURAGE

Phil Liggett in Pontarlier

Paul Sherwen, 29, one of only three British riders in this year's Tour de France, showed the sort of courage that has endeared the event to the heart of the French for almost a century when he limped in almost an hour and a half behind the rest of the field yesterday.

The Frodsham professional, who has lived in France for almost ten years, crashed and suffered a back injury immediately after the start of the 127-mile tenth stage from Epinal to Pontarlier. After finishing 23 minutes outside the time limit he resigned himself to elimination, but his determination impressed the normally immovable international referees, who after an hour's deliberation reinstated him.

Raphael Geminiani, the normally gruff La Redoute team manager, waited for more than an hour for Sherwen to arrive at the ski resort finish, gave him a dry undervest and said: 'Paul, this is your leader's yellow jersey for courage.'

Sherwen's French team-mates, Alan Bondue and Régis Simon, had tried to nurse him back to the field but, also fearing elimination, left him alone after 50 miles. 'I had to tell my team-mates to go on but I didn't want to give up what may be my last Tour,' said Sherwen, who understandably wept on hearing of his reinstatement, which was against the wishes of Felix Lévitan, the Tour director.

The referees considered his 'show of courage' and a high speed of 25 mph through the Jura mountains. Later they had no mercy for Didi Thurau, of West Germany, who was disqualified and fined £100 for grabbing and shaking the chief referee before the morning start in Epinal. Thurau was still annoyed at being penalised a minute for taking pace during Saturday's time trial from Charly Mottet, the French rider.

---

11 JULY 1983

KELLY IN YELLOW JERSEY – AND WHITE FOR ROCHE

Phil Liggett in Pau

Sean Kelly, 27, yesterday became the first Irish leader of the Tour de France for 20 years when he finished third at the end of the ninth stage from Bordeaux to Pau to take the lead by one second – the narrowest margin possible.

Kelly, who also increased his overall lead of the race on points, needed to finish third and win a ten-second time bonus to take the leader's yellow jersey, and in a confident sprint he beat 115 riders with apparent ease. 'It wasn't my intention to try for the yellow jersey, but when I knew that third place would be enough, I felt I had to do it for the publicity for my sponsors. You don't get two chances like this in a lifetime,' said Kelly.

It was an historic day for Ireland, who have only two professional cyclists, and Stephen Roche, 22, in his first Tour de France, moved to sixth place overall and into the lead of the while jersey competition for the best newcomer. Shay Elliott, who came from Dublin, is the only other Irishman to have worn the yellow jersey since the race began in 1903. Elliott took the lead at Roubaix and survived for three days before losing it at Angers.

Kelly, who claims to be concentrating on the green jersey as points leader, will not predict what will happen during the final two weeks, but he has proved before – by his stage victory in Pau last year – that he can climb the high mountains.

––––––––

12 JULY 1983

MILLAR TRIUMPHS OVER PYRENEES AS KELLY LOSES LEAD

Phil Liggett in Luchon

Robert Millar, from Glasgow, yesterday scored Scotland's first-ever stage victory in the Tour de France, after a magnificent ride across the Pyrenees between Pau and Luchon enabled him to finish alone. Behind him lay a trail of exhausted riders and more than a dozen retired, while Sean Kelly, of Ireland, lost the overall lead he had held for a day.

Millar, 24, who has never before seen the Pyrenees, spent six hours at the head of the attacks until finally he crossed the top of Col de Peyresourde with ten miles to go. A professional for three years, this is Millar's first Tour de France and he has waited with controlled enthusiasm for the mountainous stages. At the start of the day in 83rd place overall, he climbed to 27th.

'I have been disappointed with my race so far, but now I'm delighted. This is my first professional victory and to win a stage here is unbelievable,' said Millar, who rode for more than 30 miles with Patrocinio Jimenez, a Colombian amateur.

Kelly, the overnight leader, was never in a position to defend his yellow jersey, which passed to Pascal Simon, a team-mate of Millar's, after the Frenchman finished third, 1 m 13 s behind. Kelly fell back soon after the stage started on the Col d'Aubisque and finished 18th, more than ten minutes behind. But the Irishman was not disappointed, especially as the mountains claimed two of Kelly's rivals for his lead in the points classification.

––––––––

15 JULY 1983

RIDERS STAGE A GO-SLOW IN DOPE PENALTY PROTEST

Phil Liggett in Aurillac

During the past two days four riders in the Tour de France have been penalised for failing routine dope tests, and concern about the use of medicaments almost brought yesterday's stage of the 2,400-mile marathon to a premature end. The riders, in protest during the 130-mile 13th stage, from Roquefort-sur-Soulzon to Aurillac, continued for some time at only six miles an hour, and the organisers threatened to cancel the event.

Before the start, the 112 riders were annoyed that Patrick Clerc, a young French rider who was declared 'positive' on Wednesday evening, might not be able to complete the event. It was his second doping offence within 12 months, thereby invoking a month's ban previously suspended.

As the race moved off this attitude met with a terse response from Felix Lévitan, 72, the race co-director: 'Gentlemen, if you stop this race today, then I will stop the Tour de France and it will be finished for this year.' However, Mr Lévitan added that Clerc would be allowed to continue to Paris and that any discussion about his suspension would be between the French Cycling Federation and the world governing body (ICU) after the race.

It soon became clear as the field meandered through the picturesque Auvergne and the Massif Central that the stage, which should have proved decisive, was to be ruined by a go-slow situation.

The slowdown started after Patriocini Jimenez, a Spanish-speaking amateur rider from Colombia, had attacked on the ten-mile climb of the Col de Montjaux, where he hoped to out-manoeuvre Robert Millar, his nearest challenger for his King of the Mountains jersey.

Immediately the Colombian was joined by Gilbert Duclos-Lasalle, a team-mate of Millar's, and with the help of Marco Franceshini, of Italy, the amateur was persuaded to return to the field. Later the Italian was penalised ten seconds and fined £88 for touching Jimenez.

Now, thoroughly displeased by the action of the professional riders, Mr Lévitan said: 'Mr Duclos-Lasalle, I ask that you honour your profession and allow the race to develop in a correct and proper manner.' This request had no effect for some miles until Henk Lubberding, of Holland, and Régis Clere and Hubert Linard, of France, went ahead, after 50 miles, to gain the day's major prizes.

This excellent race could be further marred by doping problems for rumour was rife last night that ten more riders, having given positive samples, are now awaiting results of second tests. It is thought that among these are some of the leaders.

The four riders penalised so far have all claimed that the products they used were prescribed by their family doctors for general health. Riders usually follow general courses of vitamins and receive regular medical examinations. Joop Zoetemelk, 36, the Dutchman, was found to have used an anabolic steroid called nandrolone, a substance that was found in athletes during the 1980 Moscow Olympic Games but, at that time, was not on the prescribed list. It is the first time the control centres on the Tour de France have tested for this product.

'We lose so much weight in a race like this and you can't put it back on with just food,' said Millar in defence of the Dutchman.

'Look at Zoetemelk, does he seem like a man full of steroids? He only weighs ten stone.'

Unfortunately, there does seem to be a grey area in the method of dope testing and the race's overall leader, Pascal Simon, who has passed all the tests so far in this event, was penalised last month in the Dauphiné-Libéré race. On that occasion he had claimed to have used a product which was suitable for administration to a nine-month-old baby.

---

25 JULY 1983

FAIRYTALE VICTORY FOR FIGNON

Phil Liggett in Paris

Laurent Fignon, 22, became one of the youngest winners of the Tour de France when it ended on the Champs-Elysées yesterday after the final 122-mile stage from Alfortville had been disrupted by a number of pile-ups in the final mile.

After three weeks of hot sunshine, the first rain fell soon after the field came on to the Champs-Elysées and as the riders negotiated six 3½-mile laps a number of them slipped and slid into barriers. It was a tense, almost fitting ending to one of the most unpredictable races for years, and though no riders were seriously injured it caused a number of anxious moments for the overall leaders.

Sean Kelly, 27, who won the points classification for a second year, was denied his stage victory when Gilbert Glaus, the Swiss former world amateur champion, beat him by half-a-wheel in the final sprint. Kelly was disappointed at not having won a stage after finishing in the first six on ten occasions. 'Fignon spoiled it for me,' said Kelly. 'He attacked as we came into the finish and I had to chase him, otherwise he would have won, so when Glaus went I couldn't follow.'

Waiting to welcome Fignon after he had finished fourth on the last stage were his proud parents, who had sat in the Presidential Tribune. Also watching nearby was Bernard Hinault, winner four times in the previous five years. Fignon, a blond Parisian, gave the race a fairytale ending, because he lives only a few miles from the finish. In Hinault's absence through injury the French were expected to do poorly in their 80th year, but the opposite was true.

'I am incredibly happy, but now my quiet life is over,' said Fignon as he was being mobbed by autograph hunters. He no longer has any regret at giving up his studies as a veterinary surgeon to become a professional rider.

Cyrille Guimard, his Renault manager, who has an amazing record in the Tour de France, has now been behind three different winners. He managed Lucien van Impe, of Belgium, when he won in 1976. Van Impe may have finished better than fourth this time if he had not been in a rival Italian team.

Guimard, in steering Fignon to victory, has produced a winner that was never foreseen. His main problem now will be to integrate Fignon and Hinault when they continue together as team-mates. 'Well,' said Guimard, 'you must admit that if you have a wife and a mistress then you will always have problems.'

---

23 JULY 1984

FIGNON WINNER FOR SECOND YEAR

Phil Liggett in Paris

Laurent Fignon, 23, yesterday returned to Paris after 2,400 miles in the Tour de France as the winner for the second successive year. Fignon, the French champion, who lives in the city, set off on 29 June to face one of the most difficult routes for years, and in glorious sunshine, he was welcomed back with a time ten-and-a-half minutes better than the runner-up, Bernard Hinault.

Robert Millar, from Scotland, was fourth overall and the first Briton to win the King of the Mountains competition. Millar, 25, from Glasgow, said: 'I know it was my ambition but now I've done it I can't tell you how I feel. Next year, though, I know I want to do it again.'

Millar is the first British rider to break into the top five, and his fourth place was gained by extraordinary ability in the Alps, supported by a good defence against the challengers in the time trial. His fourth place, 14 m 42 s behind Fignon, bettered Tom Simpson's sixth 22 years ago. Simpson dedicated his life to the race in which he died in 1967.

Fignon's victory was, he said, 'the finest of my career because I beat Hinault, and to make me feel even better he still finished on the podium below me'. The two former team-mates openly dislike one another and have daily attacked each other in the press and on television. Hinault, 29, did not possess the ability, despite four Tour wins, to win. But he warned that next year Fignon's form might be different.

---

22 JUNE 1985

MILLAR – 5,000 CALORIE MAN
Michael Calvin

The hardy holiday-makers hunched against the wind which buffeted the Isle of Man yesterday paid no attention to the deceptively slight figure of Robert Millar. There was the occasional stir when an aide carried his bicycle into the hotel lobby with an incongruous sense of reverence. But passers-by continued their struggle along the seafront in blissful ignorance of the presence of one of the emerging stars of European sport.

Millar, in his fifth year as a professional cyclist, accepts his anonymity in his native Britain. Yet the shrewdest judges in his sport suspect that his appearance in the British Professional Championship on the island tomorrow will mark the end of an era. Next Friday, Millar, 26, will embark on the Tour de France, a classic test of athletic endurance which begins in Brittany and, some 4,000 km later, climaxes on the Champs-Elysées to the type of reception accorded to the liberation forces in 1945.

Millar was fourth overall on the Tour last year – the best performance by a Briton – and if he wins in 1985 he will be thrust into a millionaire lifestyle beyond the imagination of the friends he left behind in Glasgow's Gorbals. No one will ignore him again.

Although the financial rewards are spectacular, they must be earned with the acceptance of pain throughout 23 days of racing. A rider's robotic devotion to duty must combat excruciating saddle sores, aching limbs and insidious mental pressure. Millar, a vegetarian, who, paradoxically, is considering investing in a franchise for McDonald's hamburgers in his adoptive homeland of France, has wanted nothing else since, at the age of 16, he glimpsed the Tour on television. His store of physical energy is stocked by the consumption of 5,000 calories a day, and he admits that his ration of ten hours' sleep a night will be insufficient.

'People in Britain cannot relate to the style of the Tour,' he tells you without a trace of reproach. 'But for three weeks it is the most important thing that is happening in France. When you are racing for that length of time you forget what real life is like. There are times when, quite literally, you do not know what day it is. There's a certain relief when you race down the Champs-Elysées at the end. But there's also a great sense of anti-climax. You wonder what on earth you are going to do with your time.'

The winner will consult his agent, and count his winnings. Other survivors – and only half the field completes the Tour – will reflect on the cruelty of one of the most physically demanding sports.

Millar, so aware of the need for prime fitness that he sends a monthly blood sample to a specialist in Bordeaux for analysis, has an intimate knowledge of such disappointment. He was manoeuvred out of winning this year's Tour of Spain because other teams, persuaded of the necessity of producing a home triumph, openly conspired against him.

'Alliances will always be made when teams want something badly enough,' he says in a gentle Franco-Scottish accent which testifies to the complete success of his resettlement south of Paris. 'I have learnt that cycling is basically an individual sport where no one can trust anyone else.'

Riders make – and break – promises to one another on the road, and Millar, acknowledged climbing expert who won the polka dot shirt given to the Tour's King of the Mountains last year, exhibits an animal's instinct for weakness. Cocooned in concentration, he listens to every breath of his rivals, and studies whether their faces are flushed with fatigue. Then, banking on the value of surprise, he suddenly strains every sinew and sustains a 30-second burst of killing speed.

'The thing that gives me greatest pleasure in cycling is still feeling the wind in my face on a sunny day,' he reflects with a half-smile. 'But the inner satisfaction when you leave people gasping behind you is enormous. You glance over your shoulder and see them suffer. But you are also suffering yourself. You can't laugh or even smile with pleasure because of the physical effort you have put in, but inside you feel very excited.'

Millar, a self-confessed introvert, relaxes by listening to music, and lives with his girlfriend, a canteen worker in the town of Troves in the south-east of the French capital. He learnt the language on a cassette course and, as he studies Dutch to become a more complete European, he concedes that he has no affinity with Glasgow.

He cannot, however, escape the lessons of his background. He still remembers the drudgery of an abandoned apprenticeship in engineering, which remains a powerful force of motivation. The stark features of his face, soothed by a sun tan, are emphasised when he considers the enormity of the opportunity which awaits him.

He knows that cycling legends like Hinault and Fignon occasionally struggle when confronted by mass adulation and admits:

'That sort of thing worries me. When I see the big guys having trouble dealing with all the questions and all the supporters, I know I'm not prepared for life at that level. But if I have to, I will cope. Let's face it, I'm being paid to do something I would do for nothing. I know what it's like to work in a factory, so I can put up with not being just another rider.'

---

22 JULY 1985

HINAULT TRIUMPHS FOR FIFTH TIME
Phil Liggett in Paris

Bernard Hinault, 30, smiled for the first time in three weeks when he was duly crowned as winner of the 2,500-mile Tour de France on the Champs-Elysées for a record-equalling fifth time yesterday.

Hinault finished safely in the main pack after the 122-mile final stage from Orléans, which was won by Belgium's Rudy Matthijs. The Breton, who equalled a record held by Jacques Anquetil and Eddy Merckx, was cheered to the podium by the thousands of spectators who packed the capital's most famous boulevard. He had led the race since the ninth day.

In the final sprint yesterday, contested by all 144 survivors, Sean Kelly was again beaten into second place – his fifth runners-up position of the Tour, and his 14th second place since he last won in 1982. Even so it was Ireland's most successful race and Stephen Roche and Kelly produced their country's best performance by finishing third and fourth overall, with Kelly also winning the race on points. Greg LeMond, of the United States, became the highest-placed English-speaking rider when he finished second, 1 m 42 s behind Hinault.

Hinault's victory is a personal triumph after a successful fight-back from a knee injury which forced him to give up in the 1980 Tour when leading at Pau. Since then few have believed he had the resources to return to the top, though he always said he would. While Hinault was injured, France produced a new star in twice Tour winner Laurent Fignon, who pushed Hinault into second place last year.

The victory is also a credit to a dedicated La Vie Claire team formed by young millionaire Bernard Tapie, a health food chain owner. Tapie tempted Hinault away from his former team, Renault, and then weakened Renault further by offering Greg LeMond $1.5 million over four years to leave also.

Only 36 retirements in the marathon indicates an easier than usual passage for most – the organisers had anticipated about 65 – but after Hinault won the lead at Strasbourg on day nine of 22, the race centred on only a handful.

---

22 JULY 1986

LEMOND TAKES CONTROL AS MILLAR FADES

Phil Liggett at Alpe d'Huez

Three giant Alpine climbs were all that Greg LeMond and Bernard Hinault needed to put their final stamp on this year's Tour de France, and when they reached the finish of the 18th stage at Alpe d'Huez yesterday, the pair had spread-eagled the field over almost an hour.

The riders spend their only rest day at the ski station today, licking their wounds before facing the final 500 miles to Paris, after Hinault and LeMond had proved themselves to be the most outstanding riders.

LeMond, the first American to lead the race, spent his first day in the yellow jersey on the attack with Hinault, his French team-mate, and together they finished over five minutes ahead of Urs Zimmermann, who slipped back to third overall. With a piece of showmanship never before seen in the 83 years of the Tour, the Vie Claire colleagues linked arms and came up the last half-mile together. Hinault was awarded the stage – the 26th such victory of his career – and LeMond was content with second place.

Robert Millar, the Panasonic rider from Glasgow, was the main casualty of another most gruelling day and, after crossing the 8,000-feet summit of the Col du Galibier in fourth place, he faded rapidly, losing over 19 minutes and dropping back from fourth to eighth overall.

Only Hinault remains within three minutes of LeMond after yesterday's escape by the pair, which started on the rapid descent of the Galibier. Hinault was doing the aggressive work and with over 60 of the 101 miles still to go – and, more importantly, the 6,000-foot climbs of the Col de la Croix Fer and Alpe d'Huez – he attacked again, taking with him Canadian Steve Bauer, another team-mate, LeMond and Ruiz-Cabestany, from Spain.

The Spaniard and Bauer fell back as the narrow ascent of the Croix Fer began, and from this point, Hinault nursed LeMond over the mountains without requiring him to share the pace-making.

Hinault, being denied an historic sixth overall victory by LeMond, seemed to have come to terms with the great disappointment, and together they pulled clear of Zimmermann, who, LeMond felt, must have been asleep when they began their attack.

---

25 JULY 1986

LEMOND MUST TRIUMPH NOW SAYS HINAULT

Phil Liggett in St Etienne

Bernard Hinault, the defending champion who has won the Tour five times, was ready to concede victory to the American Greg LeMond last night, despite winning the 36-mile time trial at St Etienne by a scant 25 seconds yesterday.

'I have attacked since the start of this race but, although I intend to race all the way to Paris, I have lost it now,' said Hinault, after his third stage victory of the Tour, which kept him in second place, 2 m 18 s behind, with three days to go.

Hinault recorded 1 h 15 m 36 s for the hilly circuit, which included the 600-foot climb of the Côte de Rochetaillée. LeMond, as last to start, then came home 3 m 25 s after with 1 h 16 m 41 s for second place. But there was considerable doubt that Hinault would have won if LeMond had not fallen and changed bikes, losing perhaps 30 seconds.

LeMond overshot a right-hand bend after 20 miles, and fell without injury, quickly remounting. As he restarted, he noted his front brake was broken, and he stopped again to change his cycle. At the finish line, there were emotional scenes as, on hearing news of the crash, LeMond's family burst into tears. They even accused LeMond's rivals of sabotaging his machine; there was no proof of this.

With three days left, LeMond is unlikely to concede much more of his 2 m 18 s advantage; and even with today's climb of the giant Puy de Dôme mountain outside Clermont Ferrand, he will remain confident of victory. The Californian is climbing well, and after venting his anger at the finish yesterday – which was exacerbated when he cut his finger opening a soft drink can – he is likely to be suitably conditioned emotionally for a final day of attacking riding before the flat roads to Paris this weekend.

---

28 JULY 1986

LEMOND RIDES TO GLORY AFTER LATE ACCIDENT

Phil Liggett in Paris

Greg LeMond fulfilled all his promises yesterday by becoming the first American to win the Tour de France when the 2,500-mile race ended its lap of the country on the Champs-Elysées. He was only 44th in the final scramble to the line by the 132 survivors, but after a crash entering the city and two bicycle changes, he finished more than three minutes clear overall.

Perhaps the thousands who lined the gentle incline between the Place de la Concorde and the Arc de Triomphe reserved their loudest cheers for the losing Frenchman, Bernard Hinault, but there was no doubt about the strongest rider after almost 23 days of the most open racing. LeMond, 26, from California, duelled with his La Vie Claire team-mate for 2,250 miles, and it was only after Friday's time trial at St Etienne that Hinault conceded the race.

LeMond is two years older than Hinault was when he won his first Tour in 1978 almost four minutes in front of Joop Zoetemelk, of Holland. Yesterday the Dutchman, now 39, created his own piece of history when he completed his 16th Tour. The blond American, who was welcomed by his wife Kathy and baby son Jeffrey and both sets of parents at the finish line, never doubted his ability to win. He predicted his victory even before the start in Paris on 4 July, and always refused to be second best to Hinault, five times a winner of the race, even though the Frenchman did try to unnerve him.

LeMond, who lives in Kortrijk, Belgium, is already a millionaire, yet is still comparatively unknown in the United States.

---

23 JULY 1987

ROCHE BATTLES TO BRINK IN CHASING LEADER DELGADO

Phil Ligget at La Plagne

The finest sporting duel the Tour de France has witnessed for many years almost ended in disaster yesterday when Stephen Roche, the Irishman in second place overall, pushed himself to the limits of endurance and collapsed after he crossed the finish line at La Plagne. Minutes before his collapse at the 6,400-feet ski station on the Italian border, Roche had produced the most unbelievable fightback after Pedro Delgado, his only rival for the race's overall victory, had led all the way up the last mountain. Delgado, who started the day 25 seconds ahead of Roche, was hoping to gain at least three minutes yesterday, and halfway up the climb he had made almost one and a half when Roche fought back.

At the line Delgado finished fourth and Roche, who closed 45 seconds in the last three kilometres, finished fifth, losing only four seconds to the Spaniard, although he was later penalised ten extra seconds for feeding outside designated zones.

Immediately after crossing the line Roche fell into the arms of helpers and then two race doctors lowered him to the floor, where he was wrapped in silver foil against the cool air and given oxygen for 15 minutes. Roche was taken by ambulance to his hotel but not before he forced a smile and gave the 'thumbs up' sign after the most extraordinary effort the race has seen. He was later reported to be sleeping normally and will be at the start again today.

It was an act of desperation on Roche's part for, with six miles to climb to the finish, he seemed to be losing any chance of victory in the Tour after Delgado launched his calculated attack. Ahead of both was Laurent Fignon, who won the 115-mile Alpine stage from Bourg d'Oisans in a sprint finish from Anselmo Fuerte, but this was a supporting role in the real race for the leader's yellow jersey.

Fignon, who won the same stage in 1984 when he also won the Tour, also avoided disaster by inches yesterday when he crashed on the descent of the Col de la Madeleine at 40 mph. Fignon landed over a crash barrier but his bike disappeared high into a tree, from where mechanics rescued it as he shrugged off the incident with a smile.

This race has built into a battle between Delgado and Roche, with the last mountain stage to come today. The efforts by both riders so far now leave a question mark over how much strength they have left. Delgado, who saw Roche lying on the road, said: 'I tried to get three minutes today, and all I got was four seconds.'

TRIUMPH FOR ROCHE BY 40 SECONDS
Phil Liggett in Paris

Stephen Roche showed the first signs of emotion in 26 days when he mounted the podium to stand alongside the Prime Ministers of France and Ireland on the Champs-Elysées, after winning the Tour de France by 40 seconds.

His eyes filled with tears as he was hugged by the Irish Taoiseach Charles Haughey, who was among the first to congratulate Roche, the first Irishman to win the Tour. 'It's hard to believe it,' said Roche. 'There are so many people responsible, all I did was ride the bike.'

Roche's margin of 40 seconds was only two seconds away from the smallest ever, in 1968, but there was never any danger of an attack by his shadow, Pedro Delgado of Spain, who raced himself out of the picture in Saturday's time trial. Delgado was a magnificent adversary for Roche, and it was with more than just relief that Roche lifted Delgado's arm in the air after he stepped up on the podium.

Roche's prize of £75,000 is made up of an apartment, a Peugeot car, cash and a map of the route traced in diamonds. Most of his winnings will be split among his team-mates, who guided him through from West Berlin to Paris.

There were many highlights in a marvellous race, but one of the great sadnesses was the late retirement on Saturday of Sean Yates, who had finished every Tour ridden. A week after a crash, the injury turned septic and he was forced to give up his fourth Tour.

Before the race started in anger yesterday, Roche stopped by the roadside to embrace Jacques Goddet, the co-director of the race following his 52nd and last Tour de France. Mr Goddet, 82, is still an active director of the sponsoring newspaper *L'Equipe,* and has witnessed every major happening in the Tour since he followed it for the first time in 1928.

---

27 JULY 1987

IRISH EYES SMILE FOR ROCHE

PETER BYRNE REPORTS FROM DUBLIN ON THE MAN
WHO WON THE TOUR DE FRANCE CYCLE RACE

Larry Roche packed an extra item into his bags when he left for work as a security man in Dublin on Saturday morning. While all Ireland and much of Europe prepared to follow the penultimate stage of the Tour de France live on television, Larry was content to monitor the progress of his son Stephen by means of a tiny transistor radio.

One of sport's most alluring individual awards might have been about to fall to a member of the family but Larry Roche had other priorities and other business to settle. In a fashion, it fitted the mood of improbability as Stephen Roche, a 27-year-old Dubliner, achieved a special place in sporting history when he crossed the finishing line in the Champs-Elysées yesterday at the end of a punitive journey of 4,200 km.

In winning the Tour de France, Roche became only the second rider from the English-speaking world to invade the territory which mainland Europe has long regarded as its own. No less than the achievement of America's Greg LeMond a year ago, victory had come only grudgingly.

'These last three weeks have been among the hardest and most delightful of our lives,' said Larry Roche as the general classification table confirmed that his son had finally put himself beyond reach of the pursuit. 'The pressures on the family back in Dublin were considerable. God knows what they were like in the closing stages of the Tour for Stephen.'

Roche senior need scarcely have worried about the son who has matured considerably since he left home in search of fame and fortune and settled in Paris seven years ago. In June, Stephen fell foul of the partisan Italian crowds after a controversial spill had left his Carrera team-mate, Roberto Visentini, writhing on the roadside during the Tour of Italy. The Irishman was accused of sacrificing his colleague in the pursuit of his ambition. For much of the next ten days he was punched and spat at by crowds lining the mountain passes and generally vilified in a section of the Italian sporting press.

'It's at times like these that you discover how badly you want to win races,' said Roche. 'I had waited seven years for this hour – nothing and nobody was going to deter me.'

A month earlier, Ireland had followed the exploits of another of its cyclists, Sean Kelly, who led the Tour of Spain until illness put him out of the race with only days to go. That the Irish should produce two riders like Roche and Kelly was as astounding as contemporary milers of the quality of Steve Ovett and Sebastian Coe emerging in British athletics in the Seventies.

A colourful Irishman, Shay Elliott, later to die tragically, had once flirted with success at a time when professional cycling was viewed merely as a curiosity by Britain and Ireland some 30 years ago. Yet history was scarcely reassuring when Kelly, senior to Roche by some four years and later to claim a place among the ten most successful riders in history, took the emigrant boat to France in 1977. In time the two Irishmen, from widely divergent backgrounds, were to conquer Europe with their remarkable performances.

Kelly, acknowledged as one of the hard men of a sport in which courage is paramount, has headed the points table for consistency in each of the past four years. Roche learned the rudiments of the sport in the foothills around his native Dublin; yet, no less than

Kelly, from Carrick-on-Suir, County Tipperary, his competitive instincts are finely honed.

'In the situation in which Sean and I found ourselves when we first set foot in Europe, you tend to grow up pretty fast,' he said. 'For all the exploits of Shay Elliott in another era, there weren't too many clubs ready to offer professional contracts to Irish riders ten years ago. I'd like to think that between us, we have changed all that and opened a few doors for the young people coming up behind us.'

The people who package Roche commercially contend that, even at the summit of Barry McGuigan's popularity, their man is more marketable than was the former world featherweight champion. 'He's a lad who has never lost sight of his origins and that counts for much around here,' said his Dublin agent Frank Quinn.

Modern sport treats its favoured sons like kings, and the certainty is that victory in the Tour de France will bring the Irishman close on £1 million in sponsorship, product endorsement and appearance money over the next three years. It contrasts starkly with the days when the personable Dubliner earned his living as a maintenance fitter and spent every available penny on 'bikes and biking gear'. Today he lives with his French-born wife, Lydia, and their two children just outside Paris, is fluent in four languages and enjoys the lifestyle of the famous.

There had been occasions when he felt neglected by his fellow countrymen at a time when he was a cult figure in Europe. That, one suspects, will change irrevocably this afternoon when the young man, who left almost unnoticed, returns to the applause of the masses for a civic reception in Dublin. Stephen Roche has, at last, come of age.

———

19 NOVEMBER 1987

ANQUETIL, A CYCLING COLOSSUS

OBITUARY

Phil Liggett

Jacques Anquetil, who died yesterday aged 53, was one of the greatest cyclists in the history of the sport. His death has robbed France of its best-known sportsman of the 1950s and 1960s.

Anquetil was the first of only three men to win the Tour de France five times — at his first attempt in 1957 and then each year from 1961 to 1964 — and was the finest ever rider of time trials. He never, however, excelled at single-day road racing and failed to win the world championship.

The first Frenchman to win the Tour of Italy, in 1960, he matched a feat previously achieved only by Italian maestro Fausto Coppi when he completed the Italian and French Tour double in 1964.

Some felt Anquetil was strongest in adverse conditions. In the 1964 Tour de France, sapped by his efforts in Italy, he lost four minutes on an agonising climb of the Eavalira mountain in the Pyrenees, only to pull back a huge amount with a daring, head-long charge down the mountain in thick mist.

For a decade he engaged in intense rivalry with another Frenchman, Raymond Poulidor, and although Anquetil clinically beat Poulidor on each occasion, it was Poulidor — nicknamed the Eternal Second — who received more public affection. 'He won races. I got the applause,' said Poulidor.

Anquetil never again rode a bicycle following his retirement in 1969, but he retained a direct interest in the sport. He was a regular and respected commentator for radio and television on the Tour de France and he directed the Paris-Nice race, which he won five times.

This summer Anquetil insisted on reporting the Tour even though he had been advised to enter hospital. His death, at a Rouen clinic, was a result of cancer of the stomach.

A Normandy country boy whose father grew strawberries, he returned at the end of his career to cultivate the land once more, this time as a gentleman farmer and owner of a vast estate.

---

9 JULY 1988

YATES SPRINGS SURPRISE FOR EMPHATIC VICTORY

Phil Liggett in Wasquehal

Sean Yates, 28, from Sussex, yesterday surprised the more famous names in the Tour de France when he won the 32-mile individual time trial between Liévin and Wasquehal to become the first English rider to win a stage since 1975.

Yates, who has been enjoying his best season since turning professional in 1982, was the fastest rider at every check point except the first, which came after ten miles, and he finished a difficult course in 1 h 3 m 22 s to beat Roberto Visentini, the former Tour of Italy winner, by 14 seconds.

It was a stunning performance over roads which Yates came to know well when he lived and trained near Lille three years ago. His victory is the first for England since Yorkshire's Barry Hoban won a road race stage at Bordeaux 13 years ago.

---

23 JULY 1988

RIDERS DELAY START IN PROTEST OVER DRUGS CONTROVERSY

Phil Liggett in Chalon-sur-Saone

The remaining 152 riders in the Tour de France ignored the starter's flag yesterday and sat on the line for ten minutes in protest against the manner in which drug control tests have been conducted.

The riders, angry over the handling of Tour leader Pedro Delgado's controversial test, timed their protest to match the time penalty imposed on Gert-Jan Theunisse, the Dutch PDM rider. Theunisse was also fined £600 because the second analysis of his drug test proved positive, but the president of the international jury is refusing to tell the Dutchman which illegal substance he had been found guilty of taking.

The decision further aggravated the riders, already annoyed that the result of Delgado's test was leaked to the media and that the laboratory involved, because of a misunderstanding, pronounced the test positive. That finding was then changed to negative because the drug, Probenecid, will not be on cycling's banned list until next month.

———

25 JULY 1988

VAN POPPEL SPRINTS IN AS DELGADO FULFILS GOAL

Phil Liggett in Paris

Jean-Paul van Poppel, from Holland, brought the Tour de France to a stylish end on the Champs-Elysées yesterday by out-sprinting the 151-rider field to win his fourth stage of the race. Malcolm Elliott, from Sheffield, gained his best finish of the race in fourth place.

But the cheers were largely reserved for Pedro Delgado, of Spain, who took the lead at Alpe d'Huez on 14 July and never looked like losing it. He was clearly the best rider in the 2,050-mile race, having made victory his only target of the season after losing narrowly to Ireland's Stephen Roche last year. Delgado won the race with the biggest margin since Laurent Fignon four years ago and, because of the shorter daily stages, the fierce pace set the fastest average in the race's history.

In the eyes of many, Delgado's victory will always be tarnished by the 'positive' dope test he gave in the Alps. The test was later deemed negative because Probenecid, despite being on the International Olympic Committee's outlawed list, does not become a banned substance in cycling until next month.

The Spaniard vehemently denied he had used the drug to mask the use of steroids, which is one of the properties of Probenecid. He has taken a dope test every day since the Alps stages, and, so far – some have still to be analysed – all are negative.

---

30 JUNE 1989

'FANAS' LOOK FORWARD TO GREETING THEIR HEROES

JACQUES GODDET, WHO DIRECTED THE TOUR FOR MORE THAN 40 YEARS, LOOKS BACK TO ITS ORIGINS AND GREATEST PERFORMERS

A talented French writer, Tristan Bernard, wrote at the beginning of the century: 'France is on its doorstep, watching the Tour go by.' Since then, the Tour de France has become a much bigger event. Now people leave home to see the cyclists pass. They come from far and wide, crossing frontiers and seas, to join French country folk who leave their fields, children grouped round a priest on a jaunt from their summer camp.

Between 12 and 15 million people line the French roads, good-hearted people, excited and happy to be there to support the cyclists, struggling on their bicycles, dripping in sweat in the very image of modern heroes. Hundreds of thousands of *fanas* cross the Alps, Pyrenees, Auvergne and the Vosges, camping out at night by the side of the road in a narrow human corridor, cheering with enthusiasm and admiration.

Television found the Tour a perfect subject. Indeed, it would appear that the Tour de France and television were made for each other. Those coloured live images, sent throughout the world from the very moment battle commences, were previously only seen by the very few – the organisers, and now and then journalists, though they were often kept at a distance from the action so as not to get in the way.

Television has emphasised the greatness and indeed the cruelty of the effort demanded. It has also enabled us to double-check any exaggerated praise by writers. In return, the Tour has brought television a spectacular, live subject, in the varied, often grandiose setting of the French countryside.

I have followed 53 Tours de France, having lost seven during the years 1940–47. I have participated in the organisation since 1929 and have taken part fully since 1947. I have directed 42 of them. I have never tired of working on the Tour. Henri Desgrange, my mentor, created the Tour in 1903 for the daily sports newspaper *L'Auto,* founded by my father, Victor Goddet.

Thus I have known, both on the road and privately, the greatest cyclists of all time. I appreciated their athletic qualities and above all, their will-power. I daresay that the Belgian Eddy Merckx was the greatest of all, reigning undisputed on the Tour: an exceptional superiority continuously shining out. But the legendary post-war Italian Fausto Coppi was certainly the most dazzling: a morphological phenomenon with his unending legs and heron's chest, he almost seemed to have superhuman take-off capacity.

I have for long been eager to expand the area of international road racing: it has been for too long enclosed within Western Europe. For this reason, and in the tracks of the Tour de France, I created the Tour de l'Avenir. From this preparatory formation test for new and young cyclists alike, the strength of Colombian, American, Soviet and Scandinavian cycling developed and the structure of British cycling was reinforced, going back to its foundation at the beginning of the century.

Stephen Roche, Sean Kelly, Robert Millar, Phil Anderson, Greg LeMond and Steve Bauer are today among the world's leading cyclists – not forgetting Tom Simpson, who died in my sight on the overheated gravel on Mont Ventoux because he did not know how to limit his great ambition.

This precisely sums up the great step forward in world cycling, propelled by the galvanising force of the Tour de France.

————

30 JUNE 1989

FAME IS THE SPUR – PAIN THE LIKELY RESULT

AUSTRALIAN ALLAN PEIPER, A VETERAN OF THREE TOURS, GIVES A RIDER'S VIEW OF THE RACE'S GLAMOUR AND GRIND

I've ridden the Tour de France three times in my seven-year career as a professional cyclist. I wore the white jersey for the best young rider for six days during my first attempt in 1984. My second Tour was in 1985, and my last in 1986 – when I swore, 'Never again'.

My first two Tours, both of which I finished, pushed me to extremities. At that time I was with the French Peugeot team and had no specific task except to sacrifice myself to my leaders. The pressure of riding for the Dutch Panasonic-Isostar team in the 1987 Tour became so overwhelming that four days from the finish I pulled out.

What caused my surrender was an upset stomach, diarrhoea, headaches and a congested chest. The night before I stopped, I spent the whole night in bed crying. I was so broken in mind and body I just couldn't face any more pain. Admittedly, I'm not a top rider and for people like me the Tour pushes the rider to the limit from start to finish. After the 1987 Tour my health was in pieces for six months.

For a professional cyclist the Tour is the big race. Just to get into it is a challenge. The fight to get the results to gain team selection can prove exhausting before the event begins. Once the rider makes it into the Tour, a good result or a stage win is lucrative. It can mean a bigger pay packet and better appearance money in the annual post-Tour show races. Foremost in the rider's mind is the knowledge that the eyes of the world are watching so, in basic terms, fame is only a good ride away.

For the cyclist, the build-up is exhilarating. After the presentation of teams and the handing out of new bikes and clothing, everyone is anxious to start the suffering. But once the gun fires, the enjoyment quickly ends.

The cyclist is locked inside his own world of being woken up at 7 a.m., shovelling muesli and spaghetti down his throat for breakfast, followed by a car ride to the start of the day's race. After the daily torture it's time for the journey to the hotel for a shower, a wash of your clothes and then a massage before dinner at seven-thirty – and bed by ten.

Day after day for three weeks it is the same routine, as the legs get sorer and the mind weakens. All you can look forward to is the hope that you won't let the team down. There is nothing worse after a bad day, when you want to ring home, than to find that you can't get a line because there are six teams in the hotel and only two telephone lines. It seems everyone wants to seek the support of their family.

The vast majority of Tour cyclists do not see the glamour or the publicity of this three-week extravaganza. They are just fighting their own private battle to make it Paris.

So if you are watching the Tour on television – or follow it every day in the newspaper – try to imagine what it's like to be one of a hardened, exhausted bunch of 200 men summoning up their last reserves of energy and courage to keep with the pack in a 50 mph sprint finish.

Do not be fooled by the glamour of shining bicycles, sun-tanned bodies and the array of coloured team jerseys and massive crowds. The teeth-on-edge scraping of metal against tarmac or cobbles as the bunch slide into a mass crash, with the riders lying higgledy-piggledy, will provide subtler reminders of the Tour's basic realities.

They are the quest for victory, or more likely the heavenly relief of just getting to the finish line, of this, the race of races.

13 JULY 1989

DELGADO'S COMEBACK PROVES HIS FITNESS TO BE CALLED A CHAMPION

MICHAEL CALVIN ANALYSES THE REMARKABLE PERFORMANCE OF A RIDER DETERMINED TO SHOW HE WAS WRONGLY ACCUSED OF DRUG ABUSE

Pedro Delgado, cheat or champion? The question will probably never be adequately resolved in sport's new climate of secrecy and suspicion. But, by completing the most astonishing comeback in the history of the Tour de France, Delgado has at least provided his critics with evidence that his win last year was not attributable to the black arts of medical science – as some have claimed.

After making a powerful statement of intent in the Pyrenees he was content to recuperate on yesterday's stage to Blagnac, an industrial suburb of Toulouse. With his favourite challenge in the Alps to come, he is in fourth place, 2 m 53 s behind race leader Laurent Fignon.

He remains insistent that he does not deserve the stain on his character left by last summer's revelation that traces of probenecid, a drug on the IOC's list of banned substances, were found in a urine sample. Probenecid has been used in other sports, notably athletics, as a masking agent for steroids. Delgado continues to claim he accepted it from his team doctor only to reduce levels of uric acid in his muscles. He justifies himself by reminding the world that, at the time, its use was not prohibited by the cycling authorities.

This year's Tour incorporates the most extensive drug-testing system. Every day samples taken from the overall leader, the first two riders in the stage and two other competitors chosen at random, are flown to Paris and analysed overnight.

The esteem in which Delgado is held by his public, ironically, has never been higher. Spectators wave Basque flags in his honour along the route, chant his name and scrawl promises of their support on the road. When he returned to his home in Segovia he was welcomed by 350,000 people. The town's mayor announced: 'Pedro gives so many of our people a reason to live.'

The cyclist remains a turbulent figure. His victory in the Tour of Spain earlier this year was accompanied by unsubstantiated accusations that he had bribed a Russian rider to help him win. However, Delgado's strong sense of regional identity makes him a man of real social and political influence. He is an intense, emotional individual whose essential humanity makes a deep impact on those around him.

He regards the Alpe d'Huez as a shrine to his mother, who died while he was riding it during the 1986 Tour. He dedicated his victory in the stage over that famous climb to her the following year and many feel it is his destiny to reclaim the yellow jersey there in 1989.

That achievement would embellish his legend. For no one has come from 198th and last, the position he occupied after he reported late for the opening day's Prologue. A mixture of embarrassment and mental turmoil is thought to have accounted for his performance on the second day, when he was in some distress and left himself a deficit of 7 m 20 s to make up on his principal rivals.

An unprecedented comeback would honour the traditions of an event that prides itself in remaining close to its roots. With its roadside parties and hordes of schoolchildren lining the lanes it continues to be an essential reflection of French life. That was especially so yesterday when the residents of Martres-Tolosane, a village that constituted the 1,789th kilometre of the race, turned out in French Revolution dress to welcome the Tour's survivors.

Yet, slowly, the character of the event is changing. It has, thanks to the patronage of American TV and such multinational companies as Coca-Cola, become even more aware of its commercial value. The prize fund of £800,000 has increased the stakes for the riders, a majority of whom are convinced that Delgado will be taking the salute, and the first prize of £150,000 on the Champs-Elysées. He will be able to claim that as a victory with honour.

———

LEMOND STEALS VICTORY WITH BRILLIANT TIME TRIAL

Phil Liggett in Paris

Greg LeMond produced the finest finish seen to the Tour de France yesterday when he won the final time trial from Versailles to the Champs-Elysées to turn an overnight deficit of 50 seconds into a remarkable victory by just eight seconds.

It was the closest finish in the 76 years of the race, bettering the finale 21 years ago when Jan Janssen beat Herman van Springel by 38 seconds. Laurent Fignon was desperately disappointed as the American flag flew near the Place de la Concorde. He was unable to smile after he lost 58 seconds to LeMond in yesterday's time trial, collapsing as he finished in a time of 27 m 55 s.

LeMond set off two minutes in front of Fignon, needing to make up about two seconds per kilometre to win the race. It would normally have been an impossible task. Instead the American, who still carries pellets from the hunting accident which nearly killed him in 1987, produced the fastest time trial in race history to win his third stage of the race and the most important with 26 m 57 s.

The route from the chateau was the reverse of that taken 200 years ago when revolutionaries marched on the monarchy, but the inspired ride by LeMond made its own slice of history as he took on the Parisians in the biggest head-to-head the race has ever known. LeMond set the standard at half-distance with 12 m 8 s and as he sped along the banks of the Seine, he stayed on his schedule. When he entered the Champs-Elysées with just two miles to go, he led Fignon by 48 seconds — just three more required on the ride down from the Arc de Triomphe. After 2,000 miles the race was decided in the last 300 yards.

LeMond said: 'I just had to produce something special to win and I had a fantastic day. At the finish line, I was just so surprised to win. This victory will mean more in the States than my 1986 win. A lot of people said then that [Frenchman Bernard] Hinault let me win but this time I did it all on my own.'

He also felt that his unusual triathlete's handlebars had played a part in his success. 'I think they gave me something like a 12-second advantage in the time trial,' LeMond said of the loop fitted on the front of his bike, allowing him to crouch into a better aerodynamic position.

Fignon, who won the Tour of Italy before this race began, nursed a saddle boil over the last few days. He was not making any excuses, but said afterwards: 'I didn't even think I would be able to start today it was so bad.'

**CHAPTER 5
THE 1990s**

PUBLICITY STUNT THAT BECAME A NATIONAL OBSESSION

Jacques Goddet

The Tour de France is a phenomenon which has become a part of our civilisation. It was born in 1903, at the beginning of this century of progress, to promote the daily sports paper *L'Auto*, set up to rival another sports publication, *Velo*.

L'Auto's director was Henri Desgrange; sport was his gospel. He was a sportsman himself, holding a 100-km tricycle record which, given the virtual disappearance of that machine, will probably stand for ever. The paper's administrator, Victor Goddet, was a man of organisation and figures.

The former, the journalist, was my spiritual father. The latter, the financier, was my natural father. Today the idea of the Tour de France seems ingenious. At the time, though, its creation met with misunderstanding, even hostility.

Country people could not accept that their age-old customs were being violated. Scythes to the fore, they threatened the disturbing, bare-legged characters who came on their peculiar machines to upset animal life, scattering terrified chickens and ducks.

What is more, unlike today, the riders were out on their own. Stages were of between 300 and 500 km in length and random checks were carried out at night in the depth of the countryside. There was cheating and conflict, relegation down the race standings and protest. Yet the idea must have been a good one because, in spite of everything, the Tour de France survived. Interest snowballed when M Desgrange boldly decided that his heroes should be sent into the mountains.

The adventure began cautiously with the Ballon d'Alsace in 1905. Five years later the race moved into the Pyrenees where many frightened riders dreaded a close encounter with a wolf. The race's great cols became known as the *'judges de paix'* [justices of the peace], the competitors as the *'giants de la route'* [giants of the road]. A whole mythical vocabulary grew up around the race.

Over the years the Tour has become a giant, living entity — a powerful financial operation with considerable media influence, increased by the arrival of television. Indeed, television and the Tour were made for each other. In return, because of the large crowds it generates, there is a heavy contribution to the Tour stage stopovers, sponsors, companies equipping the riders, and so on. All have benefited from being seen on television screens worldwide.

Coca-Cola now sponsor the race leader's yellow jersey. But why a yellow jersey? It was only in 1919, 16 years after the Tour's creation, that the race's organiser, M Desgrange, took up a suggestion to dress the event's overall leader in a distinctive jersey. The father of the Tour chose yellow simply because the newspaper he managed was printed on yellow paper and had earned its popularity with that colour.

The Tour de France's influence extends to the authorities and political and social life of the country. Traditionally held from the end of June through to the end of July, the race comes as a kind of truce. It appeases quarrels; ensures that controversies are forgotten. Politicians await the race to call a break, the government for some breathing space.

The Tour can certainly be a para-political instrument, as my own experience tells. I am not just referring to the appearance out in the field of government or parliamentary personalities, not averse to getting into the line of the cameras to congratulate a stage winner. Rather, I allude to the battle I had to wage during the German occupation of the 1940s to prevent the holding of the Tour de France. Both occupiers and the Vichy authorities, keen to prove to the world that France was living happily under the Nazi boot, wanted the Tour to go ahead. I was alone in charge, Henri Desgrange having died in 1940. Involved in the Resistance, my position was to succeed in refusing the provisions, fuel and vehicles offered to me, resist the pressures and oppose, in every way I could, the holding of the race. In the end others got together a substitute which did not survive.

---

3 JULY 1990

PIED PIPER ON A MOPED HELPS GREAT RACE TO BEAT PROTESTERS' BLOCKADE

Phil Liggett in Nantes

The Tour de France, which operates on a budget of £10 million, had one of its more bizarre days yesterday when the 198 riders and support vehicles were obliged to follow a man on his moped on a three-mile detour along country lanes.

The richest race in the world, which brings France to a halt wherever it goes, disappointed thousands of spectators in the town of Ste Gemme, when it took extreme action to beat a road blockade that had threatened to stop the race during the stage between Poitiers and Nantes. Burning tyres, trees and manure had been placed across the route before the town, which had been shut down to watch the riders snatch their food packs after 53 miles, but an unknown group of protesters, thought to number about 30, had been thwarted by the Frenchman who volunteered to pilot the race through the lanes.

The Tour, which was also disrupted on Sunday morning by the farmers' union Paysan, when they demonstrated about the price of mutton, had received advance warnings for yesterday's protests on the 148-mile third stage. Jean-Marie Leblanc, the race director, said: 'We had heard of four likely points on the course and we had drawn up secret detours, but the fifth place was a surprise to us.' The race itself was unaffected on the three-mile detour as the field had regrouped after a particularly fast start. The riders saw the occasion as a source of amusement.

---

23 JULY 1990

PURISTS PUZZLE OVER ENIGMATIC CHAMPION

VICTORIOUS RIDER REFUSES TO SACRIFICE ALL

Phil Liggett in Paris

If Greg LeMond had not possessed a great wish to become an acrobatic skier, then he would almost certainly never have discovered the bicycle which, at 29 years of age, has made him the richest cyclist in the world. He is an enigma the Latin Europeans will never fully understand because, instead of just being a cyclist, he is a family man who loves many facets of life. Above all, he hates to train.

LeMond believes the Tour de France is his by right and, if he had not been near death after being injured in a shooting accident which lost him two years of a short career, he could have been rivalling Jacques Anquetil, Eddy Merckx and Bernard Hinault, all of whom have won the race five times.

LeMond is not a complex character, unless one is French, in which case understanding a man who plays golf, fishes, eats Mexican food and hunts when he should be training, leaves a bad taste among those who concentrate 12 months a year on preparing for a race they are unlikely to win.

The American, who lives in Kortrijk, Belgium, during the season, turned to cycling by accident after attending a ski school in Nevada for potential 'hot dog' skiers. He was advised the best training in the summer was cycling and with Bob, his father, he watched a bicycle race. From then he developed a burning desire to win the Tour de France.

Last winter, having won both the Tour and the World Championship for the second time each, LeMond signed a contract with the French children's clothing manufacturer Z for a record £3.2 million over three years, wiping away in one deal the cloth-cap image the sport had engendered from its 100 years of development around the villages of Italy, France and Belgium.

After signing the deal, LeMond gave cause for concern in March when he started the season poorly prepared. At one point he even hinted at retirement after finishing many minutes behind in every race. Roger Legeay, his team manager, sent him back to his American home in Wayzata, on the edge of Lake Minnetonka in Minnesota, with instructions just to train and rest. LeMond's poor condition, mainly as a result of the dinner round as a celebrity after being the first cyclist to be voted America's top sportsman of 1989, led Merckx to predict that he would not finish the Tour of Italy and would not even start the Tour de France.

LeMond's talent for the sport was first sighted in Europe by Cyrille Guimard, a Frenchman who had trained Hinault to Tour victory, and after hearing of the American's junior world title in 1979 he watched him in an international race in France. Riding for an American international team, LeMond joined in a breakaway and punctured without the team car behind.

He threw his bicycle into a hedge, saying he was retiring, but was asked by his team manager to continue for the sake of the team. He picked up his bike and again threw it away, watched by Guimard. 'I like you,' Guimard told him. 'You have a character, but don't you ever do something like that again in front of me when you are a professional.'

Hinault and Guimard, neither of whom spoke English, went to the United States, wore Stetsons and rode horses with LeMond before coming back with a deal for him to turn professional. But, in 1985, the rookie became as good as Hinault the teacher, and a rift developed which broke up their winning partnership.

LeMond shows no animosity towards his brother-in-law, who accidentally shot him in the back when hunting in California in 1987, weeks before he should have defended his first Tour title of 1986. LeMond's life was saved almost by chance. A rough ride over hard ground took him to the entry to the private area behind his house, where the radio calls for help were intercepted by a police helicopter. The police decided to land for LeMond rather than attend a traffic accident. Had they chosen the accident LeMond would probably have died.

Today LeMond rides with some of the 200 pellets still in the walls of his heart, but when you watch him fiercely defend and attack, driven on by the belief that the Tour de France is his until he retires, his strong will to live marries naturally with his strong will to win.

30 JULY 1990

TOUR DE FORCE

Sir,

The Tour de France seems to have gone without any of the disgraceful scenes which have marred other sporting events. The fact that the riders represented trade teams instead of national teams no doubt had much to do with the sporting atmosphere. Is there a lesson to be learnt?

E.L. Parsons
Twickenham

10 AUGUST 1990

CYCLING ENTENTE

Sir,

Now that Phil Liggett has confirmed that cycling has climbed from 30th to tenth in sporting popularity, may I offer the following as worthy of contemplation by followers of some other sports. I refer to the sincere internationalism that is innate among road racing fans – each encouraging their favourite but still clapping in genuine admiration of the other contenders.

With the crowds for the Tour of Britain now rivalling those on the Tour de France, the practice of chalking their heroes' name and national colours on the road prior to the riders' arrival is now common on both sides of the Channel. I have never heard of the need to segregate fans. In fact supporters co-operate by sharing the chalk!

Alan Stuart
Wokingham, Berks

---

24 JULY 1991

THE HILLS ARE ALIVE WITH SALUTES TO 'SINGING' INDURAIN

Ian Ridley

Eighteen days and 17 stages into the Tour de France and almost 80 hours of riding can be undone by 45 minutes of what is probably the most punishing test in sport. Alpe d'Huez makes or breaks champions.

Last night it looked to have done both as Greg LeMond, last year's winner, trailed in almost two minutes behind Miguel Indurain, potentially this year's. It will have done much to reinforce Alpe d'Huez's reputation as the most intimidating tranche of the Tour.

Its intensity and drama are why more than 500,000 people line the mountain road, enduring hours of discomfort and traffic jams to get claustrophobically close to this breed apart for just a few minutes. The stage from Gap, although previously mountainous enough, begins in reality only 15 km from the finish, at the foot of the Alp. The bunch, the peloton, were content to let Frenchman Thierry Bourguignon enjoy his day in the sun through his home area, his name painted everywhere en route. It did seem to beef up Bourguignon.

Then, after a descent for the skilled and brave into Bourg d'Oisans – great climbers can lose time descending if they lack the ability to look beyond the immediate bend – the real climbing began. A left turn out of the village and the extent of the task becomes apparent. Just the sight of winding roads almost vertically above can break the spirit. The lesser riders will be calculating how much time they can afford to lose on the leaders without being eliminated.

Television scarcely conveys the extent of the task: 21 bends rising 1,100 metres at one-in-12 over the 15 km. With only the mind racing ahead, the first three or four are said to be the worst. There are second-hand cars that wouldn't make it that far. It is not just the height but the heat. A rider is likely to lose six or seven pounds during the ordeal. Most of it is body fluid and, dangerously, he has time to consume only about a litre of water as replacement. Several have collapsed but none has died. Yet.

Bend 15 – they are counted down – can bring more demoralising moments for those weakening: the sight of the leaders a few bends up and the noise of the accompanying cheers. For the *domestiques,* the drones to the team leader's queen bee, the worst thing of all can be hearing the result. That can happen three kilometres from the finish, cruelly at the first glimpse of the summit, at the bend where the cemetery d'Huez can seem to wink at a rider. But by two kilometres he knows he has made it and relief, emotional and physical, is at hand. The one final twist is yet another hairpin bend 200 metres from the finish, followed by an uphill sprint to the line.

The tortuous nature of the experience is matched only by the extent to which spectators will go to witness it all. Thousands of them cycle the mountains in the morning for the hell of it, though at scarcely the same speed as the professionals. By 8 a.m., with the race due through at 4.30 p.m., Bourg d'Oisans is jammed with traffic. By 9 a.m. the road up the Alp is closed. Those who have located prime positions on the mountain or in Alpe d'Huez itself have been camped there for several days. It is a little like Christmas lunch: hours to cook, minutes to eat.

From Italy, Spain, Holland, the fans come. And, yes, Britain, even though only the Scot, Robert Millar, remains since the last English-man, Sean Yates, baled out the previous day. Some wear the foot-ball shirts of Liverpool, Everton and Wolverhampton Wanderers; many more wear the cycling attire of such as Port Sunlight Wheel-ers, Tyneside Vagabonds and Letchworth Velo Club.

Five coaches have disgorged a large group of Brits intending to cycle up from Bourg. The man from Middlesex Road Club is most concerned about losing his false teeth. There may be much to amuse in the chic ski resort of Alpe d'Huez but, lower down, there is only camaraderie to occupy the time. That and the thought of Eddy Merckx riding out for pleasure with his son Axel, a junior champion.

It is on the ascent that painting the road with the name of one's favourite has mostly got out of hand. Only some environmentally conscious people, such as those who etched 'Vinny Smith' on the melting tarmac, use water soluble paint. There were no words exhorting Djamolidine Abdoujaparov, the Soviet rider from Tashkent who does not speak Russian. The heat must have rendered the effort too much.

That was until dark clouds enveloped the Alp and the heavens opened. It mattered not for the leader at the end of a remarkable day. He may well be nicknamed 'Singing' Indurain.

---

27 JULY 1991

INTROVERT INDURAIN STEPS OUT OF DELGADO'S GIANT SHADOW

Ian Ridley

For a man who lives in Pamplona, it has taken Miguel Indurain a long time to learn to run with the bulls. Tomorrow in Paris should see him crowned as winner of the Tour de France, finally ready to assume the role of champion, toughness in heart and mind now matching that of his talented body.

In this sporting year of the Quiet Man, Indurain joins the list that takes in Michael Stich and Ian Baker-Finch. Actually the Spaniard is more José Maria Olazábal to Pedro Delgado's Severiano Ballesteros. Delgado, winner of the Tour three years ago, is the dashing, attacking darling of a nation. Until now, he has cast a giant shadow over Indurain. There have even been suggestions that Indurain was content to remain in darkness, unwilling because of his quiet nature to cross the divide from what golfers call the comfort zone to that possibly scary place where a major champion exists.

Indurain has hitherto dedicated himself to working for Delgado in the Banesto team. Last year, for example, he paced him to the base of Alpe d'Huez, drawing the sting from challengers. He lost 11 m 55 s on the stage to the winner by sacrificing his own ambitions. He eventually finished 12 m and 47 s down on champion Greg LeMond.

That was the best performance of a career that was not delivering its promise, at least in the Tour. The Spanish amateur champion of 1983, who turned professional two years later, did not finish his first two Tours, then finished 97th and 47th in his next two. Stage wins in the Pyrenees in 1989 and 1990, when he finished 17th and tenth overall, and two victories in the Paris-Nice classic, served notice of his prowess. Victory in the Tour of Vaucluse and second place in the Tour of Spain this year proved his growing maturity.

Indurain made the Tour de France sit up in its saddle this year when, more commonly known for his climbing, he won the 73-km time trial from Argentan to Alençon in the first week.

The Banesto team said before the Tour that the race would decide who was the team leader between Indurain and Delgado. But Indurain, it seemed, had already decided. Fittingly, he took over the yellow jersey as the race briefly entered Spain. Delgado, who had said that he would not forget Indurain's past efforts on his behalf, now rode in support. With Jean-François 'Jeff' Bernard also riding excellently alongside, Indurain has had the best protective team.

'He has been very careful with his goals and stuck to the planning of his career,' says Stephen Hodge, the Australian who rides for the Spanish Once team. 'Everyone has seen his huge potential for a long time. Now the mental toughness has come with experience. He is extremely modest and a really incredible athlete. He has a huge physiological capacity for work, probably because he is extremely tall and heavy.' At 6 ft 5 in and 12 st 2 lb, Indurain is unusually big for a top cyclist. They more often resemble emaciated greyhounds. 'He is very friendly, very relaxed and very well respected among the riders,' adds Hodge. 'Delgado is still the mega-star in Spain, but Miguel is approaching him, even if he is a little different in character.'

That difference in character worries the Spanish press slightly. They have gathered in France this week to acclaim him – 70 journalists are here already, with more descending on Paris now – but he is not very communicative. The joke goes that he nods in response to questions from radio interviewers. His trainer, François Lafarge, said: 'He has many things to say but he can't express them.'

Indurain has declared, though, that he would like to be successful enough to retire in three or four years. He turned 27 during the Tour, on the verge of his peak, so he might be able to do so. Indurain may never be another Ballesteros, but, after tomorrow, Indurain in Spain will never again be plain.

———

29 JULY 1991

INDURAIN COMPLETES PROCESSION TO VICTORY

Phil Liggett in Paris

After a week of domination, Miguel Indurain became only the fourth Spaniard to win the Tour de France when it ended its 2,400-mile journey on the Champs-Elysées. Farmer's son Indurain, 27, follows in the wheel tracks of Federico Bahamontes (1959), Luis Ocaña (1973) and Pedro Delgado (1988). Indurain, from Villava near Pamplona in northern Spain, shepherded his former team leader, Delgado, to victory three years ago, but this time the roles were reversed.

Both riders were discovered by their current Banesto team director, José-Miguel Echávarri. 'I owe Echávarri a lot,' Indurain said. 'He moulded my career both as an apprentice and a professional. He pushed me when I needed it.'

Echávarri said of Indurain: 'I saw what natural talent he had, but it's important not to look for immediate results. You can wear out a rider prematurely.' Consequently, Echávarri was cautious and only permitted him to emerge as team leader this year. 'Before, he was not ready for the responsibilities,' he said. 'It was the same with Pedro. We waited till he was mature enough. It was no problem for Pedro to work for Miguel as team leader. It's a question of loyalty.'

Referring to his replacement of Delgado as the top Spanish rider, Indurain said: 'I think he prefers to be deposed by me than by someone he doesn't like. But I don't suppose he is completely happy about it because it is cruel.'

Indurain was expertly guided through the mountains by his Banesto team – so much so that he said after the finish in Paris: 'To be honest, I didn't have to go deep into my reserves to win this Tour.'

Greg LeMond, winner for the past two years, but this time collapsing on the second day in the Pyrenees after earlier leading, finished seventh – his worst position in six Tours de France. The American, sometimes in tears in the mountains, resisted the easy alternative of giving up and showed his tenacity. LeMond said: 'I've always come into the Tour de France believing I can't lose. I put all the pressure on myself this year, so there's no one else to blame. When you're bad in the Tour, then you appreciate what it's like when you're good, and just how good you have to be.'

----

29 JUNE 1992

FRENCH STAY FAITHFUL TO THE ORIGINAL HOLIDAY ATTRACTION

THE CONTINUING ALLURE OF THE TOUR DE FRANCE

Samuel Abt

Jean-Marie Leblanc is just joking – or is he? – when he explains that the Tour de France, the world's most prestigious bicycle race, owes its immense popularity with the French to one of those small accidents of history.

When the race began in 1903, July arbitrarily became the month of its setting. 'July makes all the difference,' says Leblanc, who directs the race. 'July is vacation for so many people,' notwithstanding the foreigners' impression that France shuts down for August. 'No, no,' Leblanc explains. 'Paris shuts for August. For most of the rest of France July is vacation. So that gives us so many more spectators, more television coverage, more sponsors and more reporters. And that translates into more interest by the great riders and the great teams.'

As theories go, Leblanc's makes as much sense as any. The Tour de France has only two rivals, the Giro d'Italia and the Vuelta a España, and neither really competes in terms of interest, let alone financial reward. Perhaps that is because both are held long before the sun is hot enough to lure holiday-makers to the mountains, seas and plains that the Tour de France passes by. The Vuelta runs from late April to mid-May and the Giro from late May to mid-June.

From 15 to 20 million spectators are expected to line the race's roads for three weeks, starting on Saturday, while a global audience estimated at several hundred million will watch on television.

By today's standards, the one-column headline at the top of page one of *L'Auto* on 19 January 1903, was a minimal display: 'Le Tour de France,' it announced. Underneath, in small type: 'The greatest bicycling test in the world − a month-long race − Paris-Lyon-Marseille-Toulouse-Bordeaux-Nantes-Paris − 20,000 francs in prizes − Leaving June 1. Arriving in Paris, July 5, at the Parc des Princes.'

The impressive total of 20,000 francs, then worth $100,000, would be roughly equal in buying power now to 3.2 million francs. The 1992 Tour will award ten million francs in overall prizes.

The announcement caused 'an enormous emotion in the sports world', *L'Auto* reported the next day in a front page article signed by the paper's chief cycling correspondent, Geo Lefevre. 'Naturally, champions of the road now in Paris paraded into our offices, enthusiastic about the idea and thrilled by such a manna of prizes,' Lefevre continued.

To read *L'Auto* nearly 90 years later, even discounting the self-promotion, it is easy to see why the idea of the race was a sensation. Sportsmen in cities to be visited sent letters celebrating the news. On the other hand, the organiser reported on 25 January, many cities complained that the Tour would miss them. 'Perpignan, in a tearful letter, insists that it isn't far from the projected route,' *L'Auto* wrote. Albi, Cahors and Auch, 'with a touching unanimity', protested that they had not been included. So did Cognac, Niort and Limoges.

By May, though, barely more than a dozen riders had signed up. Without 50 riders there would be no Tour de France the paper warned. Realising that few men wanted to be away for 35 days, the organisers decided to reduce the length to three weeks, the same time-span still used. Because of the organisational work still to be completed, the race was pushed back to a 1 July start. *Et voilà!*

There are other theories, of course, to explain why the Tour is the centre of the French summer. One, much beloved by foreigners, is that the French love sports, especially when played by somebody else. They also love a spectacle and a free outing, which the Tour offers daily. Then, as the sociologist Richard Holt observed in the book *Sport and Society in Modern France:* 'To a country obsessed with a fear of demographic decline, economic failure and military defeat, the Tour de France offered a comforting image of Frenchmen as tenacious, strong and swift.'

Part of the truth is that, because of its age, the Tour, and bicycle racing in general, have their roots deep into the French soil. In Paris, the preference in sports has moved upmarket to tennis from bicycle racing which, with its emphasis on struggle and sacrifices, was an ideal sport for a country rebuilding after the Second World War. Now the mood in Paris has turned against sacrifice and suffering.

Despite their names, Paris-Roubaix, Paris-Nice, Paris-Camembert, and a handful of other races prefixed with 'Paris', start far outside the capital. Traffic problems, officials explain, but the true reason is indifference.

Outside Paris, where there is little obligation to be modern, where things chic and new are distrusted, fans still flock to races to play their own small roles. If the day is hot and a climb long and tiring, people will hold out a bottle of water to a cyclist. Pushes, even unsolicited ones, may be illegal and yet officials will often look away when a fan helps a faltering climber by shoving him uphill. In the time before a race starts, fans will circulate among the pack, seeking autographs from their favourites, posing for photographers alongside this rider or that, wishing good luck.

In the countryside, *la France profond*, vanishing France, where the old prejudices live on, the Tour de France is still paramount. Boulogne sur Gesse in the French southwest is one of those places. Boulogne is a small town (1,600 population by generous count) founded by an order of monks in the 13th century. Between then and now not much appears to have happened there, according to tourist literature. The biggest day ever arrived on 23 March 1814, when the British army under the Duke of Wellington camped there overnight on its way to fight Napoleon.

In seven centuries, Boulogne sur Gesse has produced only two persons judged noteworthy by the same tourist literature: Emmanuel Peres de la Gesse, a minor figure in the French Revolution, who advanced to become a baron of the empire, and Jacques Moujica, who won the marathon Bordeaux-Paris bicycle race in 1949. That same year he finished second in Paris-Brussels and third in Paris-Roubaix. A year later at the age of 24 he was killed in a car crash while travelling to a bicycle criterium after the Tour de France.

Moujica is buried in Boulogne sur Gesse, which mourns him still. When the Tour de France whizzed through the town two years ago on a stage from Blagnac to Luz Ardiden in the Pyrenees, journalists with the race were invited to a late breakfast/early lunch ('brunch' is a Paris word) in Boulogne and served bowls of hearty stew and beakers of heartier wine.

The reception hall, a market most other days, was decorated with posters celebrating Moujica and his feats. Scrapbooks covered display cases, as did some of his Mercier team jerseys. Townspeople sat on wooden benches with the journalists and talked about Moujica and that glorious Bordeaux-Paris race as if he had won it earlier in the season.

The mayor spoke, too. He discussed the decline of rural France, where agriculture is imperilled by rising costs and falling subsidies, and quoted Talleyrand as having said: 'Industry can only weaken the national morality: France must remain agricultural.' Everybody applauded, even the farmers, who wanted to talk bicycle racing, that elegant sport.

———

5 JULY 1992

TERRORIST BOMB FAILS TO HALT TOUR DE FRANCE

Phil Liggett

The incendiary device which destroyed three Channel 4 television cars and four other vehicles in the early hours of yesterday morning has placed the Tour de France on red alert as the 2,500-mile race began in the Spanish resort of San Sebastian.

Assumed by official sources to be the work of the Basque separatist movement, ETA, the seven cars set on fire in the small border town of Fuenterrabia, 12 miles outside San Sebastian, followed the burning of two cars near the official start line in the city on Friday evening.

The burning of three of the five British television company's vehicles happened at 2 a.m. yesterday outside the Hotel San Nicolas. The alarm was raised by a Dutch holidaymaker when a Renault Espace, rented by Channel 4 and registered in France, burst into flames. The fire quickly spread to a row of six vehicles, including the Citroën rented by me and Paul Sherwen, the Channel 4 commentary team on the race.

We saw the flames engulf first the Espace and then our car and it quickly spread to four private vehicles. Police indicated to us that the terrorists had chosen the vehicles because two of them had French plates. More than £1,700 of my personal effects were destroyed and my clothes for the television programme were also lost.

Police took the remaining two vehicles into a guarded pound in the town, where they will stay each evening until the race leaves Spain. The 14-man team reporting the race were given two cars by the organising committee for temporary use.

It is the first time the Tour de France has attempted a start in Spain and though the organisers had received a number of threats, it had been generally felt that the Basque movement would not disrupt the race after the Société du Tour de France agreed to give them a high profile by signing the route and all facilities in the Euskara (Basque) language. The political wing of ETA, the Herri Batasuna movement, had promised the race full support, but they could not account for extremist views.

On Friday, a man was arrested after being injured during the throwing of an incendiary device in which a French television car was destroyed in a car park near to where yesterday's Prologue time trial finished.

---

20 JULY 1992

A MASS WALKOUT HANDED ROGER LAPEBIE VICTORY IN 1937

William Fotheringham

A saboteur with a hacksaw did his best to wreck Roger Lapébie's chances of winning the Tour de France by sawing through the handlebars of his bike. The handlebars collapsed as Lapébie warmed up the next day but the Frenchman later arrived triumphant in Paris – with new handlebars.

The incident was typical of the acrimonious Tour of 1937, raced at a time when life was so hard for the riders they were nicknamed 'convicts of the road'. Lapébie, the oldest surviving winner of the Tour, is, at 81, small and birdlike and does not look his age. His face is deeply tanned and lean from the long hours he still puts in on his bike from his home near Bordeaux. With Gino Bartali, he is one of only two pre-War winners still alive.

The 1937 Tour reached a crisis when the entire Belgian team pulled out due to what they saw as favouritism by the French race judges. The cycling reference book, *Gotha,* describes the events:

'The decision taken by the race judges, after the Belgians' win in the team time trial, to suppress several of these stages, annoyed them in the first place. When Roger Lapébie, who had been caught taking pushes in the Pyrenees and was seen taking pace behind a car, was then only fined 90 seconds, the tension mounted. The French, who had threatened to walk out after Lapébie was penalised, claimed that the Belgian team had been helped by an individual rider [against the rules]. The 15-second penalty given to the Belgians was considered insufficient by one camp, and an injustice by the other.'

The last straw for the Belgians came when a level-crossing barrier went down just as their leader, Sylvère Maes, was returning to the bunch after a puncture. Added to hostility from the general public, the incident led the Belgians to retire *en masse* with four days remaining.

Lapébie, who in 1934 had picked up five stage wins and third place overall, had only five team-mates left by the rest day in Geneva and decided to restrict himself to going for stages. 'I wasn't sure I was able to win so I wanted to make money,' he said. 'After the Alps I won the stage from Briançon to Digne, and got close to the lead. Bartali was in the yellow jersey but he fell on that stage and abandoned the next day. The Belgian team were really strong, with Maes and Vervaecke, and were most likely to win. There were five Belgians in other teams which meant they had 15 men to control the race.'

The most important stage, according to Lapébie, was the 280-km leg from Luchon to Pau. 'It was decisive. I was either going to do OK or lose.' Then, as he was warming up before the start, his handlebars broke. 'They had been sawed part way through. It was a bit suspicious. It was sawed through by someone close to the Belgians,' Lapébie maintains.

Lapébie suffered time penalties on the stage because his new bars had no bottle cages on them and, against the rules, drinks were handed to him. He was also involved in a brush with race officials about whether the crowds had been pushing him. A dip in a roadside spring inspired Lapébie to go on and catch the leaders and take second place.

The next stage, Pau-Bordeaux, proved the end of the Belgian

challenge. 'Maes punctured, all the team waited for him, and some of the other Belgians. I attacked with the Swiss team. There was a bit of *complicité* and I had friends in the bunch. Maes lost a minute.'

Then the Belgians left the race, led by their leader, Karl Stayer, director of a Belgian paper. 'He did the selection, was a journalist, director and a big boss, and he didn't like his team to be beaten by five little Frenchmen, so they took the train from Bordeaux, and I arrived in Paris the winner,' said Lapébie.

Conditions endured by Tour fields of old were distinctly rough and ready compared to those enjoyed by today's riders. The roads, he says, were *épouvantable* – atrocious. 'There were pot-holes, which we used to call birds' nests, pebbles, dust, gravel. In those days we were given 25 pairs of shorts and 25 jerseys and changed our socks every day because of the dust and the dirt.

'We got lots of saddle sores because of the dirt and the cow dung – it was easy to get infected.' Ninety-eight men started the 1937 race; only 36 finished. The diet is one thing that has not changed a great deal. 'We ate lots of fresh vegetables, rice, fish and a lot of red meat, which we ate rare. As a result of that, in 1934 I became a vegetarian because the meat polluted our bodies and gave us boils.'

Lapébie may have been the first vegetarian winner of the Tour as well. He puts his continuing good health down to his diet, plus the fact that he has never drunk alcohol or smoked. During the race there were no isotonic drinks, no special foods. 'We drank tea and coffee, that was our form of doping. I used to take two bottles of very strong coffee with lots of sugar. We used to eat sugar and rice cake.'

What Lapébie calls 'old wives' remedies' were used to look after the riders. 'We took very hot baths, with three or four kilogrammes of sea salt and two or three litres of vinegar after a cold, rainy stage. After the bath we would have a very good, very hard massage, using a lot of seaweed. The *soigneur* [masseur] would wipe our legs with cotton, then we would put on long johns.'

Mustard plasters were another remedy, doubtless for their power to concentrate heat in parts of the body. 'American or English were best. We'd buy packets of three or four dozen in Paris and put them on our legs all night if they were painful.'

Bikes were solid, according to Lapébie, with very few light components. The bottle cage might be aluminium, but this relatively lightweight metal was avoided for bars and stem because they tended to break. In 1934 and 1935 lighter materials were used more and more. 'We started experimenting with light stuff like dural rims and bikes progressed every year.' Lapébie was the first man to win the race using a derailleur gear, which revolutionised gear-changing, as 1937 was the first year they were permitted.

For Lapébie, 1937 was his moment of glory. The following year he did not start the Tour. He was not invited, following a disagreement with race founder Henri Desgrange. In 1939 a knee injury sustained in the Bordeaux-Paris race brought a premature end to an eventful career.

---

25 JULY 1992

QUIET ACHIEVER YATES AT FINAL STAGE OF HIS CAREER

Ian Ridley

Barring accidents and illness, unlikely at this stage of the race, he should make it to Paris tomorrow having consolidated his position in the most gruelling Tour de France most riders can remember. No, not Miguel Indurain, but Sean Yates.

Yates is – and this is his description – a 'little' rider, a *domestique*, whose job is to nurse along, when needed, the team leader, in his case, Andy Hampsten of Motorola. This could be the last time though, says the 32-year-old from Forest Row in Sussex, and the passing of his unspectacular but worthy career in the race deserves recognition.

Yates is listed among the 'other placings' in the results, even if he is well known to the British cycling fraternity, of whom there are many with *Le Tour*, including a marvellous mad pair who came by tandem to Blois from Alençon yesterday.

But though he is poles apart from Indurain, the British professional champion is still a part – and he did, remarkably, win a stage four years ago – and in demand. 'I came to the decision that I was never going to be a big leader so I thought I would make the most of my talents and be a good *domestique*,' he says. 'I can only compete with the best guys when I'm screaming warm, which is about three times a year. But if you can get a good reputation as a team man you are always guaranteed a job.'

And he has a good reputation for durability and unselfishness. Nine Tours – and this should be the seventh finish – testify to him never being short of work. He is thus also well qualified to assess this year's event, the toughest he and many more have known, he says, the pace draining as much from riders as if they had also ridden the Pyrenees. The event, too, has gone from circus to zoo. 'It is the only race that everyone watches,' he says. 'It's just so big, almost too big. It feels much more of a strain than it has ever done. You can't relax for a minute. At the *départ* you used to be able to have a cup of coffee with people. Now there are millions milling around. It's just chaos.'

It pains him, he says, having to ignore people sometimes because otherwise he might never even start. 'Everyone is clambering around you, and I'm just a little rider, so you know what it's like for Indurain.'

The racing has been so fast – the pattern of modern cycling, he says – because without many riders capable of winning the race, teams often opt to try to win stages for the glory and publicity, thus the attacking is frequent. Another factor has been the Tour's progress through so many countries this year. 'When you are in Spain, the Spanish riders go much harder,' he says. 'When you are in Belgium, the Belgians; then in Holland, the Dutch; and in

Germany, the Germans.' You tell him that we therefore await the Tour coming to England when the Channel Tunnel opens, and he smiles.

The variation in weather has, too, proved punishing, and accounted for so many dropping out – 68 of the 198 starters. 'It puts more strain on the immune system. Some have got food poisoning due to general fatigue.'

Yates himself has not felt close to abandoning this year, even though he was suffering from bronchitis during the Alps, the legacy of which is a dry cough which punctuates his conversation as we speak after yesterday's sizzling time trial. 'At first I couldn't breathe. I thought I was going to drop,' he says of the mountain stages. 'But I was lucky up Alpe d'Huez. I got in with a good crowd,' he adds, sounding like someone-made-good looking back on his teens.

The climb's well in the past; yesterday was more to his taste as he raced with no opportunity to take in the beauty bordering the banks of the Loire from Tours to Blois in the 18th-fastest time, beating riders such as Pascal Lino, a former yellow jersey wearer, and Hampsten.

It was a stirring, storming performance to end on, even if it lifted him only two places to 82nd overall, and end he intends it to be. He acknowledges, though, that he does not yet know how he will cope with the 'emptiness' that a season without the Tour de France evokes. 'When you aren't there you wish you were,' says the man who once had to pull out a week from the end with an infection. 'But when you are going up an Alp you wish you were at home watching it on TV.'

Tomorrow he will wish to be nowhere except the Champs-Elysées. If, that is, he can just avoid his fate of this Saturday last year: a crash which ripped open an arm and cruelly caused his only other withdrawal. 'Still,' he says, 'I can't complain. It's a good life.'

————

12 JULY 1993

ARMSTRONG SHOWS MATURITY IN HIS MODEST DESIRES

Phil Liggett in Verdun

Lance Armstrong, 21, who was thought by many observers to be too young to ride the 2,700-mile Tour de France, saluted the large crowd in Verdun yesterday after he won the 114-mile eighth stage from Châlons-sur-Marne. The Texan, a former triathlete and a professional only since the Olympic Games last year, delivered a finishing sprint that left the rest of an experienced front group watching from the wings.

Armstrong said: 'I came to the Tour for two reasons: to learn and to win a stage, and I've achieved both.' Since the race began more than a week ago in western France, Armstrong has been viewed as a rider who should have stayed at home for one more year, but his maturity, both physically and mentally, has shown through in these opening 900 miles.

Armstrong, America's road-race champion, takes each day as it comes. If he finds the mountains, which start with the Alps this week, too hard he will be pulled out of the race in a manner similar to Swiss star Alex Zulle a year ago. Yesterday, Zulle's hopes of Tour victory took a severe setback when he was knocked off by a spectator as the race passed the Douaumont memorial to the fallen of the First World War. Last night his team were confident he would start the race today despite bruising and cuts to his right elbow and left thigh and severe bruising to his back.

———

26 JULY 1993

INDURAIN IS A CLASS APART WITH THIRD VICTORY IN A ROW

Phil Liggett in Paris

Miguel Indurain, of Spain, duly rode on the Champs-Elysées in warm sunshine yesterday afternoon to claim his third Tour de France victory in succession. He also became the first rider to win both the Tours of Italy and France in successive years.

Indurain's final margin, after leading the race for two weeks, was 4 m 59 s, 27 seconds better than last year, when he beat Italians Claudio Chiappucci and Gianni Bugno. This time he had found much harder opposition from Tony Rominger, who was the runner-up.

Dublin's Stephen Roche, who along with Sean Kelly has been one of Ireland's most successful riders since turning professional in 1981, said '*au revoir*' to the Tour de France when he finished 13th. 'It has been a fantastic period of my life, but I will not be going back on my decision to retire, although many people have asked me to reconsider,' Roche said.

Roche, 33, was the first Irishman to win the Tour de France during a magical 1987 season when he won the Tour of Italy and, six weeks after the French race, added the world crown. On that occasion, having won the previous two big Tours, he rode all day to try to help Sean Kelly win the world title for the first time. With a mile to go, Kelly missed a split in the leading group and Roche raced to his first, and only, world championship. He had achieved the cycling equivalent of the Triple Crown, a feat which had been accomplished only once before, in 1974 by Eddy Merckx.

Roche, whose career was punctuated by injury and contractual disputes, has worked hard this season to leave the sport on a high note with a string of excellent performances. He finished ninth in this year's Tour of Italy and his 13th place in the Tour de France will assure him he looks back with fondness over his final season.

28 JUNE 1994

TOUR TROUBLE

Sir,

Has anybody considered the residents of Kent whose lives will be severely disrupted by the invasion of the Tour de France on July 6? The roads forming the route of the race through Kent and Sussex will be closed, even to residents, for at least four hours.

More important, the route cannot be crossed during the closure, which will effectively isolate the north from the south of the county. Kentish Men of Newenden wishing to connect with Men of Kent in Maidstone are diverted 12 miles via the A21 and Tonbridge.

What effect will this sort of thing have on businesses, such as haulage contractors, for whom mobility is the very essence? Surely it is not worth this upset just to bring a bit of extra trade to the pubs and similar establishments along the route?

Lionel Macpherson-Strutt
Tonbridge, Kent

---

30 JUNE 1994

THE TOUR SET FOR BUMPER CROWDS

Sir,

Mr Macpherson-Strutt (Letter, June 28) complains that our roads will be closed for some four hours to allow the Tour de France to pass – a small price to see one of the world's great sporting events.

Certainly cycling is not as popular as football or cricket, but I will eat my bike if Tour enthusiasts give the police any problems, either by drinking or by hooliganism.

And, as I told a local complainer, if the sight of 200 superbly fit young men, speeding through our village, inspires only one of the local lads to take up the sport, it will be well worth it.

Mrs Pat Hill
Ashford, Kent

———

4 JULY 1994

BOARDMAN KEEPS YELLOW JERSEY AS SPRINTERS CRASH

Phil Liggett in Armentières

Chris Boardman, the Olympic champion, was thoroughly blooded into the tough world of professional racing in the Tour de France yesterday. He had to survive a long and hot opening stage from Lille to Armentières as race leader and a spectacular crash at the finish where the world's fastest sprinters collided with a policeman in the last 50 metres.

The accident happened at 40 mph when Belgian champion Wilfried Nelissen, with the complete field of 189 riders hot on his heels, hit a policeman who was standing on the race-side of the barriers taking a photograph. Then top Frenchman Laurent Jalabert somersaulted over the scene, quickly followed by Italian Fabiano Fontinelli, Russian Alexander Gontchenkov and another Belgian sprinter, Johan Capiot.

It was a grim end to a stage which saw Boardman gain another British record by holding the yellow jersey for two days since winning the opening Prologue time trial in record time in Lille on Saturday. Previously, Tom Simpson wore it for a day in 1962. Boardman, 25, who finished 29th, was warmly received by the French crowds here after the 145-mile stage, but breathed a sigh of relief as he avoided the chaos which reigned as the leaders fell in sight of the line.

The stage was won by Djamolidine Abdoujaparov, the great

Uzbek sprinter so often involved in controversial finishes. Yesterday he was totally absolved from blame as he swerved clear of the crashing riders to his right.

Jalabert, a winner of seven stages of this year's Tour of Spain, and fellow sprinter Nelissen, recent winner of the Belgian championship and an early leader of the Tour last year, were taken to hospital immediately. Jalabert suffered broken bones in his face and severe concussion, while Nelissen, who only recently started racing again after breaking his collarbone in an event in Belgium, underwent a brain scan last night.

Fontinelli walked across the line 20 minutes after the crash in a daze and was also taken to hospital, though all the fallen riders were given a finishing position in the hope that they would be able to line up today. The policeman, later criticised by Tour organisers, was also taken to hospital with rib and elbow injuries.

Abdoujaparov said: 'I don't know how the accident happened because it was a very wide road. But in any case, a sprint is always dangerous because the non-sprinters mix it with sprinters and don't know what to do. I don't know how the policeman got there but I know he shouldn't have been on the course.'

7 JULY 1994

TWO WORLDS PASS IN WHIRR

TEA AND BUNTING GREET CYCLING'S CREAM IN SUSSEX COUNTRYSIDE

Michael Calvin

Cream teas were being served in the village hall, where the Women's Institute prepared a chairobics demonstration for the unconverted. Dame Vera Lynn, Ditchling's most celebrated resident, had a suitable song for the occasion.

There *will* always be an England. Whether the Tour de France, which has crossed the Channel for the first time in 20 years, can be integrated successfully into a different culture remains to be seen. But yesterday, with the rain clouds scudding over the South Downs and Sussex self-consciously adopting the strangled vowels and tortured syntax of *Franglais,* two worlds collided with remarkably little fall-out.

The Tour, a symbol of national identity to rank with Wimbledon, the Super Bowl and a Test match at Sabina Park, is, true to Gallic tradition, self-obsessed, self-important, self-promoting.

Since its very name has its price, and we are supposed to celebrate the Channel Tunnel, *Le Tour en Angleterre* is a commercial proposition. Francisco Cabello, the unheralded Spaniard who won the first of two English stages, covering 128 miles from Dover Castle to Brighton seafront, is not complaining.

Ditchling, a dot on the Tour's landscape, is a quintessential English village, bequeathed in King Alfred's will to a cousin in the year 880. It remained in royal ownership until Anne of Cleves forfeited it on the insistence of Henry VIII. It conforms to the chocolate box clichés of half-timbered cottages and carefully tended privet hedges. Sport, staged formally once a year to coincide with England's oldest gooseberry show, extends little beyond village cricket. It has an air of timelessness. The village museum tells of a challenge match for 50 guineas between villagers and Eleven Gentlemen of Brighton on 8 July 1818.

Hilary Bourne, the museum's curator, is a bright-eyed 85-year-old. She can still point out the patch of grass at the crossroads where she played marbles, the only game in town, before the First World War. She has a collection of wooden golf clubs, battered skittles and square slack-string tennis rackets that saw service in genteel games on the green. But cycling, and the spectacle of her birthplace being over-run by Lycra-clad visitors from another planet, was beyond her comprehension. 'It's all so strange, something quite new to us,' she said, gesturing towards the High Street, decked out in balloons and bunting. 'This race has upset all our lives, really.'

Yet, just as in France, when Le Tour caravan passes through, the enterprise culture was at work. Villagers sipped Pimm's and sold maps of Pooh's Forest. They distributed crisp, dry local white wine and dispensed cured ham.

The village was *en fête*, even if local police banned enthusiasts from emulating their French counterparts by daubing the name of their heroes across the road. Fanatics were restricted to a single act of homage, messages of support scrawled on plywood tacked to a telegraph pole outside the Emmanuel Chapel. '*Vamos*, Oliveiro Rincon, *allez* Laurent Dufaux' they read. '*Forza El Diablo*, Claudio Chiappucci. Go Sean Yates.'

The most fortunate spectators sat sedately on white plastic chairs, teetering on home-made scaffolding. Others lined the narrow streets, six deep, for more than three hours before the peloton swept by. Few knew quite what they were waiting for. The driver of Sussex police van No 1837, who descended the High Street with an impromptu chant of 'Ooh ah, Cantona' over the intercom, offered no clues. The bunting, a red, white and blue signal that the *entente* had rarely been more *cordiale,* was nearly brought down by a giant cornflake packet in the pre-race convoy. Everyone waved wildly for TV cameramen clinging uneasily to the pillion seats of over-powered motorcycles.

The wait was long, the stoicism peculiarly British. Suddenly, in an all too brief blur, two riders were through. The crowd were not to know it but Cabello had passed among them. A three-man breakaway emerged two minutes later. Then, some 90 seconds behind them, the peloton surged in, covering the width of the road. In the strange silence that followed an initial cheer, all one could hear was the metallic whirr of lightweight wheels.

Within seconds they had gone, towards Ditchling Beacon, the toughest climb of the stage. Families had gathered there to picnic, just as they do on Alpine climbs and in Pyrenean passes.

'Ditchling will seem such a tame place tomorrow,' reflected one woman as she headed the 50 yards towards the village hall.

'Yes,' concurred her companion, 'but it will be such a *nice* place, won't it?'

———

9 JULY 1994

YATES JUMPS INTO LEAD WITH SUCCESS ON LONGEST DAY

Phil Liggett in Rennes

After Chris Boardman, the first leader, followed by two outstandingly successful days in Great Britain, the French (not to mention the British) were unprepared for another surprise turn of events yesterday when Sean Yates, the only other British rider in the Tour de France, became the new leader by a single second.

Not since 1962 has a British rider led the event and Yates emulated his team rival Boardman when he finished sixth on the longest stage of 170 miles from Cherbourg to Rennes to become the second home leader in the race's opening week.

Ironically, the only time a British rider has not led the Tour, which began last Saturday in Lille, has been during the two days spent in Britain. Italian Flavio Vanzella was the leader then, and yesterday he slipped back to fifth, but only six seconds behind.

Yates, 34, said: 'The day had to come when the Italian GB-MG team would crack, so we just waited and watched, and when we attacked we went flat out.' His move came about 12 miles from the end after almost seven hours' riding, and the group of seven riders, including Motorola team-mate Frankie Andreu, quickly gained over a minute.

'When the lead went up to one minute and 20 seconds, I realised I had a chance of the jersey, but I really didn't want to think about it,' added Yates, as he waited to be presented with his first *maillot jaune* in his 11th Tour.

The long haul south from Normandy to Rennes proved too much for former world champion and triple Tour winner Greg LeMond, who almost certainly said '*au revoir*' to the race which has made him a pedalling millionaire. LeMond gave up after 119 miles with no excuses, other than saying he was feeling terrible and could not explain it. 'This isn't the way I wanted to go,' he said. 'I gave it everything in the time trial [to help Chris Boardman, on whose team he rides] and perhaps I did too much.'

INDURAIN JOINS TOUR GREATS WITH POWER AND PANACHE

Phil Liggett in Paris

Miguel Indurain shook hands with his seven surviving Banesto team-mates as he cruised down the Champs-Elysées to win the Tour de France for the fourth successive year yesterday. His reward of £250,000 was the biggest prize in the history of the sport. The 30-year-old Spaniard recorded his biggest victory margin yet — 5 m 39 s — over runner-up Piotr Ugrumov from Latvia with third-placed Italian Marco Pantani, in his first Tour, more than seven minutes behind.

Indurain's triumph equals the record of four consecutive Tour de France victories set by Frenchman Jacques Anquetil (1961–4) and Belgian legend Eddy Merckx (1969–72). His aim next year will be to join those two, and Bernard Hinault, the last French winner of the Tour in 1985, on the record number of five victories.

Yesterday's final stage of the 2,500-mile race, 110 miles from EuroDisney to Paris, gave the 117 survivors the chance to relax. They even stopped *en masse* when a downpour began as they passed under a motorway bridge.

Indurain has shown that a new record of six wins remains a realistic target, though the quiet man from Pamplona, whose salary is said to be more than £2 million per year, has a more immediate target. He said: 'We will have to see about winning a fifth Tour de France. For the moment I'll take a week's rest and test to see if I am ready to try to break the world one-hour record.'

Until this year Indurain has always crushed his rivals in the individual time trial and he was surprised at this year's start when he lost the opening Prologue time trial in Lille to Chris Board-man. Conscious of poor press after his Tour of Italy defeat, Indurain told a friend afterwards that he had wanted to lead the French race from start to finish – something never achieved in post-War years.

In the end, he turned his attention to just two stages, and in 47 miles he destroyed the field with frightening displays of power which led to speculation that he would win by more than ten minutes in Paris. Spain's greatest rider is not a man of great colour but he realises a fifth consecutive win next year would make him one of the race's immortals. That, surely, will arouse some excitement within him.

———

14 JULY 1995

SCIANDRI JOINS ELITE BAND OF BRITISH WINNERS
Phil Liggett in St Etienne

Max Sciandri, born in Derby, but a permanent resident of Italy, gave Britain its first road-race stage win in the Tour de France since Robert Millar in 1984 when he sprinted clear of Colombian climber Hernán Buenahora at the end of the 11th stage, from Bourg d'Oisans to St Etienne yesterday.

Sciandri, who was granted a British racing licence this year because he holds a British passport, became only the seventh Briton to win a stage, following in the wheel tracks of Brian Robinson, Michael Wright, Barry Hoban, Millar, Sean Yates and Chris Boardman.

'This win is neither English nor Italian, it is Sciandri's win,' he said last night after finishing almost six minutes ahead of the main race leaders. 'But I would like to dedicate this win to my British supporters who were shouting my name, and not Sean Yates's, along the road. I'd like to thank them for that.'

Sciandri, who won the Tour of Britain in 1992 and a stage of the Tour of Italy last year, wants to ride in the World Championship, but despite a series of outstanding results, he has been consistently left out of the Italian team. He feels that is because he is regarded as more British than Italian.

Yesterday, the main contenders took a rare chance to relax, not reacting when a small bunch of lower-placed riders attacked. Sciandri joined in the move by eight men after 35 miles and was then the only rider able to sustain the attack on Buenahora on the climb of the Col de l'Oeillon with 26 miles left. He said: 'I had a very comfortable ride during the two days to the mountains, so I planned to start attacking from today as I wanted a stage win. I knew when I was with the Colombian that I was going well.'

---

19 JULY 1995

ITALIAN DIES AFTER CRASH IN PYRENEES

Phil Liggett in Cauterets

Fabio Casartelli, the Olympic road race champion, died yesterday in the Tour de France when he crashed on the descent of the Pyrenean mountain, the Col de Portet d'Aspet. The Italian, 24, was the first rider to die in the race since Britain's Tom Simpson on Mont Ventoux in 1967.

Casartelli crashed into a concrete post while negotiating a left-hand bend on the 55 mph descent of the 4,000-foot mountain, the first of six crossed during the 126-mile 15th stage from St Girons to Cauterets. Six riders fell, including Frenchman Dante Rezze, who plunged into a ravine off the edge of the unguarded road. Rezze was pulled back with the aid of straps and taken to hospital with a broken thigh bone, while Germany's Dirk Baldinger suffered a fractured hip bone.

Casartelli, who married last year and had a six-month-old baby, was riding his second Tour after joining the American Motorola team at the start of this season. The team left the finish in tears but decided to continue in the race after a meeting last night.

The race medical services arrived at the scene within minutes of the crash, and while Rezze and Baldinger were taken to St Gaudens hospital by road, Casartelli was flown by helicopter to Tarbes. During the flight he suffered three cardiac arrests and died later in the afternoon while the race was progressing towards Cauterets. Most riders did not know of the tragedy until the finish.

Last night, Gary L Tooker, the vice-president of Motorola, said from the United States: 'We tend to forget a rider's bravery in the face of the danger they encounter every day. He was an outstanding athlete and a courageous competitor.'

The Italian is the fourth rider to die since the race began in 1903. In 1910 Adolphe Hélière drowned while swimming during the race's rest day, and Francesco Cepeda, of Spain, died in hospital in 1935 after crashing in the Alps.

———

20 JULY 1995

RIDERS SUSPEND COMPETITION

Phil Liggett in Pau

Fabio Casartelli, the Italian Olympic champion who died on the Tour de France on Tuesday, was remembered yesterday by the 117 survivors of the three-week event when they suspended competitive racing for the day. The riders took almost eight hours to ride the 153-mile stage from Tarbes to Pau before allowing the six riders on Casartelli's American Motorola team to finish alone.

It was the greatest show of respect the race has seen. Race organisers decided to give all the riders the same time as Italian Andrea Peron, a close colleague of Casartelli, who led the field across the winning line. Peron, who lives in the Como area near Casartelli, was on the same Olympic team in 1992 in Barcelona. He won a silver medal in the team time trial, while Casartelli took gold in the road race.

After a minute's silence before the start in the morning, the riders told Jean-Marie Leblanc, the race director, that the day's prizes would be donated to the young rider's family. The race organisation doubled the amount, making £60,000 in all.

Stephen Hodge, the Australian rider for Festina, said: 'We all thought of Fabio today. It was our way of saying goodbye.' Casartelli, who will be buried in Italy today, was riding his second Tour having turned professional in 1993. The Motorola team have agreed that their prize money will also go to Casartelli's family.

---

22 JULY 1995

ARMSTRONG FINDS INSPIRATION

Phil Liggett in Limoges

Lance Armstrong, the captain of the American Motorola team, looked to the skies and saluted with both arms as he won the 103-mile 18th stage of the Tour de France from Montpon-Ménestérol to Limoges yesterday. Three days after the death of his team-mate Fabio Casartelli, Armstrong broke clear of the leading group of 12 descending the Cote de Villeneuve with about 20 miles to go, and was never caught.

The Texan, who broke down in tears after finishing, said: 'All I could think about on the ride was poor Fabio. He motivated me all the way today.' This was Armstrong's second stage win in three years and he is about to finish his first Tour when the race ends in Paris tomorrow.

---

24 JULY 1995

INDURAIN HAS TIME TO SPARE AS HE PEDALS HOME TO RECORD

Phil Liggett in Paris

Miguel Indurain duly took his place in the record books on the Champs-Elysées yesterday when, in glorious sunshine, he finished the 2,300-mile Tour de France as winner for a fifth successive year. Before a crowd estimated at 300,000 the Spaniard allowed the rest to make the running during the eight laps of the finishing circuit, observing from the back of the 115 survivors as Djamolidine Abdoujaparov snatched the stage win after 97 miles through the Chevreuse from Ste Geneviève des Bois.

Indurain, who led home the only complete team of nine, wins £300,000 and the team will have netted nearer to £1 million from prizes along the route. He becomes only the fourth member of the 'five' club, joining Jacques Anquetil (France) who won in 1957 and 1961–64, Eddy Merckx (Belgium) the winner from 1969–72 and again in 1974, and another Frenchman, Bernard Hinault (1978, '79, '81, '82 and '85).

As with all his victories, Indurain has won the race by his domination in the time trials and, since his first win in 1991, he has won ten races against the clock, but none of the massed-start road-race stages. On Saturday, he removed any doubt of a fifth win when he led throughout the 29-mile time trial around Lac de Vassivière, near Limoges.

Of all the five-times winners, Indurain is the most liked by his rivals, who are conscious of the way he tries not to humiliate them in defeat. His wins are always calculated, and this is probably why he has never seen the need to win in the road races. This year, after taking the lead in Belgium in the time trial there, he only reacted in the mountains when those nearest to him threatened his lead. He did just enough to reduce their time gains and keep his yellow jersey, but he never took away their moment of achievement, which was winning the stage.

It is impossible not to like the quiet man from outside Pamplona because he does nothing to create offence. He only gives interviews in Spanish, although he understands French, as he is afraid he will be misquoted in anything but his native tongue.

---

9 OCTOBER 1996

ARMSTRONG DETERMINED TO OVERCOME CANCER

Phil Liggett

Lance Armstrong, who in 1993 became the youngest professional world champion since Eddy Merckx, and this year was the first American to win a traditional classic race, has testicular cancer. The condition has spread into his abdomen and lungs but Armstrong puts his chances of a complete cure at between 60 and 85 per cent.

Armstrong, 25, recently signed a contract with the new French professional team Cofidis, thought to be worth almost £1 million per year. He decided to make his condition public after an emergency operation last Thursday for the removal of a testicle. He said: 'Last Wednesday I was diagnosed with testicular cancer. Before seeing my doctor I had been experiencing swelling and coughing up some blood.'

The Texan, without doubt the finest rider in the United States since the retirement of Greg LeMond, has enjoyed an exceptional season which has seen him climb to fourth place in both the World Cup series and the world rankings. He will undergo intense chemotherapy for nine weeks from his home in Austin. 'My condition is seen to be advanced,' said Armstrong, who had complained of saddle soreness and enlargement of a testicle.

Last week he talked to his team doctor Jim Ochowicz as he suspected a hernia, but a professional consultation later revealed the cancer. He said: 'I have been assured that there is no reason why I cannot make a full and complete recovery. I want everyone to know that I intend to beat it and to ride again.' Doctors have told him he can ride his bicycle whenever he wishes while undergoing chemotherapy, as soon as the operation scars heal.

Captain of the Motorola team, Armstrong has won two stages of the Tour de France, but he says his most emotional win was in Limoges last year following the death a few days earlier of teammate Fabio Casartelli, who was killed during a descent in the Pyrenees.

---

16 JUNE 1997

MEMORIAL BRINGS HONOUR TO BRITISH KING OF THE ROAD

Sarah Edworthy

Just over a kilometre from the summit of Mont Ventoux, the 6,720-foot extinct volcano that dominates Provence, a simple marble memorial marks the spot where Tom Simpson, Britain's greatest road-racing cyclist, collapsed and died among the glaring white rocks on 13 July 1967.

Although it is 30 years since his death at 29, on the 13th stage of the Tour de France, that monument is still an active shrine. Two-wheeled pilgrims drape it in cycling paraphernalia – hats, inner tubes, water bottles and brake blocks – inspired by the man who died a victim of his desperate ambition to prove that a Briton could win the Tour de France. The mayor from the nearby town of Bédoin regularly has to send up his workforce to tidy up the site.

There is also a stone in Belgium, where Simpson chose to live to facilitate a professional career that was unique for a boy from a north Nottinghamshire pit village.

In a well attended ceremony yesterday before the annual Tom Simpson Memorial Grand Prix, his family and friends watched with pride as a stone, cut in half and faced with a silhouette of a cyclist like the one on the Ventoux, was unveiled in his home village in front of the recreation ground around whose grass tracks Simpson once raced. A Union Flag was pulled off by Simpson's widow Helen, who later married his friend and rival Barry Hoban. It carries a simple message: 'In memory of a Harworth cyclist.'

The Abraham Lincoln log-cabin-to-president theme is some-thing his family want local children to relate to. 'It's about an ordinary person who achieved great things, a story about a person who really tried and made mistakes and wasn't perfect but did a lot of good and made people happy,' explained his nephew Chris Sidwells.

Why has it taken so long for Simpson's homeland to commem-orate him? And why the understatement? Those who can recall one of the bleakest days in British sport will have an inkling, but a generation has grown up curious about why this great hero of his time has 'not been remembered perhaps as he should be', as Sidwells delicately puts it.

Simpson was a remarkable athlete who burst into the headlines when at 18 he knocked out the reigning world champion in the quarter-finals of the national 4,000 metres pursuit championships and went on to take the silver medal. From there he was selected to ride in the 1956 Melbourne Olympics, where he won bronze, and later silver at the 1958 Commonwealth Games.

In 1959 he embarked on a professional career that included wins in cycling's great monuments, the Tour of Flanders, Bordeaux-Paris, Milan-San Remo, Tour of Lombardy and Paris-Nice races. In 1962 he wore the yellow jersey for one stage of the Tour de France and in 1965, having won the world professional road race champi-onship, he became world champion.

He also had charisma that shone beyond the handlebars. In 1965 Simpson was voted BBC Sports Personality of the Year (when Graham Hill and Bobby Moore were in the running) and won the Sports Writers' Association and *Daily Express* awards – a triple equalled only by the Princess Royal – for his achievements in a sport which in Britain had never generated extensive media interest.

He was a great character – 'Mr Tom' or 'Major Thompson' the French dubbed him for his patriotic pride and tendency to wear bowler hats and City suits – and his personality and determination beam even from the yellowing press cuttings of his family scrapbooks. 'He was exotic,' Sidwells states simply, recalling anecdotes such as the time his uncle picked up his mother and him in a white Mercedes, put them in the back and drove up to visit family in the North-East wearing a chauffeur's cap.

He assembled a famous collection of hats, and his family have a host of stories which illustrate his personality. There was the time he rode from Harworth to London on his bike, typically over-ambitious, to get fitted for his Olympic uniform and had to stop at Grantham on the way back and catch a train. And the time the nation feared a Communist kidnapping when Simpson failed to return from a cycling trip to Bulgaria in time to be best man at his brother's wedding; he had simply been such a success behind the Iron Curtain that he had been invited to stay an extra week.

However, the poignancy of losing this boy from the land of black mining hills to that cruel white, strength-sapping French mountain was immediately overshadowed by the fact that amphetamines were found in his blood. But his is not a drugs story and it serves no purpose to see it as such, except in as much as it explains his family's determined wish to re-establish his true importance within the history of British sport.

'It's a feeling I've always had that what he did for that race has to be judged against the background of what was happening in cycling in those days,' says Sidwells. 'There's no doubt that he saw the Tour de France slipping away from him in the year he thought was now or never and, as it's been put, sought help from outside the rules. My opinion was that he felt he'd gone too far and done too much towards his ambitions to see other people gaining from doing this. He saw it as hell but he justified it to himself that others were doing it.

'Many people have done far more and paid less. It's something that has been picked on more than his successes and it has led to him being a little bit forgotten in this country. He would have been 60 this year and we felt it was time to bring out his story to people. He was a hero. Everybody is vulnerable; he made mistakes and he paid a terrible price.'

On 13 July, Simpson's daughter, Joanne, will return with Sidwells to Mont Ventoux, to ride up the same route as a continuation of this memorial. His 14-year-old grandson Thomas will also be riding the last two or three kilometres.

The family have returned often to the Ventoux. 'It's such a long way away, though. It will be nice to have a memorial here,' said Sidwells. 'When he died it felt like some sort of light went out in Harworth.'

---

7 JULY 1997

LIFT-OFF FOR BOARDMAN'S TOUR DE FRANCE

Sport on Television by Giles Smith

The opening stages of the Tour de France had a little competition for our enthusiasm and amazement this weekend. Given that the United States could land a probe on Mars, just how impressed were we meant to be at the prospect of a bunch of blokes taking three weeks to get from Rouen to Paris by bike?

Nevertheless, Channel 4 were out there as usual, ready to play Ground Control and assemble the first of their nightly half-hour bulletins on the state of the mission. And good for them. Mars may have its fascination, but so, too, does France, where the landscape is altogether more interesting, the climate a touch more hospitable and the food a definite improvement.

On location for lift-off was the city centre of Rouen where, on Saturday evening, the Prologue time trial took place to establish the race order for the first leg. This business had apparently been going on all day but, through a piece of inter-departmental planning of which NASA would have been proud, we arrive bang on time to catch the British interest, Chris Boardman, as he levered himself out of the starter's hut and, without so much as a hand-signal, set off on his 8½-minute sprint.

It was clear immediately, even to those of us who would claim no expertise as professional cyclists, that Boardman was about to log a time to be reckoned with. After all, he was successfully holding in his wake two motorbikes, dangerously overloaded with cameramen, a police car with flashing lights and several other bicycles attached to the roof of a bright red Fiat.

But what, exactly, was he riding? A black, tubular construction, with a pair of garden shears where the handlebars ought to have been. It looked like a spare prop from Batman and Robin. It also condemned Boardman to a riding position in which his backside was at least four feet above the level of his head. Our commentator, Phil Liggett, who also excitedly alerted us to the bike's electric gear-shift, gave us an intelligent paraphrase of the ergonomic benefits accruing to Boardman from riding with his nose just above the front mudguard. It gave him 'great penetration from the air', apparently, which sounded a lot more enjoyable than it looked.

That Boardman's machine actually qualified as a bicycle we only had Liggett's word. That and the fact that the judges had not moved to disqualify it in advance, which, we were told, had happened to one of the other riders. Frustratingly, we were not given the reasons for the ban. In a world in which electric gear-shifts get the nod it was hard to imagine what, exactly, would tip a bike over the limits. Perhaps the jet engines had infringed Rouen's noise-pollution regulations.

Anyway, Boardman stormed through to take the yellow jersey despite a late challenge from the police car, which seemed to be finishing strongly but, sadly, had to brake sharply to avoid the various officials and spectators in the road beyond the finish line.

In a touching closing ceremony, our man waved aloft a gold trophy in the shape of a Coca-Cola bottle, and just in case those of us at home weren't getting the sponsor's message loudly enough, an aide hustled a red plastic Coca-Cola bottle into his other hand so he could wave that, too.

---

28 JULY 1997

NEW KING ULLRICH POISED FOR LONG REIGN

Phil Liggett in Paris

Jan Ullrich, 23, became the first German winner of the 2,500-mile Tour de France yesterday when it ended on the Champs-Elysées in warm sunshine and before a crowd estimated at 300,000.

Ullrich, who led for 11 days, is the youngest winner since Laurent Fignon in 1984 and also had the biggest margin — 9 m 9 s over Frenchman Richard Virenque — since the same year. He collects the £250,000 first prize and could be the man to beat for the next seven years. He has already predicted he will retire at 30.

The man from Rostock was riding only his second Tour after finishing second to the Dane Bjarne Riis last year. His German Telekom team scooped the major share of the million-pound prize money — as they did last year — by winning the team prize, and Ullrich's countryman, Erik Zabel, who won three stages, was way ahead in the green jersey points classification.

Ullrich, who lives in Merdingen, near the French border, is probably the last product of the East German athletics machine. He was sent, aged 12, to join the Dynamo cycling school after tests showed he had the best heart and lung capacity of all youngsters of his age. At nine he won his first race almost by accident when his elder brother took him to watch an event. A vacancy created by a sick rider gave Ullrich the opportunity to ride, and he won without difficulty.

Yesterday the fight had all gone from the other 138 competitors as they allowed Ullrich to enjoy the ride from Disneyland to Paris without the pressure he had absorbed with great maturity since taking the lead in the Pyrenees. The riders had been chatting, laughing and even drinking Champagne during the relaxed final day as there was virtually nothing except the stage win to be settled.

Ullrich's future is assured, but the same cannot be said for Riis, who started as team leader and with the unwavering support of Ullrich, only to fade to a distant seventh, almost half an hour behind.

'It is hard for Germans to understand why a Dane was leading the team and they would rather a German be the chief,' said Ullrich. 'But having said that, if Riis hadn't won last year, Telekom might not have maintained their sponsorship. Last year I'd have been hard pressed to be recognised by my postman. Now the team media centre has to field all the calls and I get some pretty odd requests!' he added.

In Saturday's time trial, Riis let his frustration show in public for the first time. He fell off after signing in for the start at Disneyland and then arrived 20 seconds late for his departure. In the next ten miles he was stopped by a puncture and released all of his pent-up emotion by throwing the £7,000 bicycle across the grass.

There were unedifying parts of the Tour, with five riders kicked out. The sixth stage was probably the race's low point, when stage winner Zabel was declassified for butting Frenchman Dominique Nazon. Belgian champion Tom Steels was thrown out for hurling his water bottle at Frédéric Moncassin in the final sprint and a crazy day culminated in three-times green jersey winner Djamolidine Abdoujaparov joining Steels after the 'Tashkent Express' failed a dope test.

————

11 JULY 1998

BUSINESS BLOOMING ALONG IRELAND'S HIGHWAYS AS TOUR COMES TO TOWN

Martin Johnson

If there is any substance to the apocryphal Irish story about lost foreign travellers, some time over the next few days a mud-splattered cyclist wearing a yellow jersey will pull up outside Flaherty's Bar and say: *'Excusez-moi,* do you know the way to the Champs-Elysées?' And, for once, the traditional response will not seem quite so Irish. 'Well, if I were you, I wouldn't start from here.'

However, starting from Ireland is indeed the plan for the world's biggest cycling event, the Tour de France. It gets under way in earnest in Dublin tomorrow, continuing on Monday down in the south-east, before the huge entourage – which stretches for 40 miles and takes two hours to pass – is loaded on to a fleet of ferries and transported to France. The last time an armada of this size set sail for the French coast, they called it D-Day.

This is always assuming that the entire invasion is still not wandering around Dublin airport trying to work out the arrivals hall notice which says: 'Exit. No Entry', although the locals are equally confused by giant banners draped across the roads, saying things like: *'Bienvenue à Kilkenny'.*

On the face of it, Ireland is an incongruous starting point for the world's most brutal cycle race, although Irish hospitality is such that in terms of feeling half-dead the morning after, it's probably the ideal venue for a rider to acclimatise for the three weeks of torture that lie ahead. It was something of an eyebrow-raiser to discover that the pubs have all been granted extensions for the Tour, which, from previous experience, can only mean that Ireland has reinvented the 25-hour day.

There are historical connections with the Tour starting in Ireland, Monday's Enniscorthy to Cork stage commemorating the 200th anniversary of the French landing here to help out the Irish – given their mutual dislike of the English – with the 1798 Rebellion. And it is down in the south-east that you get the real flavour of an Irish welcome which is costing the taxpayer £2 million, albeit for an expected return in tourism spin-offs of £25 million.

Halfway between Enniscorthy and Cork lies the small Tipperary town of Carrick-on-Suir, birthplace of one of the legends of Irish cycling, Sean Kelly. The peloton will be hurtling through the streets here on Monday afternoon, and it is not so much the spectators who will be holding their breath as the cyclists themselves, trying hard not to choke to death from inhaling the paint fumes.

There is not a wall or a building that has not been freshly emulsioned in Carrick over the past fortnight, a complete no-go area for the superstitious, as it is impossible to walk ten yards without passing underneath a ladder. In the Main Street is the Tour de France Information Centre, although it is not half as incongruous as the shop next door, which deals exclusively in the sale of Christmas puddings.

Inside Gerry's Bar (which inevitably had a paint-splattered ladder propped up against one of the lounge windows) Gerry was chuckling over the town's transformation. 'I came here ten years ago, and had never even seen so much as a single paint brush until this week.' He pointed across the street to the local hardware store. 'I don't know how much this race is going to bring in with tourism, but it won't be half the amount yer man is raking in over there.'

It wasn't so much the painting that Gerry minded, as the hanging baskets. 'We have to make the town look nice for the cameras, but jeez, all this watering is a total pain.' Mind you, compared with Enniscorthy, which has planted 10,000 flowers in French colours, Carrick is a horticultural desert, although it does have the edge in being more pedestrian friendly, having vaporised every last square inch of chewing gum from the pavements.

Most of the road between Enniscorthy and Cork has been resurfaced, while at the same time remaining largely impassable because of the invasion of council hedgerow-trimming machinery. Any cyclist leaving the road on this stage of the Tour will be comforted to know that he will be picking himself out of the neatest hedge on the entire 3,000 km.

There has also, needless to say, been an avalanche of local press coverage, with the *Enniscorthy Echo* leading the way. 'Tour Fever Grips Town!' was this week's front page headline, though judging by the other top stories – 'Train Was Late – But Nobody Cared' and 'Sheep Decline Heading For Decline' – Enniscorthy's definition of a fever is most people's idea of a runny nose.

In purely cycling terms, one item attracting attention is the sad absence of a single Irish cyclist in the 1998 rider line-up, a far cry from the days when the Dublin traffic ground to a halt because of car drivers dashing into bars to find out how the likes of Stephen Roche and Sean Kelly were doing on that day's stage.

---

14 JULY 1998

BOARDMAN HITS WALL TO CRASH OUT OF TOUR

Phil Liggett in Cork

Chris Boardman, the leader of the Tour de France since its start on Saturday, saw his race end abruptly yesterday after he touched the back wheel of a team-mate and crashed into a wall near Youghal during the second stage from Enniscorthy to Cork.

It was a sad end to Boardman's short reign in the 2,400-mile race, and after lying stunned in the road for some minutes, he was taken to Cork University Hospital with head injuries and a suspected broken cheekbone. Doctors said that there were no breaks, though he would be detained overnight. He was placed in the ambulance wearing a neck brace and had cuts to his face, while his left arm was strapped across his chest.

The accident happened as the race sprung to life 900 metres before the time bonus sprint in Youghal. As the riders strung out, Boardman appeared to touch wheels and catapult out of the pack, falling heavily. The Wirral professional, who also crashed out of the race in pouring rain at St Brieuc in 1995 during the Prologue time trial — he won this year's version in Dublin on Saturday — is the 13th leader of the race to give up since it began in 1903. He also gave up the Tour last year on the 13th stage.

----

25 JULY 1998

FEAR AND LOATHING IN FRANCE

THE TOUR STAGGERS ON AMID MYRIAD ALLEGATIONS OF DRUG ABUSE BY SOME OF THE LEADING TEAMS

Paul Hayward

Around four o'clock this afternoon, France's most sacred sporting institution is scheduled to honk and swish its way into the Provence town of Carpentras at the end of another 121-mile pageant. Most summers, they would rest a night before making the gruelling climb to the summit of Mont Ventoux, the 'Giant of Provence', past the roadside memorial to Britain's Tommy Simpson, whose amphetamine-fuelled heart gave up on him on 13 July 1967, as he made his own frantic ascent to sport's dark peak. Like mourners with a guilty secret, the riders of the 1998 Tour de France will pass another way.

They will pass the way in turmoil: a vast convoy of rage and recrimination that may not make it to the Champs-Elysées at the end of the race tomorrow week. Yesterday TVM were also threatened with expulsion after drugs were found in the hotel where they were staying and three Festina riders admitted to police that they had used banned substances to help them race. As sport's most spectacular drugs controversy found new ways to erupt, the remaining riders staged a two-hour strike before the start of the 12th stage, saying they would no longer be 'treated like cattle'.

As the morning papers hit the breakfast tables of the 20 surviving teams, the following declaration roared out from the pages of *Le Monde*: 'Who from now on could rejoice at seeing the rest of a compromised pack enter Paris, who would then be able to applaud the winner of a race without faith or law?' Thirty-one years after Simpson became sport's most famous casualty at the age of 29, drug abuse has advanced way beyond the desperate snorts of amphetamines by which Simpson tried to climb a viciously testing mountain. A sepia casualty from yesterday has become today's Technicolor nightmare.

Cut to 18 days ago, when football's World Cup was still at the semi-final stage: a 53-year-old masseur with the Festina racing team embarked on a roundabout route to Ireland. Willy Voet left the headquarters of the Tour Society in Evry, near Paris, and drove through Switzerland, Germany and Belgium before going on towards Calais en route to Dublin, where this year's *Le Grand Boucle* was scheduled to start the following day. Voet never made it. At around 8 a.m. at Neuville-en-Ferrain on the Franco-Belgian border — close to the cycling-mad town of Roubaix — customs officers opened the boot of his car and found 235 doses of erythropoietin (EPO), 82 shots of growth hormones, a packet of anabolic steroids, 60 doses of testosterone, eight vaccines for hepatitis A, masking agents and syringes.

It was like a scene from Hunter S. Thompson's *Fear and Loathing in Las Vegas,* without the comic edge. Voet's suitcase, say many in France, may yet come to be remembered as an undersized coffin for the Tour de France.

Any sport with a contestant called Bo Hamburger is plainly not for wimps and waifs. The world's greatest cycle race is supposed to be the ultimate sporting test of human endurance, a celebration of the noble art of cycling, an homage to the French countryside, and a great emotional loop which tightens around the heart of

France. They pass over snow-dusted Alpine ranges and through sunflower and lavender fields, chocolate-box villages and arid plains. Anyone who has seen a professional cycle race in motion is instantly sold on its charms. The Tour is biblical in intensity, sport beyond the edge of what should be possible. But if the current prognosis is right, we are seeing a 20th-century lunacy exposed. Is the Tour de France an event that can't be done, never mind won, without performance-enhancing drugs?

The innocent, the wiry warriors who have fought the roads of France unassisted these past 95 years, will rise up in protest. Yet the scale of what is happening to this merciless trial of physical and mental strength leads many to believe that the wheels are about to cease turning. Or maybe this is a seminal moment in sport for a different reason. The public, as much as cycling, could end up on trial in Lille. Will they continue to sign up to a sport they believe to be incurably corrupt, cramming the lanes of France to catch a glimpse of a passing pharmacy? Will they conclude that the war on drugs in sport, as in society, is unwinnable and that everybody should be allowed to take whatever they want, with the devil – and the broom-wagon – taking the hindmost?

A fortnight after they won the World Cup, the French should be returning to more traditional summer pleasures: marvelling at the stamina and bravery of the performers and enjoying the gastronomic and aesthetic delights of a country still gulping down the glory of capturing *la Coupe du Monde*. Should be. But from the moment daylight broke into the boot of Voet's Fiat, the Tour de France has been in a sort of toxic shock. There are those who believe that athletics will now be dragged into the ensuing investigation. At the end of the century, a reckoning may be upon us, started by a Customs check that shone a light on not just a narcotic stockpile but the moral legitimacy of a sport.

The peloton who will miss Simpson's memorial, and instead set off from Valreas to Grenoble tomorrow, is missing a few familiar faces. All nine Festina riders were taken into custody by French police on Thursday as part of the ever-widening inquiry into the contents of Voet's car. The authorities also swooped on the team's business manager, Joel Chaberon, and two other officials. Chaberon and three riders were later released.

These are no bit-part players on the Tour's great snaking express of 21 teams from seven countries. Richard Virenque was runner-up in last year's Tour; Laurent Brochard is the world champion; Alex Zulle is one of cycling's leading pros, and Laurent Dufaux (fourth in the 1996 Tour) the winner of this year's Tour of Romandie. Bruno Roussel, the Festina director, and Erik Ryckaert, the team doctor, are behind bars in Lille after being charged by Judge Patrick Keil under France's 1989 anti-drugs laws.

It gets worse: the Dutch TVM team may be next. In March, French customs found 104 syringes primed with EPO in a car driven by two TVM mechanics. EPO boosts the red blood-cell count and enables the bloodstream to transport more oxygen around the system. The TVM case has resurfaced with potentially devastating results. On Thursday, the Tour's rest day, police detained Cees Priem, the TVM manager, their Russian doctor and a mechanic for questioning. Laurent Roux, their leading rider, has denied that drugs are used by the TVM team. Meanwhile, Belgian police say they also want to interview Festina officials after finding documents and data at the home of Ryckaert which allegedly show that EPO is being used by Festina.

Riders, doctors, a masseur, mechanics and team managers have all been dragged into the maelstrom. When criminal charges are heard after the riders rattle up the Champs-Elysées on 2 August (assuming they do), an event that has woven its way into French culture since 1903, and a sport that harnesses man and machine without violating nature, could disappear under a mudslide of disclosures and revelations. Even the Tour's famous *omerta* may not withstand the possible prosecution of large swathes of the Festina team, who were expelled from the race amid high drama eight days ago, with Virenque, who had shaken hands with the wife of Jacques

Chirac days earlier, sobbing in front of the cameras in a French café. In a statement issued through his solicitor just hours before Festina's expulsion, Roussel admitted: 'A concerted system for supplying cyclists with drugs was organised between management, doctors, the masseur and the riders in the Festina team.'

Drugs in cycling are not new. In his book *Rough Ride,* winner of the William Hill Sports Book of the Year Award for 1990, Paul Kimmage describes the suffocating vow of silence which binds riders to the cause. Those who break the *omerta,* he reveals, are said to have *'craché dans la soupe'* (spat in the soup). Kimmage tells the story of the Frenchman, Didier Garcia, who reached the top at 19 and came under intense peer pressure to start taking amphetamines and corticoids. He consumed so much 'speed' before races that he needed Valium to sleep when they were over. In Kimmage's words, Garcia saw a rider 'go berserk at three o'clock in the morning. He smashed his room to pieces, broke the toilet bowl and was unapproachable for 15 minutes.' Garcia quit and found a job in a hospital on £700 a month.

'To survive,' writes Kimmage, 'I was forced, against my will, to take drugs. It happened three times. I was never caught. If I had been caught, I would have been branded – as all drug-takers are branded – a cheat. Isn't that ridiculous? A cheat, "an unfair player". I was never a cheat. I WAS A VICTIM. A victim of a corrupt system, a system that actually promotes drug-taking in sport.

'Before all this [his own career], I was too young and innocent. I looked into the sweaty faces of the stars through the TV screen and photographs and saw only glory. And now what do I see? I see dilated pupils and unnatural spots. I study not what they eat but what they swallow. Where once I applauded muscle, now I question its fabrication.'

The testing procedures, Kimmage alleges, were inadequate or non-existent. Team managers always seemed to know when the testers would swoop. EPO, which, in the words of one former rider, can turn blood 'to jam', and is potentially lethal if misused, is easily the most prevalent designer drug in cycling. Worse, it is undetectable.

Privately, some cyclists are saying that the problem is just as bad, if not worse, in track and field, and that outsiders cannot begin to understand the pressure that is exerted on young recruits to join the gang. The mantra is: *others are, so you have to*. And Kimmage's revelations raise the question of how much the race organisers know about it and how hard they are trying to stamp it out. A low number of positive tests does not mean that there is low usage. It can mean that the substances are undetectable, that the riders find out in advance when and where the testers will strike, or even that officialdom is looking the other way.

The evidence of the last fortnight suggests, at the very least, that the Tour's organisers have taken a less than robust stance on what appears to be an endemic problem and a serious threat to health. After Voet's arrest, Jean-Claude Killy, president of the Tour's commercial arm, dismissed the emerging Festina scandal as 'a sideshow' (Voet, hilariously, tried to convince police in Lille that the drugs were entirely for his own consumption, which, if true, would have turned him into King Kong). Even after Roussel and Ryckaert had been arrested, Jean-Marie Leblanc, the race director, declared: 'I think the Tour will quickly emerge from this dirty story. This business is incidental and has nothing to do with the race itself.'

But others are having their say. Gilles Delion, a former great French hope, repeated his claim that he was driven out of the sport after denouncing the widespread use of EPO. 'They had no choice, but the damage is terrible,' he said. 'To be caught out by a test these days, you've got to be a total idiot.' Lionel Jospin, the French Prime Minister, urged 'transparency' on the cycling world. The sports minister, Marie-George Buffet, declared: 'The biggest hypocrisy would be to believe that this is only happening in cycling in July.' Then, last weekend, the Belgian national champion, Alain van den Bossche, claimed that he had used EPO for a year with the Dutch TVM team. The team manager, taken away for questioning in the Pyrenees on Thursday, had said that Van den Bossche must have acted alone, and that the 104 vials in the back of the TVM mechanics' car had been planted.

Gilbert Collard, Virenque's lawyer, has issued a statement, saying: 'I completely contest this decision to ban Festina from the Tour. There is no proof of doping; all the tests were negative and I have doubts about the testing procedure.' But Virenque's denial was lost in a swirl of new admissions from the Festina officials behind bars. Ryckaert's lawyer told reporters that 'Festina's riders were forced to put part of their prize-money into a fund which was used to buy doping products'. These 'products', said Ryckaert, were stocked at the team headquarters near Lyon. And of the many ironies that present themselves in this saga, one will endure to the final inch of the race. The logo that appears in the bottom of our television screens says: 'Festina.' They are the official time-keepers for the Tour de France.

Cycling in Europe is regarded as a vital component of civilised life. It is part of the fabric of France, Germany, Spain, Italy and the Low Countries. The Tour de France was always one of the greatest of all sporting events – anywhere – and until now the incidences of proven drug abuse have not dimmed its astonishing popularity. But this is something different. The strike by riders at Tarasccon-sur-Ariège yesterday suggests that even they are buckling under the moral strain. If Kimmage is right, many of them are caught between callous team regimes, their own ambition, and the increasing proximity of the long arm of the law, which threatens to sweep away the whole Tour de France.

Soon we will find out whether it is drugs, rather than bicycles, that the sport has really been peddling. Simpson's shrine has been wreathed in flowers and mementos since he expired through drug-induced heat exhaustion. Mont Ventoux, appropriately, is an extinct volcano, but for cycling it might be about to blow.

———

31 JULY 1998

TRAGIC SPECTACLE OF AN EPIC EVENT BEING TORN TO PIECES

Phil Liggett

For 26 years I have followed every day of the Tour de France. I have seen cyclists die, as in the case of Italy's Fabio Casartelli. I have seen my car reduced to a spade-load of debris after Basque separatists blew it up near San Sebastian in 1992. And, above all, I have seen brave riders crawl across the finish, so that they can go through the same pain the next day.

So the events of the past three weeks will be remembered by me and many others as one of the great sadnesses in sport this decade. The Tour's history, as colourful as the riders themselves, is full of stories of human endurance, as man has persuaded his body to achieve feats which most would believe could never even be attempted.

Since the Tour started in 1903, and the early days of marathon stages, when riders would sleep on the roadside and secret controls were set up to stop cheats missing out the mountains, the event has entered the folklore of not just France, but the world.

During July, Tour fever is epidemic. A million spectators a day is quite normal and 1,000 media men are seen bizarrely charging around back roads in an attempt to beat the riders to the line. Television is live to 100 countries and all they want to see and talk about is the race's *maillot jaune*.

The Tour is no longer just a sporting event, it is part of the fabric of French culture. Yet the doping scandals and the way they have been handled these past few days have made many ask if the French themselves are trying to destroy their own heritage.

Make no mistake, some cyclists – but not all – take drugs and so do athletes, swimmers, footballers and any other sportsmen who are chasing a big cash reward.

Just now, the race is throwing up a clutch of young riders, such as the Australians Robbie McEwen and Stuart O'Grady, and the rider who is currently second, Bobby Julich. I know these guys well, and I believe they are clean, living through hateful times which, as McEwen hopes, 'will change soon'.

Jean-Marie Leblanc is a sad-looking race director, walking around this week with a frown on his face and the drooping eyes of a bloodhound. Despite friends in high places – after all, he is the only man to get the Champs-Elysées closed for anything except the Bastille Day parade – he sees his race as being under threat from the scandals which, so far, have had nothing directly to do with this event.

When the riders went on strike on Wednesday, after the TVM team had been taken to a hospital in police custody to give compulsory blood, urine and DNA tests, he launched an impassioned appeal to the riders 'as friends' and to the 20 team managers not to stop but continue in the race whatever happens. More arrests are likely today when the race returns to France, but at what stage will the police or examining judges admit why they are subjecting the riders and the race to a series of high-profile raids without apparent result?

The public continue to watch the event in massive numbers and they mainly support the riders, but if some are cheats, they must be weeded out and severely punished. In modern times, when medical knowledge seems as important as riding ability, there are always the suspicions which surround teams or riders who pay doctors a lot of money to be with them. It is a fact that those teams or individuals who have private doctors tend also to be the best performers. With the arrest of Dr Erik Ryckaert from Festina, and with the confessions which followed last week, these doctors have to fight now to regain credibility.

The International Cycling Union, the sport's governing body, have become transparent during this race and have yet to face the biggest scandal to hit the sport for many, many years. UCI president Hein Verbruggen did appear briefly to say: 'We don't know how many take dope. It could be as many as 40 per cent.'

When the latest round of arrests came, Verbruggen was on holiday in India. It is a week since the Festina riders admitted taking dope, yet there has been no announcement of long-term suspensions from the headquarters in Lausanne. In fact, some of the team are already planning their next races. The pain continues.

---

3 AUGUST 1998

SWASHBUCKLING PANTANI PLUNDERS RARE DOUBLE

Phil Liggett in Paris

Marco Pantani was crowned champion of the Tour de France on the Champs-Elysées yesterday, carrying off the £200,000 winner's prize to an enormous cheer from one of the largest crowds to watch the finish for some years. For a moment there was no thought of the drug-taking revelations which have marred the race.

Pantani, who had survived the setback of a puncture in the final stage, was welcomed on to the winner's podium by the last Italian winner, Felice Gimondi, who triumphed in 1965. He had also become only the seventh rider to win the Tour de France and the Giro d'Italia in the same season.

With the final places decided in Saturday's time trial, won by Jan Ullrich but not by enough to catch Pantani, the pressure yesterday was off. Yet this amazing race delivered one last surprise when Pantani suffered a puncture on the third lap of ten on the Champs-Elysées.

At the time it was raining heavily, with thunderclaps sounding for the last act of a race that refused to go away quietly. Pantani changed his back wheel and his team fell back one by one to pace him back to the pack. It was a moment when his 3 m 21 s winning margin over Ullrich seemed fragile, but he showed no panic and he slowly caught up.

Despite the problems of the Tour, the atmosphere on the road from Melun to Paris had the ambience of any previous race, with the riders pedalling towards the Champs-Elysées at a leisurely pace and with a smile and a wave to the public who, despite the scandals, still clearly adore the occasion.

Pantani, wearing a headscarf which brought a reality to his nickname of 'The Pirate', sipped Champagne with Andrea Tafi, the Italian champion. Pantani's six surviving team members had dyed their hair yellow overnight, while he, being bald, settled for a colour change to his goatee beard.

His achievement is all the more remarkable considering his recovery from two serious injuries. In 1995 Pantani, who looks likely to switch from Mercatone Uno to the more powerful Mapei team next season on a basic annual salary of £1.2 million, was out on a training run for the Tour of Italy when a driver ignored a red light and smashed into him. The accident cost Pantani three days in hospital and a ride in the Giro, and he had not fully recovered for the Tour de France. Yet he won two stages, beating Indurain up Alpe d'Huez and four days later taking the Guzet-Neige stage after a 42-km breakaway.

No sooner had he performed those Tour de France heroics than he encountered another Italian driver. Hurtling down a hill at 50 mph in the Milan-Turin race, he rounded a bend and hit a Jeep being driven towards him. He suffered a double open fracture of his left leg and the injury took a year out of his career.

In October, when he saw the route of this year's Tour de France, he maintained he would ride for stage wins, as the mountain stages were not difficult enough for him to gain time. In reality, he not only won two stages, but on a wet and cold day on the way to Les Deux Alpes he destroyed the field.

He attacked with such ferocity in the Alps that he left no one in a position to win the Tour. Pantani's victory that day, which ended with him nine minutes ahead of Ullrich, who would manage only 25th place, brought back memories of the old days when riders won by minutes. Ullrich was left behind by a puncture just before the last climb to Les Deux Alpes, then broke down mentally as his overall lead evaporated.

Many believed Ullrich, who won easily last year, would not start the next day, but not only did he reappear, but he attacked to such an extent that only Pantani could hold him. Ullrich was the Tour loser, but remains a great champion who will almost certainly win this race again.

———

10 AUGUST 1998

FRENCH FARCE

Sir,

As the founder of the British Professional and Independent Cycling Association in 1956 and their secretary for some years, it was my job to report on the death of Tommy Simpson who died on the slopes of Mont Ventoux in the 1967 Tour de France.

We thought, at that time, that this tragedy would expose and eliminate drug use by cyclists. Now, 31 years on, drug use has almost destroyed the Tour de France.

The world controlling body for cycling (UCI) have proved ineffective in putting their house in order regarding the problem.

To save the Tour de France and eliminate the numbers of people who would gain from the successes of 'doped' winners, it is essential to reintroduce – eliminating trade teams at one fell swoop – national and regional teams.

They would be regulated by the controlling body for the nation concerned. Therefore, riders would be under greater scrutiny by those officials, and by their team-mates who would not necessarily be in the same team for normal competition.

Dave Orford
BPICA National Secretary, 1956–62

———

SWEPT ALONG BY TOUR DE FORCE

Andrew Baker

It is hard, from a distance, to understand why the Tour de France has such a powerful hold on the people of the country through which it travels. Hard to understand from televised snatches why people should bake on a mountainside for a glimpse of their toiling heroes, or swing from lamp-posts for a better view of the peloton flashing by.

But we do not often see the carnival that accompanies the Tour, smell the local specialities sizzling by the wayside, or taste the wine dispensed by one and all to one and all. The Tour is a travelling party, the highlight of the year in every village on the route. That is why last year's drugs busts and strikes caused national trauma, why talk of a blighted future causes such gloom today.

The party passed yesterday through the town of St Lary-Soulan, which snuggles in a valley in the Pyrenees and marked the start of the final climb on yesterday's stage. It must be a woeful landmark for the riders: from St Lary to the finish in Piau-Engaly is all uphill.

This is Richard Virenque country, in the heart of the mountains that France's fallen hero considers his own. Mired in drug-related controversy, shoe-horned into the race against the wishes of the organisers, Virenque is attempting in the Pyrenees to earn back his place in the hearts of the nation the only way he knows – by conquering the climbs.

The crowd at St Lary-Soulan were not there to support Virenque. In 1997 the road would have been splattered with his name and the roadside plastered with *'Allez Richard!'* banners. Yesterday the roads were pristine and the only placard was a message popular wherever television cameras congregate: *'Salut Maman!'* This year's Tour is not about partisan fervour. Virenque races in the polka-dot jersey of the King of the Mountains but he has become the Prince of Doubt. A Frenchman has yet to win a stage and the event is led by an American who has been exchanging grumbles with the French media since the race began.

The Tour's preceding commercial caravan is like a high-speed version of London's Lord Mayor's Show, a cavalcade of outlandish floats dispensing music, propaganda and goodies from the various sponsors of the Tour and the teams. The spectators goggled at an extraordinary series of giant, mobile plastic mountains to Mammon. It was like a surreal version of *The Generation Game* conveyor belt: a space shuttle, a coffee grinder, a cheese, a mobile telephone, a dead wolf in a cooking pot, a vacuum cleaner, a watch, a sheep, a tube of pâté… all accompanied by grinning bimbos hurling T-shirts, stickers, hats and sweets into the ravenous crowd.

Such was the frenzy that you would think the inhabitants of St Lary-Soulan had never seen a promotional leaflet before. A man fell almost under the wheels of a van while he tried to grab a T-shirt, *gendarmes* struggled to restrain children crazy for lapel pins and a woman took a nasty blow from a flying mint.

The commotion had barely settled when a helicopter appeared overhead to herald the arrival of the stage leader. A hush fell over the crowd, then a great cheer broke as the slight green figure of Fernando Escartín swept into view. Two breaths and a wiggle of the hips later he was disappearing up the hill and the wait began again for his pursuers.

Alex Zulle passed through and then (to a slight escalation in cheering) Virenque, soon followed by Lance Armstrong in a group of six. But the greeting given to the leaders was not measurably more enthusiastic than that accorded to the peloton some 20 minutes later.

When the Tour passes through it is not winners that matter but those who take part, including the spectators.

———

26 JULY 1999

ARMSTRONG SEALS THE SWEETEST VICTORY OF THEM ALL

Phil Liggett in Paris

Lance Armstrong, the American who has led the 2,400-mile Tour de France for the past two weeks, was confirmed as its winner yesterday when the race arrived on the Champs-Elysées on a glorious summer's day. His final margin was a crushing 7 m 37 s over Switzerland's Alex Zulle, while the best Frenchman was Richard Virenque in eighth place.

Armstrong's win is worth £250,000, which he is likely to give to his team, as is the tradition among Tour winners, but he can expect to earn well in excess of £1 million next season. Immediately after the Tour he will ride circuit races in Holland and France, believed to be worth £60,000, and on Wednesday he flies to America, to be greeted by President Clinton in the White House on Friday.

Following the drug scandals of 1998 this was, as the organisers had hoped, a Tour of Redemption. But with reduced crowds in the mountains and still an air of suspicion on the riders' performances, many remain to be convinced. Certainly, there were sceptics in the French media. *Le Monde* and *L'Equipe* both worked hard to discredit Armstrong's victory, refusing to accept that a man once dying of cancer could win the race without resorting to drugs, and yesterday *L'Equipe* confirmed that, for the first time, the winner of the Tour had refused to grant them a final interview.

Armstrong said: 'What has happened to me is a miracle. Just because the French have had their worst Tour since 1926, they are wrong to take it out on me.' French disappointment centred on the failure to win even a single stage; their last overall winner was Bernard Hinault, as far back as 1985.

In winning the fourth stage, Armstrong joined the five-time winners of the Tour – Eddy Merckx, Bernard Hinault and Miguel

Indurain — as the only riders to have won all the time-trial stages in a single Tour.

Zulle, a rider of undoubted class whose image was tarnished after he admitted to using the blood-booster EPO during the last Tour — when his Festina team were thrown off the race — is one of the few suspect riders to have made a successful return. His Tour started well with a second place in the Prologue time trial. But he lost all hope of victory when he crashed on the Passage du Gois on the third day, losing six minutes. Zulle was forced to accept he 'had no answer' to Armstrong in either the mountains or the time trials.

Back in October 1996, when he told the world that he was fighting testicular cancer which had spread to his lungs and brain, Armstrong's doctors gave him little chance of survival. He endured five-day sessions of chemotherapy and underwent a series of operations to remove a testicle, golf-ball sized tumours from his lungs and two lesions from his brain. Yesterday, he admitted: 'When I drove away from the doctors, I thought I was going to die.'

CHAPTER 6
THE 2000s

MILLAR'S MATURITY COMES IMMEDIATELY TO THE FORE

Phil Liggett in Loudun

David Millar, 22, lived up to all of the faith placed in him by his French Cofidis team yesterday when he retained the overall lead in the Tour de France, finishing 17th on the 121-mile second stage from Futuroscope to Loudun. After winning Saturday's 11-mile time trial by two seconds, Millar's first day in the leader's yellow jersey was ridden with the professional skills of an old hand; the Scot's youth giving way to a maturity rarely seen from a rider in his first Tour de France.

His team, made up of Italian, Belgian, French and Swiss riders, rode hard at the front of the large pack all day, while Millar himself rode behind them and even added two seconds to his overnight lead. He took a small time bonus at Châtellerault with 35 miles to go and now leads the defending champion, Lance Armstrong, by four seconds.

The Malta-born Millar is only the fourth British rider to wear the yellow jersey, following in the wheel marks of Tom Simpson, Chris Boardman and Sean Yates, and becomes the first from north of the border. His fluency in French and his place on a popular French team has immediately endeared him to the crowds, who can expect him to keep the lead today on the 100-mile ride to Nantes.

When Millar started the race on Saturday his ambition was limited to finishing in Paris on 23 July, but his targets altered dramatically after he scorched around the time-trial course near Poitiers to set the best time of 19 m 3 s.

This 2000 race has attracted its best field for years, so Millar's beating of former world champions Armstrong, Laurent Jalabert and Abraham Olano and the world time-trial champion, Jan Ullrich, proved entirely satisfying. He rides under no illusions of final victory, especially as his youth and lack of stamina will count against him on the high climbs in the Pyrenees and the Alps, but his promise is such that he is being seen as a future winner.

———

15 JULY 2000

RED LIGHT AT THE END OF THE TUNNEL

Graeme Fife

Eddie the Eagle may have launched a short-lived celebrity on his incompetence as a ski-jumper, but no professional sportsman attaches any kudos to being last; except that in the Tour de France, the ultimate inferno for cyclists, the rider at the bottom of the order in each day's time classification occupies a special niche in Tour tradition. He is the *lanterne rouge,* the red tail lamp at the back of the race.

The French always billed the Tour grandiosely as an epic contest: riders battling against geography, elements and worsening fatigue over 2,400 miles of unforgiving road. It is a gruesome effort just to survive three weeks; gruelling punishment, and in popular imagination the *lanterne rouge* has become a symbol of human frailty caught up in a titanic struggle. The winners are on another planet; the *lanterne rouge* is the archetypal little guy, as brave as the rest but hanging on to his place by whatever tatters of will and strength he has left, just to escape the time guillotine.

In the past, someone usually donated a red lantern to tie under the last rider's saddle and that jokey token became a badge of the defiance that every Tour rider – and they are the cream – needs when the road takes them into the thin air of the high mountains: the 'Circle of Death' in the Pyrenees and, as in today's stage, the lunar landscape of the broken desert in the Alps.

It is not certain exactly when the tradition began but a photo from a Tour in the Twenties shows two riders side by side, holding a stick on the top of which is tied a tin can – the lantern. They are both grinning broadly, like a couple of kids on the way home from a tadpoling expedition. In those days they rode an average of 220 miles per day, doing all their own repairs, over the mountains on roads little better than rough, unpaved tracks. Hardly surprising if they sat back when they could.

In 1919, the race was particularly grisly: atrocious weather and bad crashes halved the field in the first stages and of the 69 starters only 11 reached Paris. The tail light was carried in by Jules Nempon, an independent rider. In those days, non-team men could ride and grab what winnings they could. The race director was so delighted that whereas most of the big stars had shown no stomach for the suffering and quit, the solitary hero had stuck it out, and he cheered him on most of the 210 miles from Dunkirk to Paris from his car.

Of the first two Britons to finish the race – in 1955 – Tony Hoar carried the *lanterne rouge* and was amazed at the ecstatic reception the French public gave him. But that is just part of what makes the Tour an exceptional event; and French cycle fans have always feted the riders who show extraordinary courage. Men like Eugène Christophe, who, in 1913, broke his forks in the Pyrenees, ran five miles down the mountain to a smithy where he forged a new set and rode on. He had lost hours of time and the overall lead, but finished a gallant seventh in Paris. The public adored him for that.

There are stories of riders actually vying for the red lamp – the last but one man dodging down a side street to wait for the *lanterne* to go past and then following him in. Perhaps on the basis that if you are going to be last, go the whole hog and be really last. More often, the *lanterne rouge* is only too aware of the broom wagon rumbling up the road behind him, witch's besom tied to the back, the grim sweeper into which the day's casualties of the perdition stumble, body broken, eyes dead, heart sunk. That happened to Jean Patrick Nazon the other day. Soaked and frozen by the rain through an appalling 125 miles over vicious climbs, he collapsed with fatigue and left the race; it was his first Tour. Only a week ago, when another rider, Stuart O'Grady, crashed and broke a shoulder but rode on to the finish, desperate to stay in the race, one arm draped useless over the bars, Nazon, the *lanterne rouge*, pushed him up every single little climb.

The red lamp is no mark of inferiority. One blistering day in 1969, on the Puy de Dôme, one of the nastier bits of geology on the Tour, the red lamp Pierre Matignan scorched past all the great men of the peloton to a famous victory at the summit. And in 1983, another tail light, Gilbert Glaus, cut loose to win the last stage on the Champs-Elysées and hand the lamp to someone else.

If there is romance in the idea of the *lanterne rouge*, the fact is very much grimmer. The present holder, Francisco Leon, riding his first Tour, has a wan look as the race goes into the first of three terrible days in the Alps. He is, in the parlance, 'an accordion player', meaning that he's constantly yo-yoing off the back and clawing his way on again. For him there is no red-nose jokery in the lamp; rather it is like a fierce 'stop' light shining in his eyes. A reminder that this day may be his last in the race and, if it is, no sympathy will compensate for the disappointment of abandoning.

---

24 JULY 2000

ARMSTRONG RIDING HIGH AGAIN

Phil Liggett in Paris

Lance Armstrong won his second successive Tour de France yesterday, pocketing the £250,000 first prize with an emphatic victory. Runner-up Jan Ullrich, of Germany, finished 6 m 2 s behind with Spain's Joseba Beloki third, more than ten minutes adrift of the Texan. Yesterday, Armstrong, 28, hoisted his recently born son, Luke, high above his head in an emotional end to his three-week campaign. 'It was a hard Tour. It's very special — but I'm glad it's finished,' he said.

Armstrong has become a changed person physically and psychologically since contracting testicular cancer. Until he recovered from the disease, he never expected to win the world's hardest bicycle race and always saw himself as a single-day rider in classic races. Since then he has re-appraised his targets, lost more than a stone in weight, and changed his pedalling action to become one of the strongest riders in the world. His next target will be the Olympic Games time trial in Sydney in September. Aware that his cancer can recur at any time, he cherishes every day of his life and enjoys his training and living in France with a relish he never had before.

Yesterday's final stage of 86 miles was only the second time the race had stayed entirely within the Paris area, the city closing its streets for the 128 survivors of the 180 who started in the Futuroscope theme park near Poitiers on 1 July. Stefano Zanini, an Italian in his third Tour, won the sprint from the entire field, and Armstrong cruised over the line in 76th place without even a wave to the large crowd on the Champs-Elysées.

Armstrong has not won, in his words, any 'popularity contests' with the French and still battles with the media in France, some of whom believe he could only have won the last two Tours with the use of chemical products. Armstrong retaliated by refusing to speak French, for fear of being misinterpreted, and in English has repeatedly denied using any forbidden products. 'I have been on my death bed, and I have no wish to go back,' he said.

The Tour ended on a sour note when Dutchman Jeroen Blijlevens was thrown out after what organisers said was a 'particularly serious asault' on Bobby Julich, of the United States. Eyewitnesses said Blijlevens struck Julich after accusing the American of blocking him during the sprint finish.

———

TOUR LEGEND DEFENDS HIS INTEGRITY

Owen Slot

This is weird. I am sitting at a table for two in a restaurant in Switzerland explaining to one of the most successful athletes on the planet why he lives under a cloud of suspicion of cheating.

I half-expect him to hit me, or at least storm out. He does, after all, have a reputation as a hot head. Sportsmen of this calibre tend to command a royal respect and, until recently, Tour de France winners were lauded like gods. Yet this one is reduced to a defence of his integrity based on the contents of his urine samples. He does so, however, with patience and intelligence, and he can turn on the charm when he wants to.

Four years ago Lance Armstrong required brain surgery to help him to beat a cancer so severe he was given a one-in-twenty chance of survival. He then returned to cycling and won the Tour de France twice. He is either, therefore, one of the greatest – arguably the greatest, a miracle – in the history of all sport, or he is using performance-enhancing drugs and is a liar and a cheat.

If he is the former, then it is an injustice that he is even being doubted, though as he makes his defence, he calmly claims that he is not unduly bothered: 'Whatever gets said, it doesn't affect what I've done for the world, it doesn't affect what I've done for cancer survivors around the world. For me, surviving the illness, coming back to win, I'm standing up for those people.'

And when you hear that – and the fact that his cancer charity expects to raise $5 million this year – you want to believe the miracle even more. But it is not easy.

On the Tour de France of 1998, doping was exposed as commonplace and the Festina team were famously busted en route with a travelling pharmacy of banned products. The following year, the 'Tour of Redemption' we were told would be clean and therefore slower, yet along came our man with victory at an average speed that broke all records.

Sounds peculiar? Armstrong smiles; he's heard this a thousand times. 'On the 1999 Tour, the course was one of the easiest they've ever selected,' he explains. 'There were more flat stages, fewer mountains, so of course the average speed was higher.' Next question please.

'How can I prove that I'm the pure Lance Armstrong? I have never ridden as fast as I rode last year. I rode the final time trial at 54 kph, I climbed faster than before; I did things that are faster than almost anyone has done in cycling. And we have three weeks of absolutely clean urine from the Tour. There isn't much better proof that I can give.'

Yet already we are on dodgy ground here. One day at the end of last year's Tour, a French TV crew tailed a car belonging to Armstrong's team, US Postal, and after 150 km, filmed them dumping some bags in a bin. On the back of this, a judicial inquiry was opened in France in November and frozen urine and blood samples from the Tour were taken away to be tested. Then, 11 weeks ago, Armstrong announced that the results had proved that he was clean.

However, this week we contacted the judge conducting the inquiry, Sophie-Helene Chateau, to check this and her response was: 'Armstrong is dreaming.' She explained: 'I'm monitoring the progress but I haven't received any of the experts' reports that have been requested in this case.'

This clearly came as something of a surprise to Armstrong. 'If she wants to change her story,' he replied incredulously, 'then it's she who's dreaming. But they can keep the inquiry open for ever. They're not going to find anything.'

Either way, the Tour has rules against the random dumping of bio-hazardous materials (medicines, syringes, etc). 'There was nothing bio-hazardous,' says Armstrong. According to the film crew, however, there were syringes aplenty. And why drive 150 km to dump rubbish when it could have been left in the hotel? 'Maybe it should have been. But you say: why didn't you dump it in the hotel? I say: why wouldn't you dump it on the roadside?' That is a ludicrous answer which he quickly changes. 'Whenever we leave hotels, as soon as we walk out one side, everybody walks in the other, the journalists, the fans, the maids. They're all looking for something.'

And that is the sum of the hard evidence: an eight-month inquiry that is still unconcluded (which is a scandal in itself) and some unexplained irregularities. Thereafter, we are into hearsay, such as the comments by Antoine Vayer, the former Festina trainer, in court last year.

'Armstrong rides at 54 kph,' he said. 'I find it scandalous. It's nonsense. Indirectly it proves he's doping.' And Armstrong's reaction? That if he had known French law – that you have only three months in which to sue for defamation – then he would have acted quicker. 'If he ever says that again, I will invest whatever it takes to sue the hell out of him. If anyone says that again, I'm going to go after them. This is what's happened in cycling: people are able to talk. They've never been held accountable for their words and they get paid a lot to make these comments.'

Armstrong adds: 'And how is 54 kph impossible anyway? What's his explanation? My blood was tested two days before – it was fine. My urine was tested too. There's no smoking gun. These guys are liars.'

But they nevertheless all contribute to the broad perception that doping is widespread, a perception that taints Armstrong more than anyone. Ask him how bad the problem is, however, and he will contend that cycling's problems are over-estimated.

Are doping scandals such as Festina's commonplace? 'They don't happen in cycling. Honestly, honestly. I'll bet the bank.' Which is interesting, because reams of information suggest otherwise, particularly the raid on the Giro d'Italia by 200 police only 18 days ago when it was reported that another pharmacy of banned drugs was confiscated and from which, it is believed, only two of the 20 teams are left free of investigation.

Does he believe that there will be doping on the Tour de France this year 'No.' Really? Why should they dope in Italy and not in France? 'The thing at the Giro made me absolutely sick,' he replies. 'If they've found things, then these guys should be punished big time.'

So how can you say the Tour de France will be clean? 'I want to believe it, that's what I'm saying. But would I bet my life's savings on it? No. I can't speak for rider No 137, I can only speak for rider No 1. But because of the facts with me – clean urine samples, no positive tests – people inevitably turn to asking about the sport: what about this guy, that guy, this crisis, that controversy?'

True, Armstrong cannot be held accountable for the rest of his sport, but the problem is that his answers have a history of being so inadequate. Ever since the Festina crisis, cyclists – and Armstrong is no exception – have closed ranks. They have insisted that all is well and that anyone suggesting otherwise is a trouble-maker, and this gives the impression that they have something to cover up. By claiming in this interview that Festina's was a one-off doping incident, or that this year's Tour might be clean, it is impossible not to suspect a certain amount of economising with the truth.

'Perhaps I didn't handle it right in 1999,' he says. 'Maybe I should have been more aggressive with the stance against doping. It was a very sensitive time for cycling and I certainly didn't want to be saying things I wasn't sure about.'

Just because you think cycling is tainted, is his argument, you shouldn't conclude that he is tainted too. But what can he prove? He shrugs. 'The problem in the sport now is that you can never prove you are innocent. Certainties only exist when a test shows you are guilty.'

As these arguments chase round in circles, it is worth recalling a thought from his autobiography: 'One of the redeeming things

about being an athlete – one of the real services we can perform –
is to redefine what's humanly possible. We cause people to reconsider their limits.'

With Armstrong, it is easy to lose sight of all this. And we will
probably never be sure because in the final analysis, no matter
how many clean urine and blood samples he provides, there are
always the new, smarter drugs on the market that the tests
cannot spot.

'Has it ultimately come down to that?' he asks wearily. And yes,
it has. 'At a time when someone has ridden faster than anyone in
cycling, and they've proved themselves clean of EPO, cortizone
and everything else that people can think of, is the only thing to
say: it must be something new? If that's the argument, then I can't
say anything, I can't defend that. There's just nothing I can do.'

---

17 JULY 2001

TOUR CLIMBERS SCENT SPRINTERS' BLOOD

Andrew Baker

Half-time in most sporting events is a welcome opportunity for
rest and reflection, a chance to take on some refreshment while
pretending to listen to a ranting coach. The job is half done, the
opposition a known quantity: there is nothing left to fear.

But on the Tour de France, half-time does not signify that half
of the required effort has been expended, and there is plenty left
to frighten the riders this morning as they set out on the tenth of
the race's 20 stages. Connoisseurs of this marathon of pain insist
that the Tour cannot properly be said to have begun until the
riders have met the mountains, and today that uncomfortable
introduction takes place.

The 2,000-metre Col de la Madeleine and the 1,924-metre Col du
Glandon are but *hors d'oeuvres* to the agonising 14-km slog up to

today's finish at Alpe d'Huez, a destination as revered by cycling fans as it is loathed by the riders. Previous peaks will seem mere hillocks and the whole complexion of the race will be changed, as climbers scent the blood of their sprinting brethren.

Yesterday's stage, from Pontarlier to Aix-les-Bains, will be a pleasant memory. If you imagine the route profile as an electrocardiogram, yesterday's patient was recovering gradually from a mild surprise; today's is suffering a series of massive heart attacks leading to a fatal coronary.

At least yesterday the riders could take comfort in the gentle downhill incline of the last few miles before the finish. The stage offered unusually hospitable conditions for spectators as well. Those who watch the Tour in the mountains must set out long before dawn in order to stake a claim to a precipitous patch of scree hours from the nearest refreshment station. At the finish in Aix, fans toddled up with their folding stools in mid-afternoon and settled down to read *L'Equipe* over a cup of coffee as they waited for the leaders to arrive.

In no other sport do fans adopt quite so much of the kit of their idols. Motor racing groupies sport a team baseball cap, football fans a replica shirt, but for followers of US Postal, Festina or Mapei-Quick Step nothing less than the full costume will do, complete with bike.

Hundreds of such clones were to be seen yesterday hobbling by the lakeside in their cleated shoes, the image of their heroes were it not for the added paunches and drooping muscles. Their bodies may betray them but the spirit is willing to believe: above all, that the Tour this year is clean, that innocence and fair play now reign where for so long the chemist has been king.

There are reasons why the fans may be justified in their hopes. Drug-testing is more comprehensive than ever, and the tests themselves are gaining in credibility. More effective than any tests have been the police raids on the Giro d'Italia before the Tour began, and the willingness of the French race organisers to co-operate with police and customs activity, should any be deemed necessary. Of course it is still not impossible to cheat, but it is getting harder.

Without any major scandal so far, the supporters who lined the Esplanade du Lac to cheer Sergei Ivanov home at the head of the field were able to do so with comparatively clear consciences. They come to applaud bravery, endurance, speed and skill, not pharmacological cunning, and the pendulum seems finally to be swinging their way.

David Millar, the British leader of the Cofidis team, has certainly had to display plenty of bravery and endurance as he attempts to recover from his painful crash in the Prologue to the race ten days ago. The gashes and grazes are gradually healing, and the mental scars inflicted by savage disappointment are starting to fade.

But still Millar is at the rear of the field. Yesterday morning he started 175th of 175 riders, the bearer of the *lanterne rouge*, the metaphorical red light at the end of the long and winding express train of the Tour. It is not a role without honour, and the fact that it has been filled for so long by a rider of promise rather than a plodder has earned Millar respect for his persistence and pluck.

Millar made up one place yesterday, but the bulk of the field will remain out of his reach all the way to Paris. It is a long way from red light to yellow jersey, but that is a journey that he will hope to complete another year.

---

23 JULY 2001

ARMSTRONG CLIMBS AHEAD

Phil Liggett in Luz-Ardiden

A week ago, Lance Armstrong was 35 minutes behind in the Tour de France, but that was before the crossing of the Alps and the Pyrenees. Yesterday, the American was the winner-elect, saluting the crowd as leader after crossing the two mountain ranges as the most dominant figure in recent years.

Since taking the lead on Saturday, it has all seemed easy for the Texan who has won the race for the past two years, and his advantage of 5 m 5 s over German champion Jan Ullrich should be enough to take to Paris next Sunday, where he will join the few who have won the race three times in succession.

This has been the finest Tour in years, with Ullrich, the winner in 1997, and with never a worse finish than second, always willing to attack Armstrong. Yesterday, on top of the final Pyrenean climb, Ullrich shook Armstrong's hand as they crossed the line together at Luz-Ardiden in third and fourth places.

It was a sporting gesture between two athletes who have the utmost respect for one another. On Saturday, descending the Col de Peyresourde, Ullrich went too fast into a turn and crashed into a ravine. Armstrong, who saw Ullrich's untimely exit as he descended behind him, freewheeled until the German rejoined with, remarkably, only a muddied racing jersey as evidence of a spectacular fall.

'When someone falls like that, you don't race away; you wait until he catches up and then restart the bike race,' said the American after ending up the stage winner at Pla d'Adet, near St Lary-Soulan, finally claiming the race lead that was always only a matter of time.

---

28 JULY 2001

VILLAGE AWAKES TO A TOUR DE FORCE
Sarah Edworthy

Question: When do ordinarily sane French families take to picnicking in deep roadside ditches, complete with table, tablecloth, comfy chairs, bottles of wine and food that requires a knife and fork?

Answer: When the fast and thrilling convoy that makes up the Tour de France squeezes through their narrow rural lanes.

The visit of Le Tour is a lifetime's honour worthy of celebration. Yesterday, for the first time in 37 years, it passed through Le Brethon, a sleepy village in the Allier, where Charolais cattle outnumber human beings, and drivers swerve off roads in shock at seeing an oncoming vehicle.

Gabriel Chevallier could have modelled *Clochemerle*, his comic masterpiece on French village life, on this hamlet of dozing charm complete with Chevallieresque communal WC. A region in which the tractor rules took the day off to pay tribute to the men who plough their sporting furrow on the skinniest of tyres – though only after the farmers prepared immaculate fields and verges for the army of Dutch, German and Belgium camper vans which invaded for 24 hours.

While Jan Ullrich was trying to take time out of Lance Armstrong's lead, and Andrei Kivilev was desperate to hang on to his third place on the 61-km individual time trial, *les Brethonnois* had a whole day of it. Not for them hours of waiting for a few blurred groups of speedy cyclists. They saw cyclists whooshing through at two-minute intervals from 11.20 a.m. to 4.40 p.m. when Armstrong triumphantly pedalled past in a sweat-soaked *maillot jaune*.

Le Brethon claims one 13th-century church, one school, one shop, one post office, a Hotel des Sports – two bedrooms, bar and restaurant (Chez Gilles et Pascale) whose 65-franc *menu du jour* had sold out in advance – and a 13th-century stone crucifix put up to commemorate the questionable presence of the English during the Hundred Years War (they maltreated the inhabitants and razed the chateau).

On the approach to the Foret de Tronais, from which Louis XIV's navy used to requisition their mighty masts, Le Brethon bills itself as 'the heart of the most beautiful oak forest'. The village mayor, Jean Pasquier, was found on Thursday in the Hotel des Sports bar having his lunchtime Pernod with the men of the village. He confirmed the population of 350 felt immense pride.

'It is very important for us, not because many of us are fascinated with cycling but because Le Brethon will be seen on televisions in Asia and South America and everybody will have a look at us,' he said back behind his desk after a hasty change into official uniform.

'One resident found an old bike in his cellar and turned it into this sculpture, bending an old farm instrument into the silhouette of a rider,' added Bernard Benoit, the mayor's first assistant, referring to a bike set up on a plinth and decorated with bunches of corn and lavender. And the son of a councillor, who likes cycling, has painted the road nearest to their farm with a list of his favourite riders in huge letters with a big heart around the name of Laurent Jalabert. Their land is on a long hill and he wanted to give the riders extra strength with his words. We are not a rich community. Everybody has realised their ideas however they can.'

This is not a place preoccupied with Le Tour's pharmaceutical history. Cars came from nowhere and the main street was lined five-deep with sun-worn faces intent on celebration as a helicopter buzzed overhead. Only one dissonant voice was heard, echoing the communist traditions of the area. 'How can Montlucon spend money hosting a stage of Le Tour when 30 per cent of the Allier's inhabitants still have outside toilets?' Hermione Quihampton griped.

But home improvements abounded. Previously shabby cottages and shutters were barely recognisable under new paint. To many inhabitants, Armstrong, the two-times Tour champion who prefers to be celebrated as a cancer survivor, is the prince of cyclists who has brought an awakening.

———

29 JULY 2001

TIME FOR SCEPTICS TO PAY ARMSTRONG HIS DUES

Chris Boardman

Running with the dog on the beach this morning and moaning loudly about how much my legs hurt, it is hard to believe that just nine months ago I was a professional cyclist and used to compete in what is the hardest physical challenge in mainstream sport, the Tour de France.

This year's Tour has truly been a vintage one, with drama from start to finish and welcome evidence that it has been a largely clean race. The time gaps between competitors have been perfectly believable and no team has dominated. Both of these things point to the fact that, perhaps, the war on drugs is being won.

There was certainly some fantastic racing in the first week, mostly ending in a mass sprint for the line, as the riders realised that no team was strong enough to control the race. The drama unfolded almost as soon as the 2001 race started in Dunkirk. Britain's David Millar, last year's winner of this stage and clear favourite to take the Tour's first yellow jersey, faltered under the immense pressure. He pushed it a shade too hard and crashed with just 1.5 km left. Millar battled on for a further week but eventually succumbed to the injuries he sustained and withdrew as the race entered the mountains.

On the 222-km eighth stage to Pontarlier, we saw the record broken for the largest amount of time yet gained in the race by a breakaway. The 14-strong group eventually earned a staggering 36 minutes, putting Stuart O'Grady into yellow. If the rules had been strictly applied, all of the main pack, including Armstrong, should have been eliminated.

The race took on a slightly more predictable format on the tenth stage, the first of five high mountain summit finishes. Armstrong, who had feigned fatigue in front of the TV cameras for the first few hours, launched a devastating attack at the foot of Alpe d'Huez. He took more than a minute out of all his rivals, a pattern he was to repeat for the next four stages.

Sidelined for most of the season with a broken back sustained when he fell off a ladder, Laurent Jalabert made an amazing comeback to win stages four and seven. He then went on to establish an unassailable lead in the polka-dot jersey competition for the best climber in the race, an incredible feat for a man who has twice won the green jersey for best sprinter in the Tour. For the non-cyclists among you, that's like Linford Christie winning a marathon.

This year's green jersey competition is headed by Australian Stuart O'Grady, of the Credit Agricole team. It is so close between him and former winner Eric Zabel, of Telekom, that it is likely to come down to the final sprint of the race on the Champs-Elysées, helping to make it an even bigger spectacle.

So after three weeks of eating 8,000 calories a day and more time in the saddle than John Wayne did in *True Grit,* this year's 3,500-km epic trip around France is due to end. Barring accidents or illness, it will be won for the third successive time by American Lance Armstrong. Most people know by now of Armstrong's battle with cancer and his incredible comeback to win the sport's biggest prize. I remember riding next to the aggressive young Texan in 1996 in the opening, rain-marred week of the Tour. He turned to me and said: 'I feel terrible, just . . . blocked up'.

At a time when nobody was having a great deal of fun I didn't think much more of it but, just five kilometres further on, Lance abandoned the Tour. Soon afterwards it was announced that he had advanced testicular cancer and was to start treatment immediately.

Today, five years on, he is poised to win his third consecutive Tour de France, nothing short of a fairytale, but, sadly, people have become more sceptical. Some refuse to accept that performances such as these are possible without 'help'. He is constantly shadowed by innuendo and veiled accusations by members of the foreign media.

I think it only fair to point out that, in a sport that now has more doping control procedures than any other in the world, he has never tested positive. I suspect that for a man like Lance, the more people throw insults and accusations at him, the more it will fuel his fire. Anyone who really wants to know why Armstrong is almost invincible at the moment need only to have looked at his face as he prepared to launch himself down the starting ramp in Dunkirk three weeks ago. It was a mask of concentration and aggression. It scared me and I was 600 miles away.

I know that look because I've worn one just like it. I think this mindset is perhaps best summed up as the difference between those of us who want to win and those who need to win. The latter category are not always the nicest individuals or the most mentally well balanced, but they are the ones who win because everything else in life comes second. I am amazed that Armstrong, after all he has done and been through, still has that drive, but he clearly does and, until he loses it, he will be next to impossible to beat. This year, even with a weak team, he did not just beat his rivals, he crushed them.

Can he beat Miguel Indurain's record? Is he another Eddy Merckx? Personally, I think his style is comparable, if a little more aggressive, to that of Indurain. He hits hard in the mountains, takes time out of his rivals and then defends. Indurain has said he sees no reason why Lance can't beat his record of five Tour victories and he'd know. It is natural people are sceptical, even paranoid after the drugs problems faced by cycling in recent years, but perhaps it's time we started to believe in the sport again.

————

ARMSTRONG READY TO RIDE ON

Phil Liggett in Paris

Lance Armstrong's expected victory in the 2,200-mile Tour de France, which finished in Paris yesterday, continued the remarkable life of the American champion since he recovered from testicular cancer in 1998. He won his third consecutive Tour by almost seven minutes.

Armstrong, 29, has no other ambition than to just keep on winning the world's biggest cycle race, and he sees each of his victories as a triumph for cancer survivors. His wife, Kristen, who is expecting twins in December, and his young son, Luke, joined him on the Champs-Elysées at the end of the 20th stage from nearby Corbeil Essonnes. Armstrong rode his finest race, never appearing to experience a bad day throughout his long journey across France. In the Alps, he won both stages, and in the Pyrenees allowed others to succeed while he closely marked his main rival, Jan Ullrich.

Armstrong said: 'I've really had a blast these past three weeks. Like everyone else I'm ready for it to end now, but this has been the best. The Tour hasn't killed me like in the past and I'm feeling so good. I would like to keep on winning the Tour as it's a triumph for all cancer survivors. I really have no other ambition left. When I lose my taste for this race, then it will be all over.'

Eddy Merckx, the winner on five occasions, believes that the Texan can break the record of five wins (held by four men) and go as far as winning seven, but the multi-millionaire from Austin may, indeed, have lost his appetite long before then. He is now one of only five riders to have won the race three times straight and joins another American, Greg LeMond, on the same number.

Armstrong stood between the same two riders as last year, Jan Ullrich, the Olympic champion who has now finished second four times (he also won in 1997), and Spain's Joseba Beloki, again third. Generous in his praise of his two rivals, Armstrong will be remembered for his act of sportsmanship when he waited for Ullrich in the Pyrenees after seeing the German fall into a ravine. Unhurt, Ullrich rejoined his side and then resumed the battle between them.

Armstrong wore the leader's yellow jersey for the last eight days, less than in his two previous races, but this time he had to bridge a gap of 35 minutes to take the lead after a surprise breakaway put different names on the leaderboard in the opening week. It made a better race and showed the full potential of the American.

––––––––––

30 JULY 2001

NOTHING LIKE THE WHEEL ACTION
David Millar

Three weeks ago, after crashing in the Prologue time trial, I was sitting in a hotel in Dunkirk coming to terms with the fact that my Tour de France 2001 was somewhat ruined, trying to be as philosophical as my professionalism would allow and telling myself that it couldn't possibly get any worse.

Eleven days later, I was but a shadow of myself with a new-found stoical mantra of 'It can always get worse', drained emotionally and physically to the point of complete and utter exhaustion, with no choice but to slow to a complete stop on the descent of the Col de la Madeleine and give up the Tour de France. I had refused to give up on the climb and made myself endure the humiliation of climbing the 25 km to the summit by myself at a pitifully slow speed past the thousands of spectators.

I can't explain why I didn't want to give up on the climb, but then it's hard to explain much about the Tour de France or professional cycling in general. After close to 2,000 kilometres of hell (almost all of which were spent oscillating on and off the back of the peloton), I wasn't about to be stopped by one mountain. When the time came for me to stop I would do it on my own terms, and where better than on a descent where anybody could have carried on?

The race organisation put me in the ambulance, so there need never be any images of me actually giving up and climbing in the dreaded *voiture balai,* a nod of respect from the Tour de France itself in acknowledgement of what I had put myself through the previous 11 days. Now I am sitting at home in Biarritz finally able to turn the page as the Tour is completed by the 139 riders who are left in the peloton, 50 less than rolled down the start ramp of the Prologue in Dunkirk, which I suppose is about the usual number of *abandons* for the Tour – not very many when you consider how ridiculously hard it is and the number of crashes and injuries that are endured.

To put into perspective the dangers involved you need only look at the crash that occurred a few days ago, from which six riders didn't get back up, four with broken collarbones, one with a broken wrist and the last, a friend of mine, who fractured his face and skull in five places. And that was only one crash.

All this is what makes the Tour de France what it is. It's a sporting event with no equal, beyond description and beyond comparison. It even made the Olympics an anti-climax for me, which may surprise a lot of people, but the Olympics could simply not generate the passion that the Tour does.

Riding up a mountainside with hundreds of thousands of people cheering for you is something that stays with you for ever, having them close enough to touch you and close enough to look straight into your eyes, to be able to look straight into the eyes of a Lance Armstrong in full flight.

So now to LA himself, the man, the myth. Three Tours de France under his belt and I can't see him stopping there. There is no doubt that Lance could have probably become a world-beater in almost anything he chose to do, and it's not until you get to know him a bit that you come to understand this fact.

This is why when he says that he loves cycling, I know that he means it. It's no longer the money nor the glory, these he now has aplenty. It's those moments when he's racing up a mountain pass in front of those hundreds of thousands of people, knowing he is the leader of the Tour de France, showing once again that he's one of the greats.

And just occasionally he may choose to glance at one of those many spectators and let them see into his eyes. Those are the moments that touch people for the rest of their lives, and that's what the Tour de France is about. It's a mad, mad sport, created to make a good story.

---

5 JULY 2002

TOUR DE FRANCE TOUGHER ON DRUGS

Phil Liggett in Luxembourg

It is 99 years since chain-smoking chimney sweep Maurice Garin won the first Tour de France and, under the current climate of drug busts and stringent tests, the nicotine consumed then would have probably earned him a ban now.

The race, which costs over £7 million a year to run, has assembled in Luxembourg ready for tomorrow afternoon's opening Prologue time trial. The organisers are hopeful that they have found the solution to the constant stream of cyclists caught for using drugs to gain their success.

Following a Tour of Italy last month, where former winner Gilberto Simoni and Stefano Garzelli were both evicted for using cocaine and Probenecid respectively, the Tour de France Society have more drugs tests than ever. They have already used their strength by rejecting Simoni's Italian Saeco team and this week banned Frenchman Laurent Paumier from being part of his AG2R team after he tested positive in last month's Midi-Libre race.

Up to ten riders a day will be spot-tested including the stage winner and all of the leaders of the race classifications plus others at random. Ninety riders will be tested for the blood booster EPO, compared to 72 last year. In addition, the International Cycling Union will test all 189 riders for EPO use, announcing the results by midday today. Any riders with a haematocrit blood count above 50 (indicating possible EPO use) will not be allowed to start.

Lance Armstrong, the winner for the past three years and favourite to make it four in Paris on 28 July, has only just been cleared of possible drug abuse after a two-year wait while a French drug-testing agency carried out an investigation into him and his US Postal team.

Armstrong, who is in remission from testicular cancer and hailed as a 'saint' in the United States for the millions of dollars he has raised for his cancer foundation, is not complimentary about the French, who have reluctantly announced his innocence.

'The key to my success has been intense training,' says Armstrong, 'and they [the French agency] are incapable of accepting this. They have made no effort to end the tests quickly. As in sport, you should admit when you are wrong, but they do not seem to want to admit that.'

―――――――――

29 JULY 2002

ARMSTRONG FAMILY AFFAIR

Phil Liggett in Paris

Lance Armstrong raced on to the Champs-Elysées yesterday to win his fourth Tour in a row and at the same time completed perhaps the easiest victory of them all. Spain's Joseba Beloki was second and Lithuanian Raimondas Rumšas third, but at no time during the 2,100-mile race from Luxembourg to Paris had Armstrong been under pressure. He countered with ease the few moves his rivals attempted in the high mountains of the Pyrenees and Alps and then finally crushed them in the time trial at Mâcon on Saturday.

After finishing safely in the pack behind Australia's Robbie McEwen yesterday, Armstrong stepped on to the podium especially erected on the Champs-Elysées with his wife and three children.

The Texan was given only a 20 per cent chance of living through the testicular cancer which spread through his body five years ago. Now, with a single-minded view on life and only his family and winning the Tour as his main directions, he enjoys every day as it comes. He raises millions and gives hope to thousands through the Lance Armstrong Cancer Foundation. He admits his life changed completely in 1996, but it is clear that the determination he showed then to beat the disease remains intact as he races to success each July.

He continues to mystify the French media and government, who have both led campaigns to discredit him. The finding of syringes allegedly used by his US Postal team two years ago, indicating possible use of drugs, and the two-year span of tests on frozen samples of his urine by the French drugs agency, have led to nothing. 'That's because there is nothing to find, so why don't they just apologise and admit they have made a mistake?' Armstrong says. 'If they saw how I train and prepare for the race then they would know how hard I try to win it without using banned substances.'

Armstrong has not been deceived by the drugs in sport and has made many friends, from President George W. Bush to his bodyguards who mix with the crowd every day. His £200,000 prize will go to his team, so loyal that they defend his name ferociously each time someone tries to insinuate he has cheated. This Tour, subject to final tests yesterday, has been drugs-free. The riders' faces, so often pained, indicate perhaps that the stringent tests which a cyclist now faces have hit the evil that almost brought the sport to its knees.

On Saturday, winning the final time trial after being beaten in Brittany two weeks earlier was more a point of honour than a necessity. Armstrong beat Rumšas by 53 seconds. Armstrong, in winning his 15th stage of a Tour, which is three more than any other current rider, also showed his single-minded application to this event – the only race he wants to win.

Armstrong says: 'I will be back for a few years yet, but I'm not saying I'm going to win it again as that would be suicide. I hate to sound like a broken record, but my team were the best I've ever ridden with and I hope I can ride with them again, too.'

---

30 JULY 2002

RUMSAS CENTRE OF DRUGS PROBE

Phil Liggett

Raimondas Rumšas, who on Sunday became the first Lithuanian to finish on the podium of the Tour de France when he took third place behind Lance Armstrong and Joseba Beloki, was at the centre of a doping controversy yesterday.

At the time Rumšas was racing into Paris, his wife was being arrested in Chamonix after her car was stopped by French customs and found to be carrying 'medication which could be considered as doping products'.

Lampre, the Italian team of Rumšas, immediately suspended their rider pending further investigation. The team's hotel was searched by police in Paris but nothing was found.

The 2,100-mile race from Luxembourg is being seen as the most drug-free for many years, with new controls felt to have had a great effect on the use of performance-enhancing drugs.

UNSUNG HERO WAS PRONE TO THROWING BREAD ROLLS AT OTHER RIDERS, BUT WAS STILL A BIG HIT ON TOUR

Brendan Gallagher

It is 25 years now since Barry Hoban completed his last Tour de France, but the fan letters keep arriving from the Continent and he cannot spend five minutes in France before the back-slapping and hand-shaking starts. Back home in Britain he remains unknown and unheralded.

Hoban is one of those sportsmen who lived his dream. A colliery apprentice in Wakefield, he quit his job in 1962 and moved to Arras in northern France with the crazy notion of trying to become a professional cyclist and ride in the world's greatest race. He succeeded on both counts.

Hoban was never going to win the thing outright – he lacked the all-round ability to assume the mantle of team leader and enjoy all the racing advantages that brings – but in his own way he was a star performer. He completed 11 of the 12 Tours he rode – only a handful of riders have bettered that – and won eight stages. Sponsors and team directors loved him: a team man who could also win the big sprints – all those headlines and pictures in *L'Equipe* the next day.

His first stage win Hoban never counts. It was the day after his friend Tommy Simpson had died on the scorching slopes of Mont Ventoux in 1967 and the peloton decided they would ride *piano* – slowly – the next day and allow the British riders to lead the race and claim the stage, which finished at Sète. The other seven, however, were full-blooded victories against the best riders in the world.

'The secret to completing the Tour and staying competitive is the ability to sleep,' insists Hoban, a sprightly 63 who still thinks nothing of putting in 55 or 60 miles on his bike before lunch. 'If you can sleep the body can recover, no matter how knackered. I've always been an eight hours solid merchant. I'm away from the moment my head hits the pillow. I might have been scraped off the finishing line the previous day, but I was always ready, bright and breezy, the following morning.

'I was one of the few who got fitter and stronger as the Tour progressed. I was always a slow starter but by the second half I was beginning to pick off a few stage wins. If the Tour could have gone on for another fortnight I might have been a real contender.

'Before any Tour starts there are only four or five riders who stand a chance of winning and I was never one of those. So as a middle-ranking rider, trying to earn a good living, my agenda was slightly different. After helping my team leader, I went looking for stage wins. Financially a stage win is worth ten times as much as slogging your guts around the route and finishing a worthy tenth or eleventh overall. 'Not only do you get reasonably rewarded for the stage win, but you put yourself in prime position to pick up lucrative little contracts to ride in the popular one-day criteriums that always follow the Tour.

'I was basically a conservative rider, especially in the sprints where there can be lots of pile-ups and bad injuries. The glory boys always hug the barricades by the crowd and the inclination is to slip alongside them. But in a bunch that can mean big trouble so my tactic was to take the outside route where there was plenty of road to work with, and an escape route if it all went pear-shaped.

'I never once fell in a sprint, though I had my share of tumbles elsewhere. The trick, by the way, is never to put your arms out to stop a fall – you'll lose all your skin and pop your shoulder for sure. Cover your head with your forearms and roll into the fall. It can shake you up, but I was never badly hurt.

'Descending was my great joy and the only time I took risks. For some reason I was naturally good at it. You just set yourself firm and solid in the saddle – squatting like a downhill skier – and let rip. You can struggle up a big mountain climb and claw back ten or fifteen minutes on a good descent. On the Tourmalet once I did the 25-mile descent run, including all the slow, tricky hairpins at the top, in just under 35 minutes. The occasional corner at 70 miles an hour, definitely, sometimes nearer 80. Very exciting,' he said.

'Legend insists that some of the great mountain riders, Jean Robic for one, used to take on food bags at the top of a big climb filled with lead weights to speed their descent. I'm not sure. I don't think you need to go any quicker than comes naturally.'

Hoban these days lives in an idyllic old farm cottage in mid-Wales with his wife Helen, the widow of Tom Simpson. The climb to their mountain home – named Col de Hoban by the locals – is as fierce, though shorter, as anything on the Tour, one-in-five in places. The view at the end, though, is well worth the effort, just like the Tour itself.

'It wasn't all pain, you know. My big mate was Gerben Karstens, from Holland, who was certifiably bonkers as well as being a great bloke. His favourite party trick on a quiet transition stage between the Alps and Pyrenees – with everybody in the peloton dozing or having a good gossip – was to spot a luxuriant maize field ahead, sprint hard, and then slam on the front brakes and somersault, bike and all, over the hedge to land comfortably upside down in a spongy bed of maize. God knows where he learnt that trick.

'Another little favourite was for Gerben and myself to sprint a couple of kilometres ahead – the peloton knew it was playtime and indulged us – before we would stop with a group of fans on a bend and invite ourselves to their picnic. A little bit of cheese and sip of Muscadet, very pleasant indeed. Then, when the peloton rode past, we would hurl bread rolls and abuse at them, especially all the big names. The crowd would love it and cheered us on our way as we remounted. We had a lot of fun on the way.'

NEWSPAPER GIMMICK SET WHEELS IN MOTION

Brendan Gallagher

It was Geo Lefevre, the 26-year-old rugby union correspondent of Parisian sports paper *L'Auto*, who came up with the novel idea of a bicycle race around France. He never received the credit or financial reward he deserved – his autocratic editor, Henri Desgrange, saw to that – but Lefevre is the man who put the wheels in motion back in 1903.

A century later his legacy is probably the biggest single sports event on the planet. More spectators will watch a stage of the Tour de France – any stage – than attend Wimbledon over a fortnight. Daily crowds of more than a million are not unusual – upwards of two million are expected for next weekend's Prologue and opening stage in Paris – while infamous set-piece climbs such as Alpe d'Huez or the Galibier can often attract 500,000 to that mountain range alone.

And all because two rival newspapers decided to wage war. Lefevre, ambitious and full of ideas, had been signed from rival sports paper *Le Velo,* a publication that was increasingly winning the dog-eat-dog circulation battle with *L'Auto* and threatening the latter's very existence.

L'Auto badly needed a gimmick, so Desgrange called his editorial staff around for a brainstorming session and listened as Lefevre, an accomplished amateur cyclist, outlined his idea for the ultimate test of man and bike, a circumnavigation of France in six stages. Later he and Desgrange retired to a nearby café to continue their discussion before Desgrange presented the idea – as his own – to the board of *L'Auto.*

It was a winner: *L'Auto* had struck gold. Within six years circulation had increased from 140,000 to 250,000. The paper was saved and one of the world's greatest sporting spectacles born. Lefevre was appointed official timekeeper, but the Tour de France became Desgrange's race and fiefdom.

In fairness to Desgrange he was the ideal tyrannical entrepreneur, self-publicist and megalomaniac to breathe life into such a project. His version of Lefevre's original concept was to make the race so arduous that ideally only one supreme rider should be able to complete the Tour and return to Paris. He wanted to break the human spirit, not to mention the riders' bodies.

The Tour length increased from 1,508 miles in 1903 to 3,257 miles in 1911, reaching an all-time high of 3,569 miles in 1926. The longest stage in this year's competition – 143 miles – is 24 miles shorter than the shortest stage in 1903.

The riders would start long before dawn and often finish in the dark that evening – heads bowed, arms and legs turned raw by the summer sun and crying in agony from saddle sores. The Tour predominantly followed rough tracks that would be barely recognised as roads these days, and would be tackled now only with a lightweight, multi-geared mountain bike.

The temptation to seek additional 'chemical' assistance has always been there and has often proved irresistible. Indeed modern-day distances are down and rest days have been added to try to counter that threat. The financial lure, however, is greater than ever and the race itself remains an incredibly tough physical challenge. The Tour de France, and professional cycling, is undeniably fighting a doping problem, but arguably no more so than athletics.

Not that the controversy is new, or indeed wholly unwelcome. The Tour has become an annual soap opera starring diverse and intense characters, in which the stories come at you from all angles. The politics are typically French, especially those concerning which towns and villages are granted stage starts and finishes – the going rate these days, apparently, is not far short of £100,000, which goes into the Tour coffers.

There can, however, be spectacular fall-outs among friends, as occurred in 1971 at Marseille, which had hosted the Tour more or less continuously since 1927. On this occasion the peloton – driven on by Eddy Merckx, who was attempting to regain the yellow jersey from Luis Ocaña – arrived fully half an hour before the earliest estimate. The city mayor, Gaston Deferre, was incandescent. Lunch had not yet finished, his guests were still waiting for dessert. *'C'est impossible, c'etait un scandale.'* Deferre ordered that the Tour was to be banned from Marseille henceforth, and indeed it returned only in 1989, following his death.

Then there's the mystery. What did happen to Ottavio Bottecchia, the winner of the 1924 and 1925 Tours? Bottecchia, a high-profile socialite, was found dead in a field near Peonis, Italy, in June 1927, allegedly the victim of a training accident near his home. Then a peasant farmer claimed to have stoned Bottecchia for allegedly trying to steal his grapes – in June? But a decade later in New York an Italian mafia hit man made a deathbed confession, claiming to have assassinated Bottecchia on behalf of the emerging Fascists.

There's been scandal, too. Italian winner Fausto Coppi, once a British prisoner of war, outraged much of his home country by publicly parading his mistress on the Tour before moving in with her. Even the Pope intervened and begged him to return to his wife. Jacques Anquetil, five times a winner, was for years accompanied by a blonde who deserted her husband, a doctor, every July to join him. They eventually married.

And, of course, there's been tragedy: Francesco Cepeda, of Spain, died on the descent of the Galibier in 1935; Britain's Tommy Simpson died on the Mont Ventoux climb in 1967; and Italy's Olympic champion, Fabio Casartelli, perished descending the Col de Portet D'Aspet in 1995.

Equally, there has been heroism. In 1996 Lance Armstrong was diagnosed with testicular cancer, with secondaries in his lungs and liver. Doctors put his chances of living at no more than 50–50. Armstrong begged to differ and staged one of the most inspiring comebacks in sport to win four consecutive Tours.

It is all there in the Tour de France, every form of emotion and human endeavour. It is the Olympics of cycling – time triallists, road specialists, climbers, descenders and sprinters are all thrown into the mix together. For nearly a month a nation is gripped by one of the few sporting events that, in the words of Chris Boardman, you can need a haircut halfway through.

———

28 JULY 2003

UNLUCKY ULLRICH PUSHES ALL THE WAY

Phil Liggett in Paris

Lance Armstrong duly won his fifth Tour de France in as many years yesterday, surviving the scares of his most difficult Tour when he beat Jan Ullrich, of Germany, by 61 seconds, and Alexander Vinokourov, by 4 m 19 s after more than three weeks and 2,100 miles.

At the final 20th stage, which ended on the Champs-Elysées after 95 miles from nearby Ville d'Avray, the 22 surviving winners of the 53 who have won the race were presented to celebrate the end of the Centenary Tour.

Jean-Patrick Nazon gave the host nation a perfect end to the most interesting race for many years, probably since another American, Greg LeMond, won in 1989, when he beat the Frenchman Laurent Fignon on the last stage from Versailles to win by just eight seconds.

Armstrong won the race, by far his most difficult, by the smallest margin of the five, after finishing third in Saturday's time trial from Pornic to Nantes. Britain's David Millar recovered from a fall to win that rain-soaked stage in spectacular style. Ullrich made his last, desperate attempt to win, taking great risks on the slick road surfaces into Nantes and paid the price as he skidded into straw bales. He was leading at the time with the fastest time, but finished 11 seconds slower than Armstrong.

Millar, in winning his third Tour stage since 2000, immediately criticised the course, saying that it was unfair to Armstrong and Ullrich that they should have to race the last ten miles in severe weather. He may have been right, but both gave it their best effort, as the stage would decide the final outcome in Paris the next day. On Saturday night Armstrong said: 'I've been vulnerable in this Tour and haven't enjoyed it. I'll come back next year having learnt a lot of lessons.'

———

7 JANUARY 2004

QUEASY RIDER FACES UP TO PEAK TEST

For one day every July some of the world's top cycling enthusiasts ride a stage of the Tour de France while the race proper enjoys a rest day. In a moment of madness **Brendan Gallagher** *agreed to take part*

I blame jet lag, the euphoria of Ireland's World Cup victory over Argentina and possibly that last, lingering glass of Hunter Valley red. I wasn't of entirely sound mind and in a court of law I could probably squirm out of my promise, but what the hell – life's too short.

So there I was in room 323 of the Adelaide Radisson in late October. Ireland had just clinched a glorious victory over the Pumas, acres of copy had been dispatched and, as is customary on such occasions, wine had been taken with friends and colleagues, possibly to excess. It was very late, in fact there was the smell of sizzling bacon and freshly ground coffee wafting up from the kitchen below. But life was good, not a worry in the world.

The office rang and an innocent voice gently applied the stiletto from 12,000 miles distant, where it was still a sober Sunday evening: 'We've got a company – Giant bikes – who want you to ride a stage of the Tour de France. Sounds a bit of fun. Fancy a bash? They will loan you a flash bike and you'll have to do a bit of training. Good chance to get fit, though. (*Chuckle.*) Are you up for it?'

My addled brain immediately conjured up memories of last summer and a fabulous five days covering the Tour – dazzling sunshine, snow-capped peaks, dramatic winding roads, ant-like crowds crawling over the mountains, fresh air, drama, excitement, world-class food and wine. Somewhere in the mental process, however, I forgot that I was driving a comfortable air-conditioned car and not pounding out the miles on a bike. In my mind's eye I was, of course, 25 and disgustingly fit – rather dashing, actually – as opposed to 45 and at least two stone overweight.

'Crackerjack idea,' I said enthusiastically and promptly turned over and returned to sleep and dreams of Ireland World Cup triumphs, Brian O'Driscoll scoring a hat-trick in the final and Keith Wood lifting the Webb Ellis Cup. A few hours later – black coffees and croissants all round – and I was swearing never to drink again. Why do we do it? What had I let myself in for? Messing about on a mountain bike was the full extent of my cycling experience thus far.

Every year the Tour organisers allow a limited number of enthusiastic cyclists – 9,000 this year out of 200,000 applicants – to ride the previous day's Tour route, while the peloton take a day off. This year, *L'Etape du Tour* is 150 miles of unrelenting climbing and descending, probably in temperatures touching 100 degrees. The longest and hardest Etape in history, the stage profile looks like a set of broken dentures. Only complete novices could study it without coming out in a cold sweat. Talented amateur riders will finish in eight or nine hours, hopeless hacks could take double or simply fall by the wayside.

Instinctively, and rather shakily, I rang Will Fotheringham, a leading cycling journalist and an invaluable Tour companion last summer, who doubles up as a rugby writer and is well acquainted with my state of fitness – mental and physical – and disastrous dietary tendencies.

'You're bonkers, absolutely bloody bonkers, Brendan. You must be completely insane. I've never heard anything so ridiculous. Get a grip. Phone me again when you are sober,' he said. This from a former semi-professional cyclist who has twice completed L'Etape.

I persisted, my pride more than a little dented. 'Seriously I can't back down now, I've got to go through with it. What I need is help.'

'What you need is a miracle. The ride is a complete bitch, the worst ever, and I'm going nowhere near it. The main thing is to stay alive, anything after that will be a bonus for you, Brendan. You have got to lose two stone in weight and start training in the New Year. You've got six months and we might just pull it off. Like I say, the main thing here is to preserve life.

'You need an hour on the bike every other day for three months just to get some general fitness and then start building on bike time and endurance in the spring when we get some better weather. You need some long rides in May and June, and it would help if you could nip over and do the route itself sometime. Allow two or three days, that's what most normal cyclists would reckon if they were just cycling for pleasure. You don't do L'Etape for pleasure, that only comes when you look back on it, and even then it still hurts.'

I took delivery of the bike just before Christmas: a Giant TCR Zero. It's a beautiful, sleek, lightweight, understated and possibly temperamental thoroughbred – not much change out of £2,000 – but for two weeks she lay idle at the back of my garage. Just as ocean-going liners are always female, so is my bike. No question. I'll think of an affectionate name as we grow closer and become better acquainted with each other's moods and habits. It's very early days of course but I think we'll get on just fine. She seems very nice. In fact it might be love.

For the first week I circled her warily trying to pluck up the courage to introduce myself properly, afraid of making a fool of myself. What if we didn't get on? The humiliation and rejection. And then I crashed out of action for a week with 'flu, but finally the big moment could be delayed no longer. In the end it all happened very quickly.

I strapped into the pedals and pushed off gently. With almost no apparent effort I was suddenly ghosting along at 25 mph. I barely noticed a sharp incline, which I have often laboured up on my heavy, under-geared mountain bike, and as I cautiously went up through the gears I could feel my excitement rising. I rather self-consciously shifted into the racing position and started pushing hard on a big gear. To my utter shock and surprise I over-took an admittedly cautious woman driver on the school run. This was fantastic, 40 mph without breaking sweat.

There was a downside of course. I had been warned about the wickedly uncomfortable racing saddles and, as predicted by the splendid Fotheringham, the pain started to kick in after half an hour. I can only liken it to somebody systematically sticking razor blades into your nether regions . . . and then leaving them there. My cycling guru insists there is only one solution – to ride and ride until your rump is hardened to the pain and discomfort. He is no fun.

I headed for home, grimacing hard with the effort and pain. This was agony. Just 300 yards from sanctuary and an old mate spotted me. Here it comes, I thought, the first abuse and mickey-taking of the year. I wasn't disappointed.

'Who the hell do you think you are, Lance Armstrong or some-body?' said my mate, almost choking with his own devastating wit. 'You'll be riding in the Tour de France next.' I smiled a massive smile, even through the pain. The look on his face when I told him that actually I would be riding 'The Tour' – as we cyclists call it – will get me through the next month's training at least.

———

BOTTOM LINE IS BEWARE OF VAPORUB
Brendan Gallagher

The words of George Bickerstaffe – 73 years young and still pound-ing out the miles around Oldham and sundry cycling hotspots in Lancashire – came to mind as I started training for *L'Etape du Tour* in earnest earlier this month.

'Dear Mr Gallagher,' he wrote. 'Bloody hell. I nearly fell off the lav when I saw your piece! It sounds a barmy idea and your novice status is clear. Look at your picture. The bike is all wrong. Look at the angle of the derailleur. What you need is a triple front c/ring. Good luck, though. *Daily Telegraph* cyclists want you to pull this off.'

Though mortified to have interrupted George's early-morning constitutional – can't a man get any peace and quiet these days? – his straight-talking, good humour and support struck a chord. I wasn't entirely alone in this ridiculous quest.

So down to business. Acting on the advice of my cycling guru, William Fotheringham, I am aiming to spend an hour on the bike every other day for the next two months in an attempt to gain a plateau of fitness from which I can then start training properly for the gruelling 150-mile stage of the Tour de France on 11 July.

I have therefore devised a 15-mile circular route from my house that takes in the fiercest climb in mid-Sussex, the mighty Col du Turners Hill. Anybody who has done the London-Brighton ride every June will know it as the pleasant halfway point where they dish out free strawberries and you can grab a quick pint at the Red Lion or Crown. It is, admittedly, some 4,500 feet lower than the Col du Pas de Peyrol, the high point of the *Etape* this year, but you have to start somewhere. I comfort myself in the knowledge that the gradient is one-in-six in places, steeper than anything on the *Etape*. Allegedly.

I have put in eight sessions so far. Mostly I feel terrible, but that is inevitable. I am unfit and any sporting activity – and this is fairly strenuous – would leave me panting and nauseous. In my defence, I do also try to ride flat out to make best use of limited time.

Like most bad workmen, I blame my tools. The saddle seems too high, the handlebars are definitely half an inch too low and probably an inch too far forward. Of course they are nothing of the sort. The bike is simply set up for a normally fit and limber specimen. It is up to me to become that person.

There are other obstacles to overcome, notably Mum's Café, the world's best greasy spoon, which is hidden in a quiet industrial estate just off leafy Rowfant Road at the end of my circuit. Some days – twice to be precise, M'Lud – the smell of bacon and sausages has proved irresistible. I have done a deal with myself that in future tea and toast is permissible but only on days when I double up and ride two circuits.

I've picked up a few health and hygiene tips already. Nappy rash cream is ideal for that irritating chafing on your inner thighs and crotch that plagues beginners, while Vicks Vaporub attacks those stubborn chest infections which afflict most cyclists. A word of warning, though: under no circumstances get the two mixed up, as I did one morning. The result brings tears to your eyes.

Last Monday was also instructive and encouraging. Freezing early morning fog was soon replaced by an icy drizzle. After successive rugby weekends working in Dublin, Belfast and Limerick, I was lacking motivation and the vestiges of a weekend hangover remained.

It was a 'bike day' but surely I could be excused. I had no winter training gear or waterproofs and the local radio was full of dire warnings about driving conditions. I started brewing a pot of coffee instead and sat down to read the papers but couldn't settle. Was it guilt or just stark terror at the challenge ahead? Perhaps neither. Experienced bikers speak of a strange madness, some call it an illness, that can take over when you start dabbling in the sport. Jobs and marriages are apparently cast aside in the need for a daily fix.

Whatever. The rain was getting heavier but suddenly I threw on my muddy fleece top and tracksuit bottoms. It was cold and miserable and the fleece was soon heavy with rain. I spent an eternity trying to get warm but gradually blood started to pump around the extremities and for some reason the bike was cruising along splendidly. Rain can be very comforting. For once, Turners Hill came and went without undue effort.

Very strange. I was sodden and freezing; rain was cascading down my face and neck, but this was OK. In fact it was more than OK. I was quite enjoying myself and even started whistling, for some obscure reason, *Pretty Flamingo* by Manfred Mann. Where on earth did that come from?

Exhilarated, I went around for another loop and, full of self-denial, sprinted past Mum's Café before heading home for a bath and that much delayed mug of coffee. I glowed with health – inwardly at least, as nobody else would have noticed – and was unbearably smug and good-humoured all day. Reality set in about 7 p.m. when the eyelids started feeling heavy and I began to slump over my laptop, the day's copy still unsent.

Dear Mr Gallagher. What you need is a triple front c/ring.

Dear Mr Bickerstaffe. Thank you, but what I need is 12 hours' sleep.

———

16 FEBRUARY 2004

TRAGIC PANTANI HAILED AS 'GENIUS'

Stephen Farrand

The world of cycling paid tribute yesterday to Marco Pantani, the greatest climber in the history of the sport, who died suddenly this weekend.

Although the Italian was widely regarded as the undisputed 'King of the Mountains' – particularly in his adoring homeland – the former Tour de France winner would always have to live with a tarnished record after being caught up in the drugs scandals of the late Nineties. His fall from grace would eventually lead to a great character suffering from clinical depression.

Pantani's impressive victories in the Giro d'Italia and Tour de France in 1998, combined with his shaven head and big ears, made him a household name, and he was openly adored by the passionate Italian cycling fans. They loved him for the way he raced with panache and courage, because he was never afraid to risk all in the pursuit of a lone victory in the mountains.

Lance Armstrong, the five-time Tour de France winner, led the tributes last night, saying: 'This is terrible and shocking news.' The American, who had a stormy relationship with Pantani, added: 'Regardless of our battles on and off the bike, I had a deep respect for Marco. Cycling has indeed lost a great champion and a great personality.'

Belgian cycling legend Eddy Merckx pointed the finger of blame at an overly enthusiastic Italian justice system: 'After his success in the Giro and Tour de France in the same year Pantani certainly made mistakes – but he was targeted by Italian justice who never let him go. I believe it was that that destroyed him.'

Merckx joined France's now-retired former world champion Laurent Jalabert in saying the solitary nature of the sport Pantani had chosen had played a role in the tragedy. 'Once your career is finished it's inevitable that you're forgotten. It's a case of every man for himself and God for all.' Jalabert said Pantani was 'a genius' whose memory should not be sullied by what went wrong in his life. 'It's always difficult to end your cycling career,' said Jalabert. 'Undoubtedly it hit him hard when he was thrown off the Tour of Italy in 1999.'

Jalabert said anyone would have struggled to handle the constant scrutiny of the authorities, which reached a peak when Pantani was among those targeted in a police raid of the riders' hotel during the 1999 Tour of Italy. 'It's difficult to constantly be a target of suspicion when you've been really successful, above all in Italy where the people are fanatics. Pantani was disillusioned. I think in the end he must have said to himself: "What's the point?" But Pantani was a genius. I still remember him climbing the Galibier, and even in last year's Giro, the determination on his face. It wouldn't be fair to summarise his life with issues of doping and depression.'

The whole of Italy was in a state of profound shock yesterday, the front pages filled with tributes to their fallen hero. His favourite football team, AC Milan, held a minute's silence before their match and wore black armbands in his memory.

Pantani was known as *Il Pirata* for his swashbuckling style of racing and the colourful bandanna he wore to cover his shaven head. It was the perfect moniker and the skull and cross-bones was flown with pride by his fans along the roadside. *Tuttosport's* front page yesterday read *'Addio Pirata'*, while the *Gazzetta dello Sport* headline was the poignant 'Lost Hero, We Adored You'. Flowers were left outside his home in Cesenatico and thousands are expected to attend his funeral.

Although Pantani was no longer registered with a team – he had not ridden competitively since May last year – he yearned for a return to the roads. He recently wrote on his website: 'Sometimes we close our eyes because we don't like to face reality, but if we stop communicating we stop savouring life and stop writing our life story. I speak with my bike. And I want to continue writing the chapter of my life that I've left unfinished for too long.'

----

17 FEBRUARY 2004

'THEY ONLY WANT TO PUNISH ME'
Phil Liggett

Marco Pantani, who died a sad and lonely person, should be remembered as a great athlete who conquered the heights of his sport. In reality this may not be the case in a sport in which drug-taking remains endemic and the cheats continue to stay one step ahead of the testers.

While Pantani's death was confirmed yesterday as a heart attack, his links with drug abuse are undeniably strong and next week he was to have entered a clinic in Bolivia to be treated for cocaine addiction.

He believed he was being persecuted for his drugs connections. 'They only want to punish me,' he was reported to have written on notepaper found in his Rimini hotel room. He was also alleged to have written that he was the victim of a conspiracy.

There is no doubt that drugs have played a major part in cycling, especially in the Fifties and Sixties. Since the mid-Sixties drug-testing controls have been in place and the International Cycling Union believe that the battle is slowly being won. But only 48 hours before Pantani died at the age of 34, unknown Belgian rider Johan Sermon, 21, died from apparent heart failure. There have been 100 such deaths in the last decade and all apparently from natural causes. Last year alone, leading professionals Denis Zannette, Fabrice Salanson and José María Jiménez all died under similar circumstances.

Sermon was reported to be fit and in 'peak condition' with a haematocrit (red blood-cell count) level of 40 per cent – well within the norms and not indicative of a person taking the blood-booster EPO. It is the use of EPO that is thought to have caused the deaths of many riders, but this cannot be proved.

The serious side-effects of EPO are that when an athlete later rests and his circulation, and therefore his heart, slows, the thickening of the blood because of the increased red cells can have fatal effects. It is a risk, it seems, that is still seen to be worth taking.

This season started badly when the well-respected Cofidis team in France were placed under investigation by police after the discovery of drugs at riders' and masseurs' homes. The team, as a group, have been exonerated, but charges have been laid against individual riders and helpers and have resulted in the French rider, Philippe Gaumont, admitting to the use of EPO.

The sport continues its fight against cheats and has introduced more and more tests and controls. It has forced riders to keep detailed health dossiers and record their bodily fluid levels, being obliged, if asked, to give a good reason for any violent changes, such as an unusually high red blood-cell count.

In a sport that demands such a high performance from its athletes on almost a daily basis, doctors are part of the lives of the performers. Injury and sickness must be combated to meet the demands of the multi-million pound sponsors who expect results on a regular basis. Young riders are vulnerable in the dark world of unscrupulous dealers and masseurs to whom the riders turn if the results are not coming.

Italy, where riders from many nations go to learn their trade, is perhaps the most demanding of its performers and there is little doubt that drug use is still rife there, though the authorities are working hard to stamp it out.

All of Pantani's victories were confirmed only after he had successfully passed the anti-doping controls of the day. Even so, he was stopped from completing the 1999 Giro d'Italia when certain of victory because of a high haematocrit level.

In 2000 he was charged under new Italian legislation with sporting fraud and given a three-month suspended prison sentence, the first custodial sentence imposed on an Italian athlete from any sport, but this was later successfully appealed against. Two years earlier he had been the toast of France after he won the Tour de France in the wake of the Festina doping scandal, when the complete French team had been thrown out after admitting that they had an organised doping programme.

With the Tour only five years away from its centenary and in danger of ending altogether, the organisers relied heavily on Pantani, who was in a different team, to hand the race back its credibility. He did, adding this win to that of the Giro d'Italia three weeks earlier, becoming only the seventh cyclist to do the double.

In later years, the same Tour organisers turned on him by not allowing him to ride in the event because of his links to the use of drugs. He felt that organisers, officials and the Italian judiciary were out to prove his performances were not what they seemed.

Walt Disney would have paid millions to have created a cartoon character with the features and habits of Pantani. He was hardly larger than life at barely five feet and weighing in at less then eight stones, but when seated on his small, custom-built bicycle, he was the fastest and most colourful mountain climber in the world.

He should have headed into retirement a contented man who had made millions of people happy. Instead he died a lonely and broken person in a hotel room, believing that the world had turned against him, and surrounded by prescription drugs. 'A tragic genius,' was how the great Spanish rider, Miguel Indurain, described Pantani. 'Many may have achieved more, but no one got more people hooked on the sport.'

----

27 MAY 2004

INJURY BRINGS MY ETAPE CHALLENGE TO END OF THE ROAD

Brendan Gallagher

Back in January – when I was still planning, plotting and dreaming – it seemed like the perfect destination. A week in La Manga in May to train like never before and lay the foundations for an assault on *L'Etape du Tour*, the 238-km challenge leg of this year's Tour de France, the toughest in history, with its six major climbs between Limoges and St-Flour.

Impatient to get cracking, I even sneaked out to the sports resort near Murcia for a week's holiday in early April, straight after rugby's Six Nations Championship, and put in seven days of between 30 and 50 miles of quality riding. This was new territory for my body and I was beginning to feel the impossible could happen and I stood a fighting chance of finishing *L'Etape*.

Then disaster: a horribly painful pulled groin on my return and a month of torturous inactivity just when I should have been racking up the miles. Soon it was time to visit La Manga again, but instead of upping the daily mileage to 60 or even 80 miles, hours of treatment and rehab awaited.

First came two strokes of luck. La Manga was, that very week, opening a £14 million spa and fitness centre with every conceivable facility, including a state-of-the-art gym and a brilliant Thalasso spa pool with a selection of power jets that can be directed to the precise point of maximum pain.

Second, it was my good fortune that the resort now employs Jose Ruiz Espinos, who, at just 25, is one of the most highly regarded physiotherapists in Spain and treats the world's top footballers, including David Beckham and Luis Figo, when they visit. Jose is a trained osteopath, sports massage therapist and physiotherapist, and disdains the use of anything electronic, such as ultrasound. The top surgeons in Spain often request that he sits in on their operations on sports stars so that he can assess ligament, tendon and muscle damage and plan the patient's rehab accordingly.

But then the bad news. Jose treated me for four days and immediately diagnosed a nasty spasm of the large iliopsoas muscle which runs under the stomach from hip to pubic bone. Everything connected to the muscle was tight and uncomfortable. No wonder my hamstrings, tendons and adductors were regularly going twang. It could be treated but it would take between two and six months to resolve. It could not be rushed. The condition can become chronic and there are no short cuts.

Jose worked like a demon, almost splitting me in two to stretch the offending muscle. But even he can't work miracles, and, in the short term, he contented himself with easing the acute pain.

The last day of my 'training' visit dawned and gradually the noon heat gave away to a perfect early summer's evening. I was determined not to bow out on the treatment table – I would sulk all summer otherwise – so I munched a handful of painkillers with lunch and planned one last hurrah. Jose said a gentle ride on the flat should do no further damage.

I paced around all afternoon feeling sick with nerves. Was I up for this or what? *L'Etape* had driven me half insane. All through the miserable winter months, I had battled through rain, frost and wind without so much as a muscle tweak or a sniffle. And now the long summer nights and champagne mornings were here, my body had deserted me. These should have been the good times. Blooming bike race.

There had been a few nightmares along the way. One icy morning, my back wheel suddenly shredded and I finished in a flooded countryside ditch, a rude wake-up call followed by a chastening four-mile walk home. On my earlier visit to La Manga, I had nearly expired on a 1,100-foot hill climb with Geoff Cox, who runs the local cycle hire shop, though I was proud to crest it with plenty to spare a couple of days later. Generally, though, *L'Etape* spelt pain and anguish.

Actually, it's a love-hate thing. Occasionally, I would shout for joy on those crisp winter morning spins around my local lanes and there is little to compare with lazing in a hot bath afterwards. It was brilliant to feel healthy and alive. There had been many magical moments and the odd mystery as well. At approximately 8 a.m. on Sunday 15 February, while out for an early spin, I witnessed an elderly lady apparently laying a wreath in the corner of a ploughed field and then playing a lament on the bagpipes – beautifully, as it happens. It seemed intimate and personal so I didn't linger.

Back to La Manga and my swansong ride. The pain had dulled by tea time and, after a long stretching routine, I climbed gingerly on my bike and set out on my familiar 'Breakfast Run', a 38-km round-trip to the seaside resort of Los Alcazares. Flat, fast, bleak and desolate but always beautiful. I knew every roadside pothole and derelict medieval windmill. I was almost part of the scenery – farm labourers and bus drivers had started to nod in recognition or give a friendly thumbs-up. Just a month earlier, before injury struck, I used to polish off this run before breakfast as a warm-up for a long day's training. Halcyon days. Where did it all go wrong?

I didn't care any more. It was all over, yet I felt strangely exhilarated. I had given every last ounce since early January but I knew this was the end of the road. I coasted down the long downhill stretch towards shimmering Mar Menor lagoon and quickly built up speed as I flicked up through the gears.

The adrenalin was pumping and an angry surge of power rocked my body. I ripped my helmet off – the safety gurus can forgive me just this once – and relished the feeling of freedom and the sharpening wind on my face. I swung left at the third roundabout outside Los Belones and headed off down the lonely coast road that had become my second home, picking my way through the villages of Los Nietos, Estrella del Mar, Los Urrutias, Punta Brava and the imposing rocky outcrop of El Carmol.

I was flying and it all seemed so effortless. I rode on in disbelief, waiting for the breathlessness and heavy legs to kick in. But they didn't. I hunkered down into the racing position, which I had grown to hate, and felt unusually comfortable as I pounded along the desolate straights with real pleasure. I sprinted hard, time and time again, but still my breath remained steady, though I was beginning to sweat buckets. Much sooner than seemed possible, I made the big right turn towards Los Alcazares and headed for the sanctuary of the Club Nautico and a reviving, ice-cold Coca-Cola. Incredibly, inexplicably, frustratingly and yet joyously, I had taken a full eight minutes off my personal best for the outward leg. Only when I tried briefly to dismount did reality intervene. Somebody was trying to drive a machete into my left groin, or so it felt.

It didn't matter. I was on a high and was not going to be denied my small moment of triumph. I set out on the return leg – as usual into a strong headwind – and still felt fantastic. I blasted my way back home and sank into a warm bath. I could scarcely climb out of bed with pain the next morning, but what the hell. The feelgood factor had been restored.

Hopelessly ill-prepared and short of time, I had lost the battle. In fact, I had been routed and humiliated, at least in my own eyes, but privately, this cycling novice has declared war on *L'Etape du Tour*. It has become personal. Next year, God willing, I shall return and hostilities will recommence.

———

19 JULY 2004

A CIRCUS ON TWO WHEELS OR FOUR
Brendan Gallagher

A strange thing happened the other morning as we were driving into St Flour to blag a copy of *L'Equipe* and a croissant in the Tour village. To be fair, we had been invited and the intention was also to meet a few riders who habitually go scavenging for free nosh themselves. Journalists and sportsmen often share the same thoughts – it's just their bodies that differ.

Anyway, we were speeding along a deserted back street when I spotted a youthful-looking cyclist wearing a yellow shirt and messing about with his mates. One minute he was standing up on the pedals, no hands, yawning expansively, the next he made an imaginary pillow with his hands and mimicked the need for more sleep. Flash git.

However, a second glance confirmed the startling fact that it was *the* yellow jersey, worn by France's new favourite son, Thomas Voeckler, pedalling to the start from his team hotel. We wound the window down as Voeckler – 25 years old despite his schoolboy looks – rode along companionably.

'*Comment ça va, Thomas?*'

'*Ça va bien, merci, monsieur,*' replied young Thomas cheerfully.

'How's the form?'

'A little tired, but thanks for asking. It was a tough day yesterday. Hopefully I can keep the yellow for one more day. I am enjoying the experience. Take care. Have a nice day.'

In cricket terms, our little encounter was the equivalent of throwing a few balls to Michael Vaughan at Lord's ten minutes before he opens for England against West Indies. That's the great irony, and the enduring appeal, of the Tour de France. The world's biggest annual sporting event is also the most free-booting, laidback and accessible. Everybody is encouraged to feel a part of the travelling roadshow and to contribute to the associated madness.

'Riding the route' is the biggest buzz of all. If you wangle the right accreditation you can drive the entire Tour route, sometimes just minutes ahead of the peloton. The trick is to park about 50 yards in front of the start line and then rev up and disappear in a cloud of dust as late as possible before the departure time.

The problem is that there are 4,000 accredited Tour and media cars and the subsequent carve-up is pure Le Mans with a dash of Keystone Cops. The unofficial rally provides hours of entertainment for the monumental crowds – upwards of 1.3 million yesterday – who line the route.

The ride can be the stuff of dreams, especially on the quieter sections of the Pyrenees we experienced on Saturday. World-beating countryside, no oncoming traffic, policemen smiling and occasionally saluting as you pass, people cheering and waving just in case you are somebody important. Or perhaps they are just happy.

But all good things come to an end and eventually you hit the 'junk train' – scores of small lorries, vans, quad bikes and the like distributing the Tour sponsors' goods. The 20-foot-high Grand Mère coffee pot, painted a garish red, is my favourite or, more accurately, my least hated.

You crawl along behind the pot and start examining the crowd. On closer acquaintance, large sections appear to be on mind-altering drugs or, dare one mention it, the French just can't take their drink any more. They dress up like the Brits going to a Headingley Test but with even less taste, play dare with the oncoming traffic, ride horses alongside the peloton, climb telegraph posts and throw water bottles at press cars and generally contribute magnificently to the madness.

Eventually you pull over at the finish and much later still, the stage done and dusted, you head for a distant B&B along an obscure mountain road. You finally relax and start planning the evening meal. But wait, what's that around the corner ahead of you glinting in the setting sun? It looks like a massive coffee pot. Surely not?

You can rant and rave or simply take heed of the splendid Voeckler. Take care and have a nice day.

---

26 JULY 2004

ARMSTRONG WINS HEARTS WITH HISTORIC TRIUMPH

Phil Liggett in Paris

In October 1996, Lance Armstrong sent out a press release announcing that he had testicular cancer in a very advanced stage, and that he would fight it with the same spirit he had shown when he became cycling's youngest world champion three years earlier.

Yesterday, on the Champs-Elysées on a perfect summer's afternoon in Paris, the Texan saluted a huge crowd as he became the first man to win the Tour de France six times. He compounded his feat by doing it in six successive years.

Since 1903 only five riders have managed to win the Tour five times and, in moving into his own exclusive club, Armstrong has won the hearts of both the Americans and the perhaps more cynical French.

After stepping down from the podium, a hastily erected covered lorry trailer pulled across the Champs-Elysées moments after Belgian Tom Boonen had won the final stage from Montereau, he smiled. That was something the American rarely does in the heat of battle, but now he smiled and said: 'It's special to stand on the most famous boulevard in the world and have your own country's national anthem played six times in six years.'

Armstrong, who at 32 is the second-oldest post-War winner, triumphed with ease. Having looked fallible for much of last year's event, this time the man from Austin, Texas, was always in control. His winning margin was a massive 6 m 19 s over German champion Andreas Kloden and 6 m 40 s ahead of Italian Ivan Basso.

Armstrong's secret is that he races to win only one event per year, while the others perform around the world. Instead, he studies the route and then rides all the sections he sees as strategic points. He then learns them by heart, and his stage win at Villard de Lans came because he remembered the sharp turns into the finish there.

His ability has never been in doubt and he spends long hours perfecting his racing equipment, hand-picking his team, all of whom finished the three-week race, and above all looking after his body, which is tuned to winning the Tour de France in July. Calories taken in must equal calories given out.

He becomes annoyed and animated when people accuse him of taking drugs and at no time has there ever been any proof of this. He is offended by comments such as those made by Greg LeMond, the American who won the event three times. 'I'm sorry and disappointed about what Greg has been saying,' he said. 'If we are all drugged then why is it that Greg still holds the record for the fastest time trial, done back in 1989?

'Sure, I do have fun and I do prepare well, but then I love my job and I love my team,' said Armstrong, who celebrated his win with actors Robin Williams and Will Smith, and his girlfriend, the rock star Sheryl Crow. He also took a congratulatory phone call from President Bush after leaving the podium.

Armstrong could be said to have come of age in the Tour de

France on Saturday, when he won his 21st stage since first taking part in 1993. At the same time, he rubbed salt into the wounds of his rivals, who arrived in Paris broken and many minutes behind this most remarkable champion.

---

26 JULY 2004

LEADER

TOUR DE FORCE

It is the magnitude of his victory that one marvels at: the achievement of, the mastery of the thing. The Tour de France is one of the most gruelling of sporting events. To ride 120 miles at speed is beyond most of us. To repeat the task day after day is awesome. Many professional cyclists aim simply to complete the course. To win is magnificent. To win six times in a row, as American Lance Armstrong has done, stands at the very edge of human accomplishment.

It is hard to think of a precedent. While all sports have their legendary figures, many of them are little noticed outside their own countries. Don Bradman may have done mighty deeds. But, beyond the Commonwealth, his feats are no better known than are, say, César Rincón's four consecutive triumphs at the Madrid bullring in 1991 outside the Hispanophone world.

Armstrong's singular achievement has been to universalise his sport. Until very recently, the Tour de France was largely the preserve of French, Belgian and Italian cyclists. But Armstrong has become a global figure, showing such determination and single-mindedness (he very rarely competes in other races, for example) as to win even the grudging respect of the host nation. Like his namesake and countryman Neil Armstrong, he has marked a milestone for all mankind.

END OF THE ROAD FOR MILLAR AFTER BAN

Brendan Gallagher

David Millar, Britain's top road cyclist, may be facing the end of his career following his admission that he took the blood-boosting drug erythropoietin (EPO). Yesterday, British authorities banned him for two years and stripped him of his world time-trial championship after his admission to French police last month.

Millar was set to become a household name with the strong possibility of winning two Olympic gold medals in Athens – in the individual time trial and the 4-km team pursuit – but is now left wondering whether to quit the sport altogether.

The Scot, who took the world title in Hamilton, Ontario, last October, has no right of appeal to the British Cycling Federation but may appeal independently to the Court of Arbitration for Sport. Ahead of yesterday's decision there had been fears of a life ban so Millar, 27, and his management team may decide to bite the bullet.

Millar has indicated recently that he would be keen to work with the British cycling authorities, addressing young cyclists on the pitfalls of becoming part of the doping culture which exists in road racing. He first admitted his guilt to a French judge, Richard Pallain, on 1 July this year, after two syringes containing traces of EPO were found in his Biarritz home during a police raid. The Scot told Pallain that he had taken it on three separate occasions, an admission he repeated to police on 20 July.

'I had always dreamed of becoming a world champion,' Millar said. 'I had reached that aim but I had cheated. I took EPO when I was in Manchester and the two syringes found at my home were those I injected myself with in Manchester. I drugged myself because I was a prisoner of fame and money. I believe that those two syringes were the witnesses of how ashamed I felt to have used drugs. I am not proud to have drugged myself; I am not happy about it. I was a prisoner of the person I had become.'

Millar told the police he had been introduced to EPO by a Cofidis team-mate before the 2001 Tour of Spain. 'I took EPO because I knew the Cofidis team were going to Spain for the Vuelta on the condition that I would do it and get a result. I could feel the pressure,' said Millar, who has subsequently been sacked by the team. Prior to that, Millar had been struggling with injuries, glandular fever and problems in his personal life.

----

25 JULY 2005

ARMSTRONG DEPARTS A TRUE CHAMPION

Phil Liggett in Paris

Lance Armstrong dodged the slippery streets of Paris yesterday to claim his seventh victory in the Tour de France in seven straight years. He stepped off the winner's podium and into retirement with no regrets at leaving the sport he has often referred to as 'the greatest in the world'.

Afterwards, he spoke movingly about the race, which now enters a new era without him. Armstrong paid tribute to Ivan Basso, the Italian rider who was second and is a close friend. 'He is the Tour's future,' said Armstrong. He nominated Jan Ullrich, who was third and has three times finished second to Armstrong, as 'my greatest competitor'. Then, in a pointed message to the journalists who have worked overtime to attempt to prove that he has won his races by using drugs, he also had a direct message: 'To the cynics and sceptics, I say I am sorry that they can't live a dream, or believe in miracles, as there are no secrets to my success. *Vive le Tour.*'

Armstrong confirmed his win over Basso by 4 m 40 s in Saturday's time trial at St Etienne, which he took by 23 seconds, from

Ullrich. The German rider had returned to the form which saw him almost beat Armstrong in 2003. 'If Jan had brought this form to the start of the Tour that he has shown at the end, I would have been in trouble,' Armstrong admitted.

After three weeks and more than 2,200 miles, Armstrong said the race could not get better for him or his Discovery team. They won four of the daily stages, have the best young rider in newcomer Yaroslav Popovych, and, in all, Armstrong won his 83rd yellow jersey to move into second place behind Eddy Merckx in the winner's list.

The time-trial victory before the long journey to Corbeil Essonnes for yesterday's stage was special for Armstrong after his three children arrived with his mother, who nursed him through his testicular cancer, and his rock star girlfriend, Sheryl Crow. In the car behind him during the race was Senator John Kerry, who was the Democratic candidate in last year's Presidential election.

'I hope that Lance goes into politics and chooses the right party,' Senator Kerry said. 'He has focus, strategic ability, is not afraid to make decisions and is intelligent. His sporting accomplishment is one of the greatest of all times and he's a great ambassador to his country. His future is limitless.'

---

31 JULY 2005

ARMSTRONG IS GREAT, BUT NOT FOR CYCLING

Sir,

I would take issue with your placing Lance Armstrong above such great cyclists as Bernard Hinault, Jacques Anquetil, Miguel Indurain and Eddy Merckx, who each won the Tour de France 'only' five times (Sport, 24 July).

Armstrong only ever trained and raced for that yearly exclusive win in the Tour and never had to wrack his body through the anguish of a full year's racing programme.

Merckx, in particular, won seemingly everything, everywhere, all year and still had sufficient strength to power off the front of the entire peloton alone, riding away to win on his own by a massive margin, something Armstrong has never done.

Armstrong has definitely earned his place among such other inspirational names as Douglas Bader and Simon Weston, by being a beacon of strength and providing massive hope for all cancer sufferers. For this reason alone his name should be feted.

Kevin N Ward,
Bromsgrove, Worcestershire

I JULY 2006

LEADING RIDERS SENT HOME OVER DRUGS RAID LINKS

Phil Liggett in Strasbourg

Ivan Basso, Jan Ullrich and Francisco Mancebo, the three outstanding favourites to win the Tour de France when it starts here today, were sent home yesterday after their names were linked to a drugs syndicate in Spain.

Guilty by implication rather than any solid proof, the three riders have all denied any link with the drugs raid five weeks ago which was known to Spanish police as *Operación Puerto*. Their names appear on an official list sent to the Tour organisers late on Wednesday.

Spanish police investigating a doctor, Eufemiano Fuentes – accused of trafficking in all types of performance-enhancing drugs, including growth hormones and the blood booster, EPO – released the list of up to 58 names of riders accused of visiting his premises in Madrid. Christian Prudhomme, the deputy Tour director, said: 'We will fight doping all the way. Cycling is a wonderful sport, but doping is our enemy.'

David Millar, of Britain, back after a two-year ban for using EPO in June 2003, said: 'I feel ashamed, but I lied and cheated. Now I want everyone to know I am riding this race clean.'

---

25 JULY 2006

LANDIS EMERGES AS THE TRUE KING OF PAIN

Andrew Baker

Adversity attends every thrust on the pedal for the rider in the Tour de France. The awful and awesome history of the great race is speckled with the blood of the fallen and remounted, shot through with the pain of illness, exhaustion and over-medication.

Lance Armstrong beat cancer to become a multiple victor, and his absence this year might have robbed the race of romance. But his compatriot and successor, Floyd Landis, also has a tale to tell of suffering surmounted.

Landis confirmed his triumph on the Champs-Elysées on Sunday, at the head of his Phonak team. It was the end of a dramatic, unpredictable contest, during which the eventual winner had suffered staggering setbacks and demonstrated immense resolve to overcome them.

But then Landis needs determination every time he throws a leg across his bike. It has to be the right leg: he cannot board a bike with his left. He walks with a limp, cannot cross his right leg over his left when seated, and plans to undergo hip replacement surgery in the autumn, before – he hopes – resuming his career. The problem is medically defined as advanced osteocronosis with superimposed osteoarthritis. In layman's terms, the ball of his right hip is deteriorating because the blood supply to it is restricted by scar tissue. His right leg is two inches shorter than his left. All of this is the result of a training crash in 2002, when he fractured the hip.

If that seems mundane, this is what it feels like: 'It's bad, it's grinding, it's bone on bone,' Landis told the *New York Times* during this year's Tour. 'Sometimes it's a sharp pain. When I pedal and walk, it comes and goes, but mostly it's an ache, like an arthritis pain. It aches down my leg into my knee. The morning is the best time. It doesn't hurt too much. But when I walk it hurts, when I ride it hurts. Most of the time it doesn't keep me awake, but there are nights when it does.'

Millions of people all over the world deal with arthritic pain in their daily lives and, with courage and medicinal help, try to ensure that it does not interfere too much with their routines. But in the routine of a top cyclist pain is a constant. Every competitor during the Tour wakes with the certainty that before the day is out he will be in agony. Landis has had to live with the waking knowledge that for him, the pain will be worse than for all the others.

With the hip replacement operation scheduled for the autumn, he might have decided to skip this year's Tour and hope for a pain-free attempt next year. But two considerations made him press on. The first is that the outcome of major surgery is never predictable. Landis, now 30, may go on to enjoy a successful post-operative career. On the other hand, he may never be able to ride a bike in competition again.

Furthermore, the retirement of Armstrong, for whom he had ridden shotgun on previous Tours, left a gap for a successor. And when the field was further depleted by the enforced withdrawals of Jan Ullrich and Ivan Basso after a Spanish doping investigation, it became clear that this was to be the most open Tour de France for years. For Floyd Landis, it was now or never.

Landis was raised in Farmersville, Pennsylvania, as a Mennonite, a member of a conservative Protestant community which discourages many manifestations of modern society, including – crucially for Landis – Lycra cycling shorts. So the teenaged Landis was obliged to take part in his early mountain-bike races wearing tracksuit bottoms. These failed to disguise his talent, and before long he was recruited into road racing and ultimately, in 2002, into Armstrong's US Postal squad.

The streak of stubbornness needed to defy his upbringing was to serve Landis well on this year's Tour. On the 16th stage he appeared on the point of collapse on the gruelling final climb up to La Toussuire, dropping ten minutes to his rivals over the final, agonising ten kilometres. Many observers scoffed, and the French sports newspaper *L'Equipe* crowed '*Landis a craqué'*.

But Landis knows more than most about cracks and how to repair them. The following day, with a breathtaking display of courage and determination, he sprinted away from the field with a long-distance counter-attack that cut his deficit to the leaders to 30 seconds, broke their resolve and set up his final victory.

Time, and the surgeons' skill, will tell whether or not Landis will return to defend his title next year. Every year, the best climber on the Tour is awarded the title of King of the Mountains. Landis has been invested, in perpetuity, as the king of pain.

---

28 JULY 2006

THE QUESTION IS WHY, WHEN HE KNEW HE'D BE CAUGHT

Phil Liggett

My first reaction to the news that Floyd Landis had returned a positive test during the 17th stage of the Tour de France between St Jean de Maurienne and Morzine was one of extreme sadness, and the huge question: 'Why?'

In Strasbourg at the *grand départ,* the Tour had seemingly handled the sending home of pre-race favourites Jan Ullrich, Ivan Basso and Francisco Mancebo, among others, well, and the stage was set for 'the cleanest Tour in years'.

The organisers had sent out a clear message that dopers would not be tolerated, even though those sent away left protesting their innocence, and still do. This year's Tour seemed 'clean' as riders had good days and bad, something which doesn't always happen if the drugs are kicking in. Landis himself collapsed on stage 16 to La Toussuire in the Alps and then, rehydrated overnight, won the fateful stage 17 to Morzine by almost six minutes. Even seven-time Tour winner Lance Armstrong was moved to call Landis at his hotel that night and congratulate him at 'having big balls' to do what he had done after such a defeat 24 hours earlier.

There are many questions to be answered before Landis is condemned. The first is: why win the stage knowing that the winner is automatically drugs-tested and when finding unusual testosterone levels in a testing laboratory is an easy thing to do? Landis would have also been tested at least three times previously as race leader, too, and these presumably have been negative, as only stage 17 is under discussion.

The quiet but determined American was genuinely happy when he finished at Morzine. He arrived punching the air. Landis has never failed a drugs test in his career and this season was enjoying his best run of victories yet, all of which would have carried compulsory drugs tests. His wins in America and France since February have all been achieved despite a dying femur bone which will mean a replacement hip soon. As winner of the Tour de France he could have expected annual earnings in the multi-million pound bracket, even though there is the risk that his hip operation might mean he never races at the same level again.

They say that drugs have been in cycling for more than 100 years. At first it was simply alcohol – a tot of brandy did wonders on a long climb in adverse weather. Then came amphetamines, which were found in Briton Tom Simpson when he died on Mont Ventoux during the Tour in 1967. Now, with the help of unscrupulous medical experts, growth hormones, steroids and blood changing is available for those who can afford it. But the doping agencies, International Cycling Union and the Tour de France all agree that drugs must be stamped out.

The Tour de France organisers have been 'saddened' by yesterday's revelations, but the second test has still to confirm the first. There is a possibility that Landis has over-produced testosterone and, if so, I hope he will be completely vindicated. If, however, he is guilty, then he will lose the Tour de France, receive a life ban at the Olympics, a two-year ban from the sport and a four-year ban from riding on a Pro Tour team. In short, he will never race again.

————

5 OCTOBER 2006

WHY PAIN WAS NEVER A BARRIER FOR FAST EDDY

Brendan Gallagher

He looked like a young Elvis Presley, rode like a runaway steam engine and, God bless him, enraged the French year after year by winning all their big races and grinding their high-profile superstars into the dust.

Lance Armstrong may have earned the worldwide headlines, notoriety and small fortune, but the Belgian with the swarthy Mediterranean looks remains cycling's *non pareil,* indeed one of sport's legendary figures. Such was his voracious appetite for devouring opponents and spitting them out on the roadside that Eddy Merckx became known as 'The Cannibal' and the nickname has stuck.

There were 525 wins in his 1,582 career races, a 33 per cent success rate and on average a win every week for ten years. Five Tour de France titles, a record 96 days in the yellow jersey and 34 stage wins. Five titles in the Giro d'Italia and 24 stage wins. Seven Milan–San Remo Classics, three world championships, three Paris–Roubaix … There just isn't space to list his honours. And all this despite a chronic back condition that should have left him on a walking stick for the rest of his life.

Back in 1969 – soon after his first sensational Tour de France title when, uniquely, he won the yellow jersey, green jersey (sprints) and the polka-dotted jersey (mountains) – Merckx was involved in an horrific crash. He was being paced by a motorbike in a 'derny' race and a cyclist fell in front of Merckx's pacer, who was killed instantly. Merckx suffered bad concussion, cracked a vertebra low in his back and his pelvis shifted horribly. It should have been the end of his career, but Merckx begged to differ.

'Cyclists live with pain; if you can't handle it you will win nothing,' he told me. 'If you don't want to suffer, take up another sport. Winning big Tours and stage races is often about pain management. When the terrible accident occurred at least I escaped with my life. I was the lucky one, that was my reaction. I was positive and having worked so hard to succeed in cycling I was determined not to give up.

'I was only young, and the injuries were to haunt me for the rest of my career, but I got through. I had to adjust my position on the saddle and I was always needing massages and manipulation. But I got through. In the end I grew philosophical. I could still turn the pedals, the bike still went quick. Not as quick, but still very quick. The only difference between me and my opponents was that I started most races in pain, they hit the wall three-quarters through or at the top of a big climb.

'I began to use it to my advantage. Being in pain from the start made me sharp and on edge and well motivated. I had no fear of what lay ahead. I was already suffering. My opponents had all that to "look forward" to, but they didn't know when it would ambush them in the race.

'Sometimes, also, it was very bad and it was as if I raced so fast just to get the race over so I could stretch out on the floor or the bed to get comfortable. The mind can overcome great setbacks and make a person very strong.'

Merckx – now 61, always approachable on the circuit and notably lacking the preening ego of many, far inferior, ex-riders –

has always enjoyed hero status in Britain. His all-out aggression and panache – termed *'merckxismo'* by the French media – are understandably revered, but his staunch friendship and support of Britain's own cycling hero, Tom Simpson, is also recalled.

Merckx and Simpson were team-mates for two years at Peugeot BP before Simpson's death on Mont Ventoux on the Tour de France in 1967. The post-mortem indicated that the use of amphetamines could have contributed to the dehydration which saw him cycle into unconsciousness in the 55-degree heat of that stark Provençal mountain. Merckx was the ambitious tyro, Simpson the seasoned pro and former world champion. Simpson was re-motivated by his young room-mate's energy and drive; Merckx soaked up sundry lessons from the Brit who had learnt everything the hard way, making his way in a foreign country.

'He was very British and a gentleman but he also had that Continental love of just racing and getting on a bike. He was one of the British trailblazers but took to it very quickly. He was a complete natural. He was a very considerable star, but I am not sure if British sports people realised exactly how big.

'I was shattered when he collapsed and died on Ventoux that dreadful day. 13 July. We all remember the date. Tom was always so strong and spirited, very brave. If he could die on a climb we could all die in a race some day. I made a point of getting over to Britain for his funeral. Because the Tour was continuing and I was not racing I was able to attend and perhaps represent those who couldn't get across. It was an emotional day. I was very proud to know Tom Simpson.'

He added: 'When the young pros ask about the old days they are always curious to know about the man whose memorial is high on Ventoux. I tell them all I know. It was an older brother-kid brother relationship. It must have been three years after his death, yes 1970, when we rode back over the mountain during the Tour and the memorial his family erected was up by then. I was in the lead and it felt natural to doff my cap and make the sign of the cross.'

Merckx is still cycling these days, an operation two years ago to cure a long-standing stomach problem giving him a new lease of life. He has been logging up the miles and has lost over three stones in weight. His enthusiasm for the sport seems undiminished despite the battering it has received this summer in the wake of the Landis affair and the banning, before the Tour, of Ivan Basso and Jan Ullrich because of their alleged connections with a doping ring.

'Cycling sometimes gets a bad press, but it always comes through; in fact I am very optimistic at present,' says Merckx. 'Its dope testing is the most severe and frequent in the world, much more than any other sport. No wonder we catch people. Cycling has identified many culprits and they have been dealt with. Other sports lag behind and perhaps they have tough days ahead.

'Cycling is a sport of the people. How many people in the world have never been on a bike? Not many. It always comes through and always will. It is unstoppable. What we must do is to make sure it is well managed and policed. After that it has a dynamic of its own. I have no worries for cycling. It remains a great spectacle and a passion for many.'

———

27 FEBRUARY 2007

ULLRICH RIDES OFF PROTESTING HIS INNOCENCE

Brendan Gallagher

Jan Ullrich went into cycling as an angry teenager with attitude, and he quit the sport yesterday a bitter man. It has been a rough but exhilarating ride, often shrouded in controversy – not unlike the sport at which he excelled.

The second-greatest cycling talent of his generation, it was his extreme misfortune to be a contemporary of Lance Armstrong. Ullrich has lived much of a considerable sporting life in the shade, and ends it under a dark cloud. Announcing his retirement, Ullrich protested angrily that he had never cheated during his long career, and the fall-out of last year's extraordinary Tour de France continued.

The powerful German was withdrawn by his T-Mobile team from the Tour the day before it started in Strasbourg, after his name was linked with *'Operación Puerto'* in Spain. Ullrich was allegedly one of around 200 individuals from a cross-section of professional sports – although only the names of cyclists were leaked – being advised by a Spanish doctor, Eufemiano Fuentes, who allegedly ran a blood-doping ring.

Last May, Spain's Civil Guard raided addresses associated with Fuentes and found anabolic steroids, blood transfusion equipment and dozens of bags of frozen blood, labelled with the names of the 200 athletes.

After being thrown off the Tour, Ullrich was sacked by T-Moblie and has been charged with sports fraud in Bonn, though he has yet to be charged with a specific doping offence. Earlier this month he gave a DNA sample for comparison with the blood found in Spain.

'I still don't understand why I was not allowed to compete in the Tour last year,' Ullrich insisted yesterday. 'My life as a cyclist collapsed that day. I've been painted as a criminal, while I've done nothing wrong. I never once cheated in my cycling career. At the start of this whole affair it was difficult to take, now it's just sad. I will continue my involvement in cycling. I couldn't live without cycling. It's my passion and my life,' said Ullrich, who is to act as an adviser to the small Austrian Volksbank team.

Thus ends a riding career in which he won the Tour de France once and finished runner-up on five occasions. He was fourth in 2004 and third in 2005, won the world time-trial championship twice and the Olympic road race in Sydney in 2000.

For Ullrich it all started in Rostock, in the then East Germany, where he was born into poverty in December 1973. His father left home when Ullrich was three and he never forgave him – an experience he shares with Armstrong.

Ullrich was identified as an outstanding talent and trained under the Communist system. Representing the reunified Germany, he was amateur world champion in 1993 – the same year that Armstrong took the world professional crown – and announced his arrival as a Tour de France rider in 1996 when he finished runner-up on debut to the Dane Bjarne Riis.

When Ullrich won the Tour the following year, it appeared to be the start of a long reign – but, atypically, he cracked on the massive Galibier climb the following year and finished second to Marco Pantani. He missed the Tour in 1999 through injury, atoned by winning the Tour of Spain, but when he returned to the Tour de France in 2000, Armstrong was in full flow.

Ullrich, having suffered in his early years in a bankrupt Communist state, was inclined to enjoy the fruits of capitalist success to excess, and in 2002 was convicted of drink-driving and using amphetamines. He fought a constant weight problem, and often used the first week to ride himself back to full fitness deep in the peloton. Armstrong would often chide Ullrich for his lack of discipline and inability to turn up race-fit, but he always acknowledged the German as his most dangerous rival, a rider of extraordinary power and tempo on the flat and a survivor in the mountains.

Ullrich's focus now is to clear his name. In contrast to his riding career, there can be no glory in defeat.

---

25 JUNE 2007

THE ALPS CERTAINLY TOOK MY BREATH AWAY

James Cracknell

The Tour de France may start with the opening Prologue on the streets of London on 7 July, but Le Tour really gets going in the

Alps, as I can testify after being given the opportunity by the T-Mobile team to attempt one of the famous race's most gruelling stages.

The 159 kilometres of stage nine start from Val d'Isère, but our plans for a room near the start-line were dashed as seemingly all the hotels were shut for the season changeover – when the ski room presumably readies itself to welcome hiking boots and bikes. However, nobody had told the weather it was the time to stop covering the slopes with snow and bathe them in glorious sunshine. Our route up the Col de l'Iseran, the mountain pass above Val d'Isère, was blocked with snow.

The last time the Tour crossed the Iseran, in 1996, terrible weather forced the riders into their cars and the climb was abandoned. As the same thing had happened to the professionals, what else could I do except get in the car and drive round the mountain? Until Roland, the German driver/mechanic/motivator of the T-Mobile team who was to be guiding/feeding/picking me up from a crumpled heap throughout the day, said: 'It's sunny, let's give it a go, the snow might not be so bad.'

Between stages eight and nine there is the first rest day, and the riders will need every bit of down time they can get as this year's Tour contains more *hors categorie* (beyond classification) and category-one climbs than any race since 1987. To empathise fully with the riders, I took a day off, but thought doing the previous eight stages was taking journalistic responsibility a step too far, especially as stage nine contained two *hors* and a category-one climb.

Let me put these Alps into perspective. Ben Nevis stands at 1,344 metres (4,406 feet). Val d'Isère is the start and is at 1,885 metres; from there the first 15 kilometres of the stage are uphill/mountain to the Col de l'Iseran, which, at 2,770 metres, is the second highest climb in the Tour's history and, to be honest, no place to be cycling.

I cut the corners of the hairpins pretending I was leading the field up the mountain. Twenty minutes later the image in my head had changed – I'd been spat out the back of the peloton and was left struggling up on my own. Despite seeing Val d'Isère in the beautiful valley far below me I struggled to enjoy the view. My pulse was thumping behind my ears and my breathing was frantic as I struggled for oxygen. With each hairpin I hoped to see either the summit or a snowdrift.

For turn after turn I saw neither. I was cursing the course designer for starting the stage with such a steep climb and even more the accompanying guide which said the Iseran comes 'too early in the stage to make any difference'. My legs disagreed. Eventually the summit came, but there was no celebration – I still had 144 kilometres of the stage left and was already exhausted. I headed down the other side, trying to enjoy the speed of the descent, the sunshine and the number of Alpine villages I passed through. Except I couldn't, because I had a big physical and mental block – the Col du Galibier which lay ahead.

Before I got to the base of the Galibier I had to climb the Col du Telegraphe, a category-one climb up to the Fort du Telegraphe, built in 1896 but also part of the Maginot Line in 1940. I underestimated this climb. It was the hottest part of the day, I wasn't in the cooler air at altitude and I hadn't drunk enough water on the descent. I plodded my way up the hill to a sign pointing straight up the road – and up the mountain – which read Col du Galibier 17 km.

I had a 40-kilometre ride to the finish after the summit, but that was mostly downhill and I would worry about that later. Until this ride I'd never paid attention to percentage gradients; it wasn't a factor that affected my rowing. The average gradient of the Galibier was 6.9 per cent. The first three kilometres seemed pretty flat, so my basic mathematics told me the average had to be made up elsewhere.

This was a different climb from the Iseran; the bends were sweeping, I couldn't focus on one hairpin at a time, I could see hundreds of metres to the next bend and they were taking ages to arrive. The realisation of what the riders go through hit me, not the riders at the front, who seem to dance up the mountain, but those who have blown their legs out helping the team leader and have been left to struggle, or the sprinters who just want to survive the mountains. For them it isn't a case of just finishing, they have to finish within a certain time limit – if they're outside it their race is over. They've gone from racing the first week of the Tour to just trying to survive every day.

I'd run out of gears on the T-Mobile team bike so there was nothing for it but to push harder with the legs, and one line from the course guide kept popping into my head: 'The Galibier rears up horribly for the final eight vertiginous kilometres.' The trees had given way to grass and the grass to snow – surely I was near the top. I wanted nothing more than to get off and walk.

Four days earlier I was knocked out in a charity boxing match, but this time I wasn't battling a 2½ st weight disadvantage but a 2,500-metre mountain and, given the choice, I'd take the punch every time. In the ring I had no choice – he hit me and down I went; against the Galibier I had to hurt myself to get to the top. Every push of the pedal was a matter of pride. I wanted to get to the top as quick as I could and the only person who could stop that happening was me, and psychologically that's a tougher situation to be in.

The last kilometre is over a ten per cent gradient. The photographer jumped out of the van and ran past me to take a picture. I swore as he ran passed. How slow was I going? 'Don't worry, they do it to Lance!'

I appreciated the line but neither felt better nor believed him. But I could see the top. If I were watching on TV, by now I'd be yelling at the rider who had let the guy in front sprint away so close to the summit, but can now understand why he had no response. When your legs have gone, they've gone.

I stopped at the top, taking great pride looking back down the valley, but there will be none of that for the riders on 17 July – they will power over and race the last 40 kilometres to Briançon.

My descent was more leisurely and with five kilometres left a rider passed me. I must have been a great target. Decked out in T-Mobile's unmistakable magenta with a matching van, he must have thought he was going to scalp one of their team testing the route. I tried to chase him down before the finish in the town centre; the mind was willing but unfortunately the legs had been left on the Galibier.

———

5 JULY 2007

ROCHE RECALLS HIS SUMMER OF SUCCESS

Brendan Gallagher

When you cast an objective historical eye over cycling's pantheon, Stephen Roche, by his own admission, probably tops the second division – the best of the rest, as it were. His achievements in the Tour de France are praiseworthy but comparatively modest when set against those of Eddy Merckx, Italy's Fausto Coppi, the legendary French riders Jacques Anquetil and Bernard Hinault, and the all-conquering Americans, Greg LeMond and Lance Armstrong.

But exactly 20 years ago, the dapper Dubliner did enjoy one remarkable season that eclipses anything achieved by the others (save for the incredible Merckx, who frankly seemed to be from another sporting planet altogether, and it is almost unfair to include him in any list containing mere mortals).

In 1987 Roche overcame his mutinous, largely Italian, team and the wrath of the Italian public, to win the gruelling, mountainous, three-week Tour of Italy before riding the canniest of races in the Tour de France to romp home in Paris as well. And, just when his cup was running over, Roche happily pitched up at the world championships in Austria to ride in support of his friend and compatriot Sean Kelly, the overwhelming favourite, and was so strong that he simply pedalled away from the field on the last lap of the race.

There is evident steel in those sparkling Irish eyes – now as well as then – and though he claims never to dwell on the past, Roche can become very animated when recalling his year of destiny. The memories burn bright.

'Putting those three massive wins together was a minor miracle, frankly, and involved a good deal of luck, not to mention some bloody hard days in the saddle. I still can't tell you exactly how it all happened, except to say that God must have been looking down on me and the talent that I do possess blossomed fully that summer.'

Roche admits: 'It had been a disastrous winter. I had struggled the previous season with my left knee and went in for a serious operation which took a long while to come good. I had missed months and months of background training yet, come the spring, I felt incredibly fresh and strong. It makes you think, doesn't it? Perhaps sometimes we overdo the training. Anyways, I was flying during the early season and hit the Giro [Tour of Italy] running, but there was a huge problem. My Italian team, Carrera, also included the current Giro champion, Roberto Visentini, and there was huge pressure to ensure another Italian triumph took place.'

Roche took the pink jersey – the equivalent of the leader's *maillot jaune* in the Tour de France – early on but his colleagues, with one notable exception, declined to defend it for him. Eddy Schepers, a tough old Belgian pro who had learned his trade in service to the great Merckx and knew when a rider was being stitched up, rode his heart out for Roche and kept him competitive.

Eventually, however, the favoured Visentini was installed as race leader, at which point Roche produced the race of his life to destroy the Italian on the mountainous stage to Sappada, beating his colleague by eight minutes. Roche regained the pink jersey, which is just as well because without that kudos and protection he would probably have been sent home altogether, or fired.

For the remainder of the race Schepers and Scotland's Robert Millar formed a protective blanket around Roche as Italian fans hurled abuse and spat mouthfuls of masticated rice in his direction. Victory was hard earned, but sweet.

Roche recalls: 'I was very strong mentally going into the Tour de France, even if I started only 80 per cent fit physically after working so hard at the Giro. I had to box clever. Apart from the political issues within the team and their decision not to ride for me for much of the Giro, I doubted our ability as a team to defend the yellow jersey for a prolonged period.

'We were a talented group individually but didn't have the obvious team make-up to produce a Tour winner. I adopted a softly, softly approach, keeping out of trouble and saving my resources.'

Roche was true to his word, waiting until stage 19 to Villard de Lans in the mountains to make his move to claim the yellow jersey from François Bernard. He defended that stoutly on Alpe d'Huez, heroically at La Plagne — where he needed oxygen after his sensational effort — and applied the garnish at the crucial time trial in Dijon. There were extraordinary scenes as 250,000 delighted Dubliners lined the streets for his homecoming the following week, and it took the returning hero fully five hours to travel from the airport to the city centre.

Today, Roche divides his life between homes in Paris and Nice. He remains fit and trim and still hops on a bike at every opportunity. 'I pile on the pounds if I slob around but I'm not prepared to deny myself the pleasures of the French table any more. So the compromise is I must get out there regularly and do a bit.'

He adds: 'My cycling life has turned full circle. I'm now cycling again for the sheer pleasure and child-like fun of getting on a bike. In between times I became a club rider, dreamt the unthinkable dream of becoming a professional, travelled to France, worked hard, immersed myself in the culture, got my break and fulfilled my dream. Now I just like pottering around country lanes. Some days I feel brilliant. I've got my racing legs on, and I up the tempo. But most of the time I'm a 47-year-old ex-pro with dodgy knees, and I ride accordingly.

'There have been some hard times and disappointments along the way. I had knee injuries which were very tough and demoralising – I lost the best part of five years in total – and it was a huge blow personally when the Fagor "Superteam" of largely British and Irish riders I helped put together fell apart in my absence, injured again in 1988. But when I look at my basket of achievement, as it were, it's pretty full. I'm very content. Generally, I never look back but I am making an exception this summer.'

---

9 JULY 2007

LONDON PASSES TEST WITH FLYING COLOURS

James Cracknell

This was a huge weekend for London. Following the previous week's terrorist attacks, the second anniversary of the bombings of 7 July 2005, had even more resonance. The capital had to prove it could put on a major sporting event in spite of the threats that exist today. But it wasn't just one big event: there was Live Earth at Wembley, tennis at Wimbledon and the Prologue of the Tour de France around Westminster, Hyde Park and Buckingham Palace.

Afterwards, Ken Livingstone, the Mayor of London, admitted they had been stretched, but the city had delivered. It had to, because there was another anniversary this weekend, one that will always be forgotten because of the 7/7 attacks – London beating Paris for the right to host the 2012 Olympic Games. Saturday was the first big test for the capital since we won the Games and it is ironic it was with France's most cherished event.

The crowds – as we knew they would – turned out in huge numbers, over a million lining the 7.9-km course, and the conditions were perfect. All the day needed was a British winner.

Of the five British riders in this year's Tour, two were genuine contenders: David Millar and Bradley Wiggins. In 2000 Millar became only the fourth Briton to wear the yellow jersey when he won the Prologue, and the Scot is fighting hard to re-establish himself after a doping ban. It's always difficult for sportsmen to come back in at the same level after a ban, first because they were cheating to reach that level in the first place and, second, because the momentum of their career has been halted.

Wiggins had a real chance because the Prologue suits a rider who can get close to sprinting speeds and maintain them – typically a velodrome pursuiter, and they don't come better than Wiggins, who is world and Olympic champion. The only question was whether it was too long for Wiggins – his Olympic record for the four-kilometre pursuit is 4 m 15 s. Saturday's winning time was expected to be under nine minutes.

Wiggins may have been the emotional favourite racing in his home town, but Fabian Cancellara was the man most tipped to win. The Swiss won the Prologue in 2004 and is the current world time-trial champion.

I got a rider's eye view of the course following Vladimir Gusev around. The Discovery Team rider rolled down the start ramp and took off; the car accelerated hard to catch up with him. The crowd was a wall of screaming noise flashing past and I couldn't believe we hadn't caught him up yet doing this speed. Then I looked out of the windscreen and realised that we had caught him up – it was just that he was going 60 km/h. Even the tight right-hander at Parliament Square barely slowed him down as he lent the bike over an alarming amount considering the tiny contact area his tyres had with the tarmac.

Just under eight kilometres sounds like a day off compared to the 3,570 kilometres the race covers, but nine minutes is a long time when you're at near maximum heart-rate, trying to maintain technique, steer a tight line and forcing your legs to keep pushing when they're screaming 'no'. Gusev went through the line in an exhausting 9 m 15 s, the fastest time so far.

Things were hotting up. German Andreas Klöden set a blistering 9 m 3 s, which again questioned his decision to join the Astana team as a support rider to pre-race favourite Alexandre Vinokourov. Klöden came second overall in the Tour in 2004 and third in 2006, and could have been a team leader elsewhere.

Vinokourov, from Kazakhstan, produced an impressive 9 m 20 s for seventh place, but the day he wants to be wearing yellow is on the Champs-Elysées, not the Mall, and he looks to have the form and the team – which is inevitably known as 'Team Borat' (because of Vinokourov's nationality) – to do it.

American George Hincapie, who supported Lance Armstrong in every one of his seven Tour de France wins, was desperate to improve on second place in last year's Prologue, but could only just beat Discovery team-mate Gusev by two seconds.

At 5.49 p.m. Millar rolled off the top of the ramp. He was riding smoothly but at halfway was 11 seconds down and he ended up 20 seconds behind in 13th place, but afterwards insisted he was 'going to win a stage'.

Wiggins started six minutes after Millar and you could hear the wave of noise from the crowd that travelled with him. There was a groan on the Mall when he was down on Klöden at halfway, but the noise grew and grew as he shot past Buckingham Palace and turned on to the Mall. He hadn't closed the gap but it was an impressive performance and he finished a fraction of a second behind Hincapie.

Meanwhile, Cancellara was tearing up the course in the rainbow jersey of the world time-trial champion. More powerfully built than the lithe Wiggins, Cancellara was seven seconds up at the interval and sprinted through the finish line in an amazing 8 m 50 s – 13 seconds ahead of Klöden with Hincapie in third and Wiggins just behind in fourth. Maybe the double motivation for Cancellara of wanting to cement his reputation as the world's best time-trialist and needing a new jersey after his luggage got lost at Heathrow was too strong to match.

———

14 JULY 2007

FRANCE ACCLAIMS THE HEROICS OF A LOSER WHO WON

Brendan Gallagher in Bourg-en-Bresse

It was not Mont Ventoux, nor was it 54 degrees. But it was 13 July and it was the Tour de France. Britain's Olympic pursuit champion, Bradley Wiggins, flew the flag proudly for five hours and 190 kilometres yesterday and proved that just occasionally losers can sometimes be winners as well, especially on the Tour de France. One fancies that Tom Simpson would have been proud.

When Wiggins finally trailed in behind the peloton in Bourg-en-Bresse yesterday he was greeted by a media scrum the like of which we had not witnessed before on this Tour. On the 40th anniversary of Simpson's agonising death, the French public, romantic fools that they are, were desperately hoping for a defiant gesture from one of Britain's five riders on Tour. They were not disappointed.

As he surveyed the scene — stage six winner Tom Boonen slipped past relatively unmolested — Wiggins insisted that his incredible solo break was not deliberately undertaken to commemorate Simpson's anniversary, nor indeed his wife Cath's birthday back home in Preston. But if Wiggins was called upon to appear in the latest revival of *Mastermind* tomorrow, his specialist subject would undoubtedly be the history of British road cycling since 1960. He is a world leader on the subject. And if he could have one wish every morning when we meet him in the Tour Village for a *café noir* and a gossip, it would be to have his wife and two children with him.

'She will have been watching at home with the kids on TV, so today was the closest I could get to spending the day with them,' he explained in fluent French afterwards. Mums preparing tea for their brood across France will have shed a quiet tear as they caught the TV coverage.

Make no mistake, yesterday was a very special day for one of Britain's most likeable champions, and if he was going to write his name large in the Tour's history, the timing was perfect. Wiggins does not do histrionic and boastful, and certainly made no grand claims ahead of the stage, but he was revved up for this one. Indeed, he said earlier in the week that he was disappointed the Tour wasn't going over Mont Ventoux to mark the anniversary. And that from a rider who hates the mountains more than most.

He and four others went after just two kilometres – only 197½ km to go – and engaged a big gear, but very soon he found himself alone. It rarely, if ever, works out like that in the Tour, but when it does you hit the green button and go.

The peloton were lethargic after a manic final hour on Wednesday's stage and Wiggins offered no threat to the general classification. It was the first really hot afternoon of the Tour and nobody felt like mounting a serious chase.

Thus began the longest day. It was like one of those childhood afternoons in front of the TV and/or radio when England mount a brave rearguard action on the final day of a Test, usually at Trent Bridge or the Oval if memory serves. You expect the worst – in fact, you make a point of loudly telling everyone in earshot that it just cannot happen – but secretly hope for a miracle, and at the very least for that extraordinary prospect to be prolonged as long as possible.

Onwards, onwards, ever onwards. For more than five hours the cycling world was held captive. There was no escape. The French television cameras, beaming pictures to more than 100 countries, had to concentrate on a British rider, miles ahead of the peloton. In the Tour de France on 13 July. Everybody on the roadside knew the date's significance and clapped their approval.

Cofidis, who have supported Wiggins's track ambitions as well, were equally delighted. Advertising like this would cost a small fortune and Wiggins's ride yesterday repaid his salary fivefold.

Onwards, ever onwards, but the lead was tumbling. A spoke on his rear wheel broke and was thrown into the undergrowth. Suddenly Wiggins began to zig-zag with a horrible sense of *déjà vu,* but no panic: he was just searching for shade. The headwind blew, the peloton closed and seven kilometres out the game was up. 'Magnificent but suicidal,' said former Tour de France winner Stephen Roche in the studios. It was and it wasn't, for which we give thanks.

---

16 JULY 2007

ONE SAVAGE WORD WHICH TURNS A DREAM TO TEARS

Brendan Gallagher in Tignes

Abandon! The most hated word on the Tour de France, but the unspoken fate that hangs over – and also unites – all 189 riders who lined up in London last week. Injury, illness, a nasty crash, sheer fatigue, loss of morale and confidence, missing the time-cut one day or simply being unable to rise from your bed on another. There but for the grace of God . . .

Even young sprinter Mark Cavendish, who was strictly here for the first week and whose team had pre-booked his ticket home today, will find quitting the Tour emotional and tearful. Cavendish has put his heart and soul into the first week and loved every moment. The young British rider endured wretched luck with two painful crashes beyond his control in stages in which he had realistic chances, and was thwarted in a third when Tom Boonen's pedal ripped out the spokes of his front wheel a kilometre from glory.

Two top-ten finishes are still a fine effort and T-Mobile, as they always promised they would, spared Cavendish the Alps proper and Pyrenees to come. At 22, time is most definitely on his side.

Cavendish has stacks of sprinting to come this season, not least in the Tour of Britain, and he will return older and stronger next year when he will, hopefully, nudge his way over the first mountain range – the Pyrenees in 2008 – and live to fight another day. And many more days until one year he gets all the way to Paris and challenges for the green jersey.

Eminently sensible and logical, but there will be days back home in the Isle of Man this week when Cavendish will ache for the heat, excitement and the pain and searing lungs of the Tour de France. Seriously.

TIME IS UP FOR THE DRUG CHEATS

Brendan Gallagher on Col d'Aubisque

Is it the beginning of the end for the Tour de France? Or, perhaps, were yesterday's extraordinary events evidence of a sport finally getting to grips with a drug problem that has polluted its history for 104 years?

These were the massive questions hanging over the Tour last night after the most remarkable day in its history. Certainly the most dramatic and thought-provoking, as the purge of drug cheats gathered pace.

The unprecedented expulsion by his own team of the yellow jersey holder Michael Rasmussen, who had virtually sealed overall victory with a stage win on the Aubisque yesterday, is a massive embarrassment as the sport appears to go into meltdown. Conversely it can also be seen as the strongest message ever sent out by cycling as a sport that the days of doping or any ambiguity over testing are over. There is now, clearly, no room for cheats to prosper in cycling and the Tour de France.

As the remarkable news broke, it was not clear if Rasmussen's team Rabobank simply stopped believing his confused stories about two, three, or was it four, missed tests and his whereabouts in June and decided to sack him forthwith – or if Tour organisers finally lost patience and made it clear what the Dutch team were expected to do. One suspects the latter.

Earlier in the evening Tour officials had acted decisively to kick out Cofidis, a favourite French squad among the home fans, after Cristian Moreni had tested positive for testosterone. One of the innocent casualties there was Britain's Bradley Wiggins, whose reputation as a clean rider is respected around the world and who is now denied the chance of winning a stage by the end of the week.

The Tour's decision was in keeping with their move earlier this week to kick out Astana after Alexandre Vinokourov had tested positive for blood doping. Zero tolerance towards drugs is an easy approach to talk about, but a difficult policy to enact. Belatedly, cycling appears to be grasping the nettle, but have they left it too late? It could be touch and go.

The day had started with Christian Prudhomme, the Tour director, again spelling out what the Tour must do, although at the time he was reacting to Vinokourov's expulsion the previous evening. Little did he know what lay ahead. 'This has to change now,' he insisted. 'The re-conquering of cycling has to be done with the Tour de France. I started this job believing that we could change this system, but it's not enough – there has to be a revolution. And if you go to war on drugs, there will be casualties.'

There you have it. The casualties are coming thick and fast. Cycling's governing body, the UCI, might technically govern cycling, but the Tour de France is the dominating force and public face of the sport. The Tour must change, and not just the riders and their anonymous and often sinister associates.

The Tour remains full of contradictions. When two German terrestrial TV stations packed their bags in disgust after it was revealed that Patrick Sinkewitz of T-Mobile tested positive before the Tour, a deal was struck with an eager German satellite station within minutes, rather than hours. French TV, meanwhile, reports their best viewing figures since accurate figures have been available with an unprecedented 52 per cent audience share every afternoon. Yesterday a staggering 1.8 million fans lined the course. It didn't seem like an event in terminal decline.

The French public staggered a little last year when the winner Floyd Landis tested positive for testosterone – this was a direct attack on the dignity of the race itself, and they were distinctly lukewarm when it arrived back in France after the triumph of the London *départ*. But the status quo has quickly returned and that is dangerous. Doping cases are considered on a par with their politicians admitting to mistresses and financial irregularities. They are expected, debated and even welcomed in a macabre kind of way. That will have to change if they want their Tour to survive.

Tour de France officials are not just fighting the cheating tendencies of one rider, there is an entire drug culture and public love of sporting scandal in France that is part of the Tour's DNA. Prudhomme and the Tour have made a good start despite the critics. The drug testing now is ferocious and targeted and could be stepped up two or three notches next year with daily tests of all riders.

A coalition of six professional French teams and two German squads – the self-styled Movement for Credible Cycling – have combined to make their views known and staged a disorganised protest before yesterday's stage.

The impact, however, is massively diluted by the fact that two of the eight – T-Mobile and now Cofidis – have riders implicated in positive drug tests.

------

30 JULY 2007

CONTADOR VICTORIOUS AT TOUR DE FRANCE

Phil Liggett in Paris

Alberto Contador, 24, became the youngest rider to win the Tour de France since Jan Ullrich a decade ago as he cruised home on the Champs-Elysées yesterday in the closest ever finish between the first three riders. Contador beat Cadel Evans, the first Australian to reach the podium, by 23 seconds and his Discovery Channel team-mate Levi Leipheimer by 31 seconds. Yesterday's final stage was won by Italian Daniele Bennati in the expected bunch sprint.

The race for the overall title was won in the time trial between Cognac and Angoulême on Saturday, which Leipheimer won, setting the fourth-fastest average speed in race history over the 34 miles when he recorded 1 h 2 m 44 s. Leipheimer came to the race as leader of his team but was forced to help Contador when the Spaniard established himself in the mountains.

Lance Armstrong, the seven-times Tour winner and part owner of the Discovery Channel team, arrived on Saturday to follow Contador in the time trial. It was all the inspiration the baby-faced newcomer needed to force his lightweight body through the most important day of his life. He started the time trial 1 m 50 s ahead overall of Evans and, although the Australian closed in to be just 23 seconds behind, Contador had demonstrated he was the worthy winner.

Armstrong said afterwards: 'We have seen Alberto Contador emerge and we have seen the future of cycling. He's a complete rider – he can climb, time trial and is completely poised as a rider, so I'm proud of him.'

Cardiff's Geraint Thomas, at 21 the youngest rider in the race, finished 140th overall and is also a fresh face in the sport. He is the renaissance rider that the organisers and world drugs agencies are hoping to see, and there is every reason to be optimistic.

After the huge crowds in England, the public continued to come out in greater numbers than for many years and they did not diminish after the disqualification of pre-race favourite Alexandre Vinokourov, caught blood doping, or the rejection of race leader Michael Rasmussen for lying to his team about his whereabouts when called for out-of-competition tests.

Next year there will be changes, but the feud between the organisers and the International Cycling Union (UCI) must end. The world body has, for whatever reason, tried for three years to lower the importance of the Tour de France and formed the ProTour, a circuit in which the Tour de France has no interest, but has been forced to be part of.

The UCI president, Irishman Pat McQuaid, was at Angoulême wearing a badge given to him by a French television network and he pointedly spoke to none of the organisers. They do, however, agree that there is no place for drugs in this sport and this is the common ground that could heal the rift.

---

5 JULY 2008

BERNARD HINAULT – THE BATTLING BRETON WHO MADE YELLOW HIS OWN

Brendan Gallagher in Brest

The Tour has returned to Brittany – the home of powerful brooding Celts and cycling fans second to none where, in sporting terms, 'The Badger' rules all that he surveys. Disturb his sett at your extreme peril, as countless cyclists discovered to their cost.

I refer, of course, to Bernard Hinault, a rider of volcanic temperament hewn from the granite blocks that make up Brittany's spectacular coastline. The very toughest of the tough and a feared warrior who in the opinion of many heads the phalanx of stellar riders tucked in behind *non-pareil* Eddy Merckx in cycling's Hall of Fame. Extraordinary to relate, he is the last French rider to win the Tour de France, 23 long years ago in 1985.

It's not all about statistics – everybody knows that – but Hinault's chapter in the record books stacks up impressively alongside the man himself – a fearless, proud, obstinate Breton who never took a backward step in his life.

Between 1978, when he made his Tour debut and caused a sensation by winning the whole shooting match, and 1986, he won five Tours and was again leading and wearing yellow in 1980 when he was forced to abandon with knee problems after battling the odds. He also claimed two second places in the remaining two races. In his pomp he was positively Armstrong-esque in his dominance of the race, both in his ability on a bike and the force of his personality. A supreme time-triallist – 13 of his 28 stage wins on Tour were time trials – but he could also hang very tough in the mountains and had a kick on him as well, if he found himself in a sprint. This is the man who also won both the green jersey (1979) – traditionally won by sprinters – and the polka-dot, King of the Mountains, jersey (1986).

Away from the Tour he was much more versatile and hungry for racing than Armstrong. He won the Giro d'Italia three times, the Vuelta a España twice, he won the Grand Prix des Nations on five occasions and took a cluster of the great spring classics such as Paris-Roubaix, Liège-Bastogne-Liège, Gent-Wevelgem and the Amstel Gold Race. Only Merckx can boast a Palmares to surpass that.

'I raced for pleasure, the pleasure of winning, that can never be denied,' says Hinault. 'That's not to say I raced to have the most victories. I didn't set out to collect victories. If that was the case I would not have retired at 32 in my prime with a couple of good years left. But when the opportunity presented itself I gave it everything.'

Did he ever. Hinault crashed frequently for a rider of his class – then again he rode harder and more aggressively than most – but he always climbed back up from the ravine or picked himself up from the tarmac before remounting to complete the race. Black eyes, broken teeth, smashed bones, blood everywhere and, on one occasion, even frostbite during an epic snowbound Liège-Bastogne-Liège classic. Nothing ever stopped him. The tougher the going, the more he enjoyed himself.

Hinault – nicknamed 'The Badger' when he was a tyro by old training partners George Talbordet and Maurice Le Guilloux because they could never shake him off – could be unpredictable and react viciously when challenged, and not just by fellow riders. When a gaggle of protesters – in France somebody is protesting about something, somewhere, most days on the Tour – lined themselves defiantly across the route one day Hinault was not amused, got up on his pedals, built up pace and charged into their midst, scattering them to the four winds, reckless of any physical hurt he may inflict, or indeed incur. *C'est magnifique, ce n'est pas la guerre.*

Not that he was averse to a little protest himself. During the Tour in 1978, he, like many others, was outraged by the extra demands being put on the riders which included one day that featured two separate stages. He stepped forward to organise a riders' strike – at a time when the Tour was much more dictatorial – at Valence d'Agen and from that moment onwards he was installed as 'Le Patron' of the peloton.

The boss. You had better believe it. With his natural air of authority and peerless record among his contemporaries, Hinault ruled with a rod of iron, perhaps the last great patron the Tour has known. Self-policing is now frowned upon in these more transparent and accountable days. If Hinault decided it was too hot or too wet and plain dangerous to race flat out, the race tempo slowed. If a young rider showed reckless disrespect to him or his friends they were quickly put in their place.

But there was generosity as well. Teams or individuals badly in need of a win to make ends meet after a poor or unlucky season were given their heads on meaningless transition stages, as long as they didn't take liberties and try to affect the general classification. Hinault may have been a benevolent dictator but he was a dictator nonetheless.

The son of a railway worker whose parents dreamt of him working in a bank, Hinault could have been a top quality runner. As a 14-year-old he finished tenth in the French junior cross-country championships in Compeigne against older runners, but his genius on a bike soon became evident as he made the daily trip from his home town of Yffinac to school in neighbouring St Brieuc, which was founded by a Welsh monk. The Celtic roots run deep here. Don't dismiss these ancient connections – Hinault not only demonstrably looks like a Celt, he shares their *hwyl* and passion and potential for the spectacular. To be in his presence, physically, is to be reminded of Gareth Edwards – bristling, latent athleticism and fury.

A force to be reckoned with. Some years back the Tour's organisers decided to get Hinault involved again. He had taken to breeding cattle in Brittany during his retirement and was getting a tad bored. Something of a poacher turned gamekeeper scenario, but it has worked nonetheless. His public duties are mainly as 'meeter and greeter' to the great and good and organiser of the podium party, but his most significant contribution is as a trusted adviser on the Tour's route. Hinault helps ensure the correct balance between climbs, sprints and time trials and knows instinctively when a route has become too hard or too soft and needs to be adjusted. Frankly, if anybody should know, he should.

---

13 JULY 2008

DRUG SCANDALS REFUSE TO DIE

Brendan Gallagher

For some it is the first swallow that heralds the onset of summer. For cycling fans these days it is the first positive drugs test on the Tour de France. It duly arrived in Aurillac on Friday, and yet again the world's biggest annual sports event has been left reeling. Spain's Manuel Beltrán, a former colleague of the Tour's seven-time winner Lance Armstrong, tested positive for the banned blood-booster erythopoietin (EPO) less than a week into the Tour.

The organisers await confirmation of Beltrán's guilt, but another confirmed positive result would constitute a nightmarish scenario, especially because the last two Tours were marred by drugs scandals. The world's greatest test of physical endurance is also testing the patience of its supporters.

'When are these idiots going to learn that it's over?' said Pat McQuaid, head of the International Cycling Union, yesterday. 'They continue to think that they can beat the system. They're wrong. The system is catching up all the time.' On last year's Tour it was also the 'old brigade' who were caught out, riders who competed when the drug culture was absolutely the norm. But the use of drugs has always haunted the Tour.

The Tour's future is on a knife-edge. The sporting world still loves it, but desperately wants it to put its house in order. A record 186 countries are taking television coverage and more than 30 million spectators will watch at least one of the 21 stages. Goodwill abounds in the cycling 'business', but it could all come crashing down unless the Tour can eliminate drugs cheats. An industry that promotes recreational cycling for its good health has become increasingly at odds with a profession that sinks so low.

―――――

22 JULY 2008

LONG JOURNEY ENDS WITH SNAPSHOT OF A DAY TO REMEMBER

LOUISE BUTLER BLOGS ON WHAT IT MEANS WHEN THE TOUR VISITS HER 'HOME' TOWN

I suspect that when the majority of ex-pats are asked: 'Where are you from?' the answer would be the place they were born, rather than where they live now. But for me a transition has been made that has ended with a small town in Hertfordshire being replaced by Cahors in southwest France as 'home'.

It's been a long journey but I can pinpoint one event that completed it: the day the Tour de France came to town. As an aspiring photographer, hearing that the 18th stage of the 2007 Tour would start just ten minutes (by car) from my doorstep, gripped me with excitement.

July 27 arrived and the town was bathed in sunshine. I was given a lift in, then strode across the Pont Louis Philippe over the River Lot into the tree-lined Boulevard Gambetta.

Even with more than two hours still to go, the sense of anticipation was palpable. I met some fellow ex-pats, complete with five children under the age of 10, and the fun began in earnest. We exchanged excited grins as the Caravane Publicitaire whizzed by; cars and vans dressed up as giant tyres, watches and washing powder boxes, adorned with dancers and sound systems pumping out some serious decibels. The kids started to leap up and down and wave in their attempts to procure some of the goodies being thrown to the crowds (at one point tussling with a fully-grown man, who really should have known better).

As we neared the start line, the crowds gathered in earnest. I found a perfect platform – a concrete plant pot, above the crowds and 20 metres from the start. I was hot and uncomfortable, but I wasn't giving up my spot for anyone.

The tension built as the start time drew near, then at 12.15 the riders set off – so quickly that I feared all I would manage would be a couple of blurred snapshots. But just a few metres down the road, there was some kind of hold-up. All the riders came to a halt right in front of me. I snapped away to my heart's content. Obstruction cleared, the riders moved on again as the delighted crowd clapped and cheered. The bikes shot down the boulevard in a vibrant blur, and were gone.

I scrambled down from my vantage point and was immediately swept along by the departing crowd with a huge grin on my face. My lift home was in the opposite direction, but I didn't care. I had the shots I'd dreamt of, and I felt such pride as I thought to myself: 'The Tour de France came to my home town, and I was there.' And then I realised: Cahors had become my home town.

———

28 JULY 2008

CARLOS SASTRE TRIUMPHS

TOUR ENJOYS FEELGOOD FACTOR AFTER
TESTING TIMES

Brendan Gallagher in Paris

Rafa Nadal and Wimbledon, Euro 2008 and now, in Carlos Sastre, a third consecutive winner of the Tour de France. King Juan Carlos should probably call another national holiday but, frankly, the Spanish get away with murder already. Just enjoy.

Enjoyment, that's the key. Ambience and mood colours our perception of everything, not least the Tour. You could argue that nothing much has changed for the better. Four riders, including Dmitry Fofonov on the final day, were drummed out as drug cheats after testing positive and another sacked by his disgusted team, statistics that are on a par with 2006 and 2007 which were considered low points in the sport.

But the Tour de France has rediscovered its confidence and is busy accentuating the positive. The sight of talented riders regularly being blown out the back or suffering horrific days when they look no better than the sport's weekend warriors has convinced many observers this is the cleanest Tour in years.

Britain's Mark Cavendish may have torn the field to shreds with four withering sprint victories, but he still finished last in the mountains and got blown away on a humble category-four climb on his last day before abandoning.

This is how big Tour cycling is meant to work. Sprinters aren't designed to trek around Europe's glacial peaks like mountain goats, and the climbers shouldn't regularly be contesting bunch sprints and time trials.

When Spaniards Moisés Dueñas Nevado and Manuel Beltrán got caught with their snouts in the EPO trough there was no hysteria, just satisfaction that the system was working and they had got their comeuppance. And when Ricardo Ricco, Italy's new climbing sensation, tested positive for a sneaky third-generation mutant version of EPO called Cera, there was universal celebration that the new tests put in place had worked. Good work by the boffins, disgrace for Ricco. Bravo.

The emergence of Cavendish is a godsend. Aside from Sastre, he is the biggest name to emerge from this Tour, a 'bums on seats' rider and an athlete the organisers and peloton believe in, even if the latter occasionally curse at his impudence and excellence.

Britain's influence on the Tour is growing apace. The *grand départ* in London last year was a huge morale booster for a beleaguered sport, and the prospect of a GB national team competing in 2010 is also welcomed. Such squads — Australia have similar plans — would be tightly controlled and tested by their national federations and Olympic committees, and would only add to the clean profile of the Tour.

Team Columbia, backed by the North American leisurewear giants, are committed to clean racing and have been notably successful in picking off stages, mainly for Cavendish, while Garmin have thrown in their lot with Slipstream, who are so confident in their squad that journalists are invited to stay with the team and even share rooms with the riders.

There are still cheats to be routed and the power struggle between the UCI and the Tour is getting a little boring but, somewhat against the odds, the Tour de France is doing OK. Meanwhile, what odds Cavendish for the green jersey next year?

———

25 SEPTEMBER 2008

ARMSTRONG'S RETURN TO TOUR DE FRANCE ONE OF SPORT'S GREAT QUESTS

Brendan Gallagher

No doubt for a future encore he will join King Canute and turn back the tides. Impossible is a word he neither recognises nor acknowledges. About to turn 37 next week, Lance Armstrong is intent on becoming the oldest Tour de France winner in history next summer after fully three years out of the sport. Don't bet against him. There is a comic-book quality to Armstrong's sporting life that rules nothing out and makes the extraordinary seem mundane.

Two major thoughts occur. Armstrong has clearly missed the Tour desperately and has manifestly failed to fill the void in his life that retirement prised open. Frankly, that was always on the cards. He devoted his sporting life to the Tour de France – not just 23 days every July – and winning the Tour was a 24/7 preoccupation for the other 11 months every year.

No rider has targeted the Tour with such a single-minded obsession – even his detractors have to concede that – and his days must have seemed empty in recent years. He will have badly missed his team-mates and even the peloton banter, albeit that he used to dish out plenty of stick to lesser mortals.

By all accounts he remains a doting father to his three children, he has worked hard with his cancer foundation and kept in shape running marathons and messing around on his mountain bike. There have also been a series of high-profile relationships – Sheryl Crow, fashion designer Tory Burch and actress Kate Hudson – in the aftermath of his divorce from wife Kristin, but in the three years since he 'retired' nothing has brought him complete fulfilment and certainly nothing has remotely sated his smouldering competitive instincts.

Secondly, he 'ended' his Tour de France career entirely on his terms, after a seventh consecutive, almost routine win. Before his cancer he was vulnerable; after coming back in 1999 he never cracked, not once. The Tour never defeated him, either physically or mentally. He starts with a clean slate and his return next year – the build-up, the early races and the Tour itself – is going to be one of sport's great modern-day quests. I sniff another best-selling book around the corner.